CAMBRIDGE TEXTS IN T
HISTORY OF PHILOSOPH

====

RALPH CUDWORTH
*A Treatise Concerning Eternal and
Immutable Morality*
with
A Treatise of Freewill

CAMBRIDGE TEXTS IN THE
HISTORY OF PHILOSOPHY

Series editors
KARL AMERIKS
Professor of Philosophy, University of Notre Dame
DESMOND M. CLARKE
Professor of Philosophy, University College Cork

The main objective of Cambridge Texts in the History of Philosophy is to expand the range, variety and quality of texts in the history of philosophy which are available in English. The series includes texts by familiar names (such as Descartes and Kant) and also by less well-known authors. Wherever possible, texts are published in complete and unabridged form, and translations are specially commissioned for the series. Each volume contains a critical introduction together with a guide to further reading and any necessary glossaries and textual apparatus. The volumes are designed for student use at undergraduate and postgraduate level and will be of interest not only to students of philosophy, but also to a wider audience of readers in the history of science, the history of theology and the history of ideas.

For a list of titles published in the series, please see end of book.

RALPH CUDWORTH

(1617 – 1688)

A Treatise Concerning Eternal and

Immutable Morality

[c. 1662] of p. xx

1st published 1731 — p. xxx ii

WITH

A Treatise of Freewill

EDITED BY

SARAH HUTTON

University of Hertfordshire

CAMBRIDGE
UNIVERSITY PRESS

Published by the Press Syndicate of the University of Cambridge
The Pitt Building, Trumpington Street, Cambridge CB2 1RP
40 West 20th Street, New York, NY 10011–4211, USA
10 Stamford Road, Oakleigh, Melbourne 3166, Australia

First published 1996

Printed in Great Britain by Bell & Bain Ltd., Glasgow

A catalogue record for this book is available from the British Library

Library of Congress cataloguing in publication data

Cudworth, Ralph, 1617–88.
[Treatise concerning eternal and immutable morality]
A treatise concerning eternal and immutable morality; with, A
treatise of freewill / Ralph Cudworth; edited by Sarah Hutton.
p.   cm. – (Cambridge texts in the history of philosophy)
Includes bibliographical references and index.
ISBN 0 521 47362 4 (hardcover). – ISBN 0 521 47918 5 (pbk)
1. Christian ethics – Anglican authors – Early works to 1800.
I. Hutton, Sarah, 1948– .   II. Cudworth, Ralph, 1617–88.
Treatise of freewill.   III. Title.   IV. Title: Treatise of freewill.
V. Series.
BJ1241.C8   1996
241–dc20   96–10996 CIP

ISBN 0 521 47362 4 hardback
ISBN 0 521 47918 5 paperback

Contents

Acknowledgements

There are three particular debts of gratitude which I would like to express: first to Erik-Jan Bos, for his assistance in preparing the text of *Freewill*; secondly to the University of Utrecht, for it was during my tenure of the Belle van Zuylen Visiting Professorship that the main groundwork for this edition was done. Last, but not least, I am grateful to the University of Hertfordshire for allowing me leave to take up the Belle van Zuylen chair.

Abbreviations

AT   *Œuvres de Descartes*, ed. C. Adam and P. Tannery, rev. B. Rochot (Paris, 1964–76)

TIS   Cudworth, *The True Intellectual System of the Universe* (London, 1678)

EIM   Cudworth, *A Treatise Concerning Eternal and Immutable Morality* (London, 1731)

CSM   *The Philosophical Writings of Descartes*, trans. J. Cottingham, R. Stoothoff and D. Murdoch, 3 vols. (Cambridge, 1984–91)

Introduction

Ralph Cudworth is a philosopher who spans the Renaissance and the Enlightenment. In an age of intellectual ferment, when the strident new philosophies of the seventeenth century announced their modernity by repudiating the past, Cudworth is a figure of continuity. This is symbolized by the fact that one of his major philosophical works, his *Treatise Concerning Eternal and Immutable Morality*, was published in the eighteenth century (1731), while the only major work published in his lifetime, his *True Intellectual System of the Universe* (1678), is steeped in the humanistic scholarship of the Renaissance. If the former has ensured that philosophers still pay some attention to Cudworth even today, the latter has helped deter them from close acquaintance, for Cudworth's reputation for learning has gone before him. The encrustation of erudition which clogs the pages of his *True Intellectual System of the Universe* has resulted in his being set aside in this century as an antiquarian.

None the less, modern neglect of Cudworth belies the enduring legacy which his writings enjoyed in the eighteenth and nineteenth centuries both at home and abroad. He was held in high regard by many, including John Locke, John Ray, Shaftesbury, Price and Reid. His *System* was reprinted twice, in different formats, in England in the eighteenth century.[1] In 1733 Johan Lorenz Mosheim published a Latin translation of Cudworth's works in Germany. Mosheim delayed publication of his translation in order to be able to include *A Treatise*

---

[1] First in an abbreviated version by Thomas Wise with the title, *A Confutation of Atheism* (London, 1706, repr. 1732), and then in a complete edition by Thomas Birch (London, 1743, repr. 1839).

Concerning Eternal and Immutable Morality, thereby ensuring a European-wide diffusion for *The Treatise* alongside Cudworth's *True Intellectual System*.[2] Selections from his works were published in French translation in Jean Le Clerc's *Bibliothèque choisie*, whence they became the centre-piece of a debate between Le Clerc and Bayle. Cudworth's doctrine of 'Plastic Nature' continued to be discussed in France through the Enlightenment and well into the nineteenth century.[3] An Italian translation of Cudworth's works by Luigi Benedetti was published in Italy in 1823.[4] Continuing interest in Cudworth in nineteenth-century Britain can be gauged from the publication of an edition of his *System* and *Treatise* by John Harrison in 1845, and the printing of one of his unpublished manuscripts as *A Treatise of Freewill* by J. Allen in 1838. Ever since Martineau's discussion of Cudworth in 1886, there has been a succession of short discussions of and extracts from *Eternal and Immutable Morality*. The most important study of Cudworth this century, J.A. Passmore's *Ralph Cudworth: An Interpretation* (1951) focuses on those writings not published in his lifetime, *A Treatise Concerning Eternal and Immutable Morality* and the unpublished manuscripts on free will.[5]

Cudworth is chiefly remembered today as a leading member of the group of seventeenth-century philosopher theologians now known as the Cambridge Platonists. This group includes such figures as Nathaniel Culverwell (d. 1651), John Smith (1618–52) and Peter Sterry (d. 1672), as well as the other philosopher of the group after Cudworth, Henry More (1614–87). Their sobriquet derives from the fact that they were all educated at Cambridge and they all, to different degrees, drew on the philosophy of Plato and his followers in preference to the Aristotelianism of the schools. As a group they are characterized more by a common outlook than a rigid set of doctrines. Their liberal theological temper was matched by a broadly syncretic approach to philosophy. Their insistence on the importance of reason in matters of religion was

---

[2] *Systema intellectualis huius universi* (Jena, 1733, repr. Leiden, 1773). For this edition, Mosheim also translated Cudworth's sermons and printed his university dissertation, *Dantur boni et mali rationes aeternae et indispensabiles* (Cambridge, 1651).

[3] Luisa Simonutti, 'Bayle and Le Clerc as Readers of Cudworth: Elements of the Debate on *Plastic Nature* in the Dutch Learned Journals', *Geschiedenis van de Wijsbegeerte in Nederland*, 4 (1993), 147–65. See also Paul Janet, *Essai sur le médiateur plastique de Cudworth* (Paris, 1860).

[4] *Sistema intellettuale del mondo*, 5 vols. (Pavia, 1823).

[5] Passmore accepted that British Library, Add. MSS 4983, 4984, 4985 and 4988 attributed to Cudworth were by him, but internal evidence does not, to my mind, bear this out.

harnessed to a tolerant religious outlook. While their academic learning ran deep, it went hand in hand with an emphasis on practical morality and serviceable knowledge.

Cudworth: life and writings

Cudworth was born in Aller, Somerset, in 1617, where his father, also called Ralph, was a minister. His father died when he was young and he was brought up by his stepfather, John Stoughton. In 1632 Cudworth was admitted pensioner at Emmanuel College, Cambridge, where his father had been a fellow, and where he was himself elected to a fellowship in 1639. Cudworth was to remain a member of the University of Cambridge for the rest of his life. His early academic career coincided with the turbulent years of the Civil War and its aftermath. Although he did not share the rigorous Calvinism for which Emmanuel College was noted, he appears to have had sympathy for the Parliamentary cause. The year 1647 was a turning point in his career. In that year he preached a sermon to the House of Commons, and was appointed Master of Clare Hall and Regius Professor of Hebrew. Seven years later he became Master of Christ's College. During the interregnum he evidently enjoyed the patronage of Cromwell's secretary of state, John Thurloe, whom he advised on suitable candidates for 'civill employments'. He was consulted by Cromwell on the question of the re-admission of the Jews to England. In 1656 he was nominated to advise parliament on a new translation of the Bible. His link to the republican regime of the Commonwealth did not prevent him from retaining his position as Master of Christ's and as Professor of Hebrew at the Restoration, posts which he held until his death in 1688.

Cudworth had several children. None of his sons survived him – one died on an expedition to India.[6] It was his daughter, Damaris, later Lady Masham, who became guardian of his philosophical legacy. Not only did she inherit his papers, but she took it upon herself to defend her father against his critics, including Leibniz. She was also the only one of his children to become a philosopher in her own right. As such she embodies the link between Cudworth and the Enlightenment, for

---

[6] Cudworth's daughter, Damaris, told Locke of the departure of her brother for India in 1684. See E.S. de Beer (ed.), *The Correspondence of John Locke* (Oxford, 1976), letter 731. Venn, *Alumni Cantabrigienses*, notes that one Charles Cudworth died in India in 1684.

she became a friend of John Locke and proponent of his philosophy.[7] It was Lady Masham's connection with Locke that led indirectly to the happy accident of Cudworth's manuscripts being mistaken for papers of John Locke's. As a result they were acquired by the British Museum (now the British Library).[8] According to Edward Chandler, the first editor of *A Treatise Concerning Eternal and Immutable Morality*, it was at the behest of Lady Masham's son, Francis Cudworth Masham, that the treatise was published in 1731.

The one work which Cudworth published in his lifetime, his magisterial *True Intellectual System of the Universe*, is an anti-determinist treatise, which seeks an accommodation of theology and philosophy. It is in large part devoted to a philosophical refutation of atheism, and a demonstration of the true idea of God as essentially good and wise. This was originally conceived as a work containing three books, of which the second and third were to deal, respectively, with the existence in nature of moral absolutes, and with freedom of the will – the subject matter of the two treatises in the present edition, *A Treatise Concerning Eternal and Immutable Morality* and *A Treatise of Freewill*. In his Preface to *The True Intellectual System*, Cudworth admits to having been surprised at how long the first book turned out to be.[9] But he defends its coherence as a single volume, in spite of the fact that he had not completed his original project. And he points out that Book 1 of his *System* touches on the themes projected for the second and third books. Thus Cudworth's treatises of *Morality* and of *Freewill* stand in integral relation to his *True Intellectual System*, for not only do they overlap at some points with the latter but, in all probability, they constitute the basis of the books on morality, liberty and necessity, originally intended for inclusion in *The True Intellectual System*.

According to his Preface to *The True Intellectual System*, Cudworth certainly intended to publish the unfinished parts of his philosophical project.[10] The question why he never completed his *System* and never published any of the manuscript works is impossible to answer satisfactorily. In the case of *Eternal and Immutable Morality*, there is

---

[7] See Luisa Simonutti, 'Damaris Cudworth Masham: una lady della repubblica di lettere', in *Studi in onore di Eugenio Garin* (Pisa, 1987), pp. 141–65, and Sarah Hutton, 'Damaris Cudworth, Lady Masham: between Platonism and Enlightenment', *British Journal for the History of Philosophy*, 1 (1993), 29–54.

[8] See the Preface to Allen's edition of *A Treatise of Freewill*.

[9] *TIS*, Preface, sig. A3⁴.   [10] *TIS*, Preface, sig. A3⁵.

evidence that he thought his work had been undermined by Henry More's publication of his ethical treatise *Enchiridion ethicum*.[11] And the manuscript evidence of his work on *Freewill* suggests that he could not decide on a suitable format for presenting his argument: the three manuscript treatises on the subject overlap considerably with one another, and could not have been intended for publication together. Lack of industry was certainly not the problem. In addition to the writings mentioned, he also prepared a monumental commentary on the Book of Daniel, which has still not been published.[12] So busy was he with his studious projects that the ecclesiastical visitors of the Parish where he had a living complained in 1686 that he neglected his Hertfordshire living.[13] It is sometimes suggested that it was Cudworth's duties as Master of Christ's College which distracted him from completing his projects. But public duties did not prevent other contemporaries of his from publishing books. On the other hand, according to his friend and colleague, Henry More, it was pressure of college and domestic business which prevented him from publishing a second volume in 1678.[14] It is not beyond the bounds of possibility that a combination of native caution along with political and ecclesiastical factors served to exacerbate his painstaking and prolix manner of argument, and thereby delay publication.

Although he enjoyed the patronage of the influential Finch family (his *System* is dedicated to the Lord Chancellor, Heneage Finch), and retained his mastership of Christ's College at the Restoration, his links with the republican regime of the interregnum were not forgotten.[15] Furthermore, his liberal theological temper was one which was out of tune with that of the Restoration ecclesiastical regimen: although he remained a member of the re-established Church of England, his extreme latitudinarianism, his theological leanings towards the het-

---

[11] See J. Crossley and R.C. Christie (eds.), *The Diary and Correspondence of John Worthington*, 3 vols., (Manchester: Chetham Society, 1847–86), vol. II, pp. 157–73.

[12] London, British Library, Add. MS 4987. According to Birch, Cudworth originally intended to publish this in 1658.

[13] MS Tanner 30, fo. 45. Cited in J. Spurr, *Restoration Church of England, 1646–1689* (New Haven, Conn., 1991).

[14] Henry More to Edmund Elys, 2nd June 1678. E. Elys, *Letters on Several Subjects* (London, 1694), pp. 28–9.

[15] M.H. Nicolson, 'Christ's College and the Latitude Men', *Modern Philology*, 27 (1929–30), 35–53. On the Restoration reaction to latitudinarianism in Cambridge, see John Gascoigne, *Cambridge in the Age of Enlightenment* (Cambridge, 1989).

erodox ante-Nicene father, Origen, and his strong millenarianism probably did not endear him to his peers in the Church hierarchy. While his anti-Hobbism may have counter-balanced his latitudinarianism in the eyes of Restoration Church hierarchy, his historico-philosophical method was soon to be regarded as outmoded.[16] Whatever the theological politics of Cudworth's position, in philosophical terms, Cudworth kept his finger on the pulse of new developments in philosophy: in addition to addressing the philosophy of Descartes and Hobbes, *The True Intellectual System* contains a refutation of Spinoza's *Tractatus theologico-politicus* (1670).

Although *A Treatise Concerning Eternal and Immutable Morality* was not published until 1731, it probably circulated in manuscript before then. Its publication history therefore gives it a somewhat unusual position in relation to the history of philosophy because it was published in a very different context from that of its original production. It was retrieved from manuscript obscurity by Edward Chandler, Bishop successively of Lichfield and of Durham, and published at a time of lively debate on ethical rationalism, the nature of moral obligation and the foundations of moral certainty, a debate which was sparked by Samuel Clarke's Boyle lectures.[17] When Cudworth wrote *Eternal and Immutable Morality*, the Church of England had still not reached a satisfactory accommodation with religious dissent. It had not worked out the latitudinarian compromise, which took it into the eighteenth century. The political upheavals of the Civil War and interregnum were fresh in people's memories, as were the theological debates occasioned by the predestinarian Calvinism which characterized establishment Puritanism of those years. On the philosophical front, Cartesianism was still a relatively new phenomenon, as was the philosophy of Thomas Hobbes, who already bore the brand of atheist materialist. The Royal

[16] A decade after the publication of *TIS*, Cudworth's erudition met its match in Richard Bentley, who neatly exposed Cudworth's lack of historical and philological rigour in his *Epistola ad Millium* of 1691. See A. Grafton, *Defenders of the Text* (Cambridge, Mass., 1991), pp. 15–17. On the abandonment of the Platonizing *prisca sapientia* by the next generation of theologians, see S. Hutton, 'Henry More, Edward Stillingfleet and the Decline of *Moses atticus*', in R. Kroll, R. Ashcraft and P. Zagorin (eds.), *Philosophy, Science and Religion in England* (Cambridge, 1992), pp. 68–84.

[17] Clarke's Boyle lectures were given in 1704 and 1705, and published as, respectively, *Demonstration of the Being and Attributes of God* (London, 1706) and *A Discourse Concerning the Unchangeable Obligations of Natural Religion, and the Truth and Certainty of the Christian Revelation* (London, 1707).

Society, founded in 1660, was in its infancy. John Locke had not yet made his mark as a philosopher, and Isaac Newton (1642–1727) was still a young Cambridge don. When *Eternal and Immutable Morality* was eventually published, the Hanoverian succession was already into the second generation, monarchical government and Protestant ascendancy thereby secured. Thinking theologians had had to face a new philosophical challenge in the form of Locke, whose *Essay Concerning Human Understanding* (1690) had swept aside the traditional grounds of religious apologetics and the innatist epistemology that underpinned it. Newton was assured a place in the pantheon of the great and the good, his scientific theories having been put to the service of Anglican apologetics in the face a new enemy, deism. Cudworth, the rational apologist for religion who was convinced overwhelmingly of the importance of philosophy for theology, re-appeared at a time when the philosophers seemed to have successfully undermined religious belief. Cudworth, who had sharpened his arguments on the flintstone of Hobbes in the 1670s, re-emerged into debates that could be traced back to the challenge of Hobbist relativism. He emerged alongside the ethical rationalists, Clarke, Balguy and Price, that is, as a posthumous participant in the debates on the foundations of morality whose terms he had helped to shape. His first editor, Edward Chandler, indicated the relevance of the *Treatise* to eighteenth-century issues, as he observed in his Preface to the 1731 edition:

> It is well known, that the loose principles, with regard to morality, that are opposed in this book, are defended by too many in our time. It is hoped also that the new controversies springing up, that have some relation to this subject, may be cleared and shortened by the reasons herein proposed.[18]

In order to understand how *Eternal and Immutable Morality* could find a place in such a different world, it is important to recognize that the Cambridge Platonist label which attaches to Cudworth does not denote a mystical movement isolated from the pressures of the time, nostalgically taking refuge in the idealism of Plato and the arcana of Plotinus. On the contrary, the Platonism of the sobriquet extends to the philosophical core of Plato's dialogues and represents only one aspect of the philosophical formation of the group with which Cudworth is

---

[18] *EIM*, p. xi.

associated. The Cambridge Platonists were well acquainted with developments in seventeenth-century philosophy and science. They were whole-hearted Copernicans, who had read Bacon and respected Galileo and Harvey. It was a Cambridge Platonist (Henry More) who was the first proponent of Cartesianism in England. Cudworth read and criticized not just Descartes, but Hobbes and Spinoza as well. The philosophy of spirit which More and Cudworth formulated was not a retreat from modernity, but a contribution to contemporary debates about the viability of the mechanical philosophy.[19] Cudworth's arguments for the natural basis of morality are directed against the materialism and ethical relativism of Hobbes. Although he denied that the mind was a *tabula rasa*, his epistemology contains some striking parallels to John Locke.

When reading Cudworth it is important to recognize that he was a theologian as well as a philosopher. For Cudworth philosophy and theology are intimately interconnected. His theological priorities interact with his philosophy in a number of ways. First of all, like the other Cambridge Platonists, he accorded reason a significant role in religion. As a religious apologist he employed philosophical argument in support of the fundamentals of religious belief. Secondly, he was profoundly aware of the theological implications of philosophical positions – for instance, he argued that materialism undermines morality and leads to atheism. Conversely, he saw that theological doctrines had implications for philosophy: he was especially critical of voluntarism, that is the doctrine that the divine will is the fundamental determinant in God's government of the world. Against the voluntarists he maintained that 'there is a nature of goodness, and a nature of wisdom antecedent to the will of God, which is the rule and measure of it' (p. 187). To subordinate divine wisdom to God's will among the divine attributes destroys certainty and leads to scepticism. This was a position which Cudworth maintained against theologians and philosophers alike. Apart from a minor figure mentioned in *Eternal and Immutable Morality*, Joannes Szydlovius, he does not name his Calvinist opponents; but he could well have had in mind Cambridge theologians like William

---

[19] See A. Gabbey, 'Cudworth, More and the Mechanical Analogy', in R. Kroll, R. Ashcroft and P. Zagorin (eds.), *Philosophy, Science and Religion in England* (Cambridge, 1992), pp. 109–21. T. Gregory, 'Studi sull'atomismo del seicento: III, Cudworth e l'atomismo', *Giornale critico della filosofia italiana*, 46 (1967), 528–41.

Perkins (1558–1602) and Anthony Tuckney (1599–1670). The philosopher whom he criticizes for attributing too much to the divine will is Descartes. The concomitant of Cudworth's theological anti-voluntarism is his insistence on the freedom of the will.[20] This is a tenet which he shares with the other Cambridge Platonists, and other liberal opponents of hard-line Calvinists, in particular the Dutch Arminians. This emphasis on freewill is probably indebted to Erasmus. It also accounts for Cudworth's admiration for Origen. Furthermore, Cudworth's concern with seventeenth-century theological issues explains not just his interest in the problem of freewill, but the fact that his writings on the subject address the issue in scholastic terms, debating topics such as indifferency of will, and whether it is the will or understanding that decides how we should act.

The dominant themes of Cudworth's writings are ones which racked the Church in England in his youth: debates about freewill and predestination had been such hot topics that they were proscribed by royal proclamation in 1626. The apparently intractable theological problems of the pre-Civil War acquired a new edge with the appearance of challenging new philosophical forms of determinism: the mechanical philosophy of Hobbes and Descartes, and the material pantheism of Spinoza. For Cudworth, philosophical determinism was the counterpart of predestinarian voluntarism in theology. Not only did he, like Henry More, see these philosophies as having atheistical implications, but also as having implications for moral conduct. Against the relativism of Hobbes he argued that goodness and the principles of morality are absolute. As he put it in one of his unpublished treatises on freewill, 'one of ye greatest Arcanums both in Phylosophy and Morality' is 'y^t there is in Nature an αὐτὸ ἀγαθόν and Ipsum Bonum an absolute good and perfection which is ye standard and measure both of Power and Liberty and also wisdome' (Add. MS 4979, fol. 38).

One difficulty in reading Cudworth and assessing his philosophy is that he often presents his philosophical arguments in antique dress, citing precedents from ancient philosophy and arguing against particular classical philosophers. None the less, it is also important not to be

---

[20] On divine will and providence, see F. Oakley, *Omnipotence, Covenant, and Order* (Ithaca, N.Y., 1984); A. Funkenstein, *Theology and the Scientific Imagination* (Princeton, N.J., 1986); M. Osler, *Divine Will and the Mechanical Philosophy* (Cambridge, 1994). Also, V.J. Bourke, *Will in Western Thought* (New York, 1964).

deceived into thinking that Cudworth was a mere antiquarian, or at best a doxographer. To those inducted in twentieth-century approaches to philosophy, it seems strange to discuss issues in contemporary philosophy by examining ancient philosophy – yet this is precisely what Cudworth does in the case, for instance, of Protagoras, whom he presents as a materialist relativist and treats in *Eternal and Immutable Morality* as a kind of stalking horse for Thomas Hobbes. Underlying Cudworth's approach is his conviction that truth is one and that philosophy is a unified system through which to arrive at knowledge of the truth: 'it is but one truth and knowledge that is in all the understandings in the world' –

> when innumerable created understandings direct themselves to the contemplation of the same universal and immutable truths, they do all of them but as it were listen to one and the same original voice of the eternal wisdom that is never silent, and the several conceptions of those truths in their minds, are but like several echoes of the same *verba mentis* [conceptions] of the divine intellect resounding in them. (see below, p. 132).

So, while Cudworth was receptive to contemporary philosophy, he did not accept its claims to novelty, but underlined its continuity with the past. As Passmore put it, Cudworth's view of philosophical debate was that

> the contestants might change their name, or might improve their technical apparatus, but they could not seriously modify the fundamental structure of their arguments. He was impressed by the recurrence of certain patterns of philosophical controversy; he was not impressed by the claim of his contemporaries that they had shaken themselves free from tradition in order to embark upon an enterprise quite novel, in a manner untrammelled by the errors of the past. In an age which insisted above all upon originality, he insisted upon the importance of tradition.[21]

Cudworth's understanding of philosophical tradition was one very much moulded by the Renaissance notion of *philosophia perennis*, or perennial philosophy. Among the figures who did much to shape the history of philosophy attaching to this idea was, first of all, Marsilio Ficino, who construed it rather as a *prisca theologia*, or ancient theology, a pagan tradition of revealed truth derived from Moses and imparted by

[21] J.A. Passmore, *Ralph Cudworth, an Interpretation* (Cambridge, 1951), p. 13.

succeeding generations of philosophers. Also important for constructing this pedigree of ancient wisdom was the third-century historical doxography of philosophy, Diogenes Laertius' *Lives of the Philosophers*, the Greek text of which had been recovered and translated by Ambrogio Traversari in 1472. In addition to offering a model for the history of philosophy, this was an important source of Epicurian thought and Stoicism. Besides using Diogenes Laertius as a source, Cudworth also draws on Sextus Empiricus, whom he uses both as a source of sceptical arguments and as a means of supplementing his knowledge of ancient philosophy from sources other than Aristotle and Plato. It is Cudworth's treatment of all philosophies as participants in *philosophia perennis* that enabled him to write about Cartesianism in *Eternal and Immutable Morality* as a modern manifestation of Democritean atomism. Likewise, in *The True Intellectual System*, Hobbes is seen as a materialist after the model of Anaximander, and Spinoza as a hylozoist. In *Eternal and Immutable Morality* the debate with Hobbes is set up, through a discussion of Plato's *Theaetetus*, in which Protagoras figures as an ethical relativist and materialist to boot. It might be added that Cudworth interprets Plato with one eye on Sextus Empiricus, a factor which distinguishes his reading of Plato from that of his Renaissance forebears. Cudworth was conscious of the difference between his interpretation of Platonic philosophy and that of the great translators and editors of Plato in the Renaissance, Marsilio Ficino and Jean de Serres, who, he notes, wrote before the recovery of corpuscular philosophy.[22]

Another important element in Cudworth's philosophy is Stoicism. Although he was highly critical of many aspects of Stoicism (such as the doctrine of repeated cycles of existence of the world), Cudworth is indebted to the Stoics for key terms in his conceptual vocabulary. This is most strikingly evident in the two treatises reproduced here, that is to say, in his epistemology and his moral psychology. Three examples might be singled out for particular mention: first of all his use of the Stoic concept of the common notions (*koinai ennoiai*) or innate principles of knowledge in the soul. He also adopts the Stoic term *prolepsis*, or 'anticipation', for the innate properties of the mind whereby it is predisposed to understand the world. The key concept in his account of freewill is that of the autonomy of the individual soul to

---

[22] See below p. 37.

direct its actions towards the good. The term he adopts to express this concept of 'self-power' is the Stoic *hegemonikon*, denoting the ruling principle of the soul.[23] In Cudworth Stoicism is blended with Platonism: for example, he integrates the Stoic common notions with the Platonic theory of recollection (*anamnesis*); in his account of the operations of the soul he deploys the terminology of Plotinus; and it was from Plato that he derived his term *ectype* to express the relationship of the physical order to the intellectual. Cudworth undoubtedly found a precedent for combining Stoicism and Platonism in the early Church Fathers, notably Origen. His debt to Patristic thought is borne out by his use of the term *schesis*, a key term in his epistemology, which he uses in the Patristic sense of 'relation' rather than the ancient Greek sense of 'condition' or 'habit'.

A Treatise Concerning Eternal and Immutable Morality

In 1664 Cudworth told John Worthington that he was working on a treatise of 'Natural Ethicks ... which I began above a year agoe'.[24] This information suggests that *A Treatise Concerning Eternal and Immutable Morality* was probably begun around 1662. The ethical position which Cudworth takes in the treatise is strongly anti-relativist. At the beginning he argues for the existence of moral absolutes, that good and evil, justice and injustice, as well as 'Wisdom, knowledge, and understanding are eternal and self-subsistent things', existing independently of the mind and of the physical world. This is a position which Cudworth had maintained from an early point in his academic career. (In 1644 he had defended the thesis that the principles of good and evil are eternal and indispensable.)[25] The main emphasis of *A Treatise Concerning Eternal and Immutable Morality* is, however, epistemolo-

---

[23] Although Cudworth's application of Stoicism is far more developed than theirs, other Protestant theologians had employed the terms 'common notions' and 'prolepsis' in their discussions of the rational soul, most notably Philip Melanchthon. Their source was probably Cicero. See J.E. Platt, *Reformed Thought and Scholasticism* (Leiden, 1982). In antiquity, Stoic epistemology was taken up by several of the later Platonists, such as Antiochus of Ascalon (b. 130 AD). See J. Dillon, *The Middle Platonists* (London, 1977), chapter 2. On Stoicism, see J.M. Rist, *The Stoics* (Berkeley, Los Angeles and London, 1978).

[24] See Worthington, *Diary and Correspondence*, vol. II, p. 158.

[25] 'Dantur boni et mali rationes aeternae et indispensabiles', published in 1651 (British Library, Thomason Tracts).

gical: the treatise contains the fullest discussion of innatist epistemology to emanate from England in the seventeenth century.

The treatise is divided into four books. The first of these poses the fundamental question asked by Socrates in Plato's *Euthyphro*: whether God wills things because they are good, or whether things are good because God wills them. Cudworth's position is that God, being supremely good, wills things because they are good. After a brief history of the opposing view, where he groups Hobbes with Protagoras and Epicurus, he denies that right and wrong are relative notions, and that the principles of right and wrong are conventional in their basis. He also argues against those who, like Descartes, found the principles of right and wrong, as well as truth and falsehood, in the will of God. Instead, he argues that moral principles are such by nature and not by authority; that they are founded in the goodness and wisdom of God, not the will of God.

The second book continues the argument for the immutable nature of all things by dealing with the sceptical issues implicit in the philosophy of Protagoras as represented in Plato's *Theaetetus*. Cudworth argues that Protagoras' sense-based epistemology and his subjective principle that 'man is the measure of all things' destroy all certainty and undermines the basis of morality. He then gives an account of the 'mechanical or atomical philosophy' of Descartes and Gassendi, which he sees as a revival of ancient doctrines, and which explains all things in terms of the primary properties of corporeal extension (shape, size, position and motility), deduced by reason and not from sense impressions. In Cudworth's view, the mechanical philosophy gives an intelligible account of the natural world, because it is coherent and accessible to reason.

In the third book Cudworth commences the account of his epistemology with a discussion of sense knowledge. Here his debt to Descartes is most apparent, particularly in his distinction between sense and intellect, in his account of the relation of soul to body, and in his discussion of sense perception. Cudworth's reservations about sense knowledge are consistent with the underlying Platonism of this thinking. He argues that knowledge derived from the senses is not true knowledge. Sense impressions are received passively. The data acquired in this way can only furnish us with particularities and superficial appearances. Moreover, the senses do not perceive external objects as they are, but, according to the mechanical hypothesis, they represent them as movements or impressions of one kind or another. Such data have to be processed by the mind before they can be understood. Knowledge is produced actively from within the mind, not received passively from without. A sensation is 'a passion in the soul', the result of corporeal movements, and perceptible by virtue of the 'natural sympathy' which the soul has for the body. Such impressions are involuntary: that is, the soul has no control over them. At best sensation is 'a certain kind of drowsy and somnolent perception' of the soul (p. 56). Although Cudworth regards sense-knowledge as inferior to knowledge generated by the mind, his position is not anti-empiricist. On the contrary, he specifically acknowledges the adequacy of the senses for providing knowledge of the external world and of the body, as well as for assisting the mind in framing hypotheses (see below, p. 57).

Book IV is the longest of the treatise, longer than the first three put together. In it Cudworth elaborates his theory of knowledge in order, he says, 'to confute scepticism or fantasticism' (the materialist view that reduces all knowledge to sense experience). Much of this section is an expansion of arguments sketched at the end of the *True Intellectual System*. Cudworth distinguishes two types of perception: one belongs to the lower part of the soul as a passive receiver of corporeal impressions; the other is a higher 'energy' of the soul, which reflects on itself and its own ideas, and compares the intelligible components of data received via the senses (what he calls the 'scheses' of external objects). All knowledge, he argues, involves the activity of mind; 'knowledge is an inward and active energy of the mind itself' (p. 73). The mind is furnished with the concepts (*noemata*) needed for arriving at knowledge. 'The mind', Cudworth writes, 'cannot know anything, but by something of its own, that is native, domestic and familiar to it' (p. 74). Cognition entails anticipation: Cudworth employs the Stoic term *prolepsis* but links it with Plato's theory of *anamnesis*, for knowing involves recollection (rather as when one recognizes the face of a friend in a crowd). But this is not simply a process of matching the ideas in the mind against external objects. Not all knowledge is external in its origins: many ideas (e.g. wisdom, honesty and justice) are generated by the mind itself. Knowledge is acquired deductively, not inductively: the mind, to use Cudworth's expression, *descends* towards particulars; and, in comprehending the external world, the mind perceives not the external appearance of things but the relational constants which reveal their immutable essences.

To illustrate the activity of the mind, as opposed to the passivity of the senses, Cudworth employs several key images: first a clock reflected in a mirror, seen by an eye, and seen by an eye attached to the mind (p. 85). In the first it is merely reflected; in the second case, the eye registers the colours as well. But it is the mind which registers the disposition of the parts and their function. By perceiving the relationship between them (for which Cudworth uses the Greek term *schesis*), the mind can recognize the object as a clock and not just a conglomerate of colours and metals. Similarly, words on a page of a book are just inky scrawls to an animal or to an illiterate (p. 99), but to someone who knows how to read, the words have meaning. The argument has an aesthetic dimension: to an animal music is mere sounds, to the rational listener these sounds are harmonious. The beauty of a beautiful landscape or picture is lost on animals, but apparent to the human mind.

Knowledge of the external world is possible because the world is intelligible, it bears 'the stamp of intellectuality'. Cudworth illustrates this by extending his book analogy to become the metaphor of the book of nature: the literate mind could not read meanings in a book unless they had first been put there. Likewise, the natural world, in its orderliness and in the disposition of its parts, contains meaningful signatures, the meaning having been placed there by the creator. Another analogy which Cudworth employs for this is architectural (p. 92): a palace is not a pile of bricks but an architecturally designed edifice. The order and relationship of the parts which make it a structure rather than a fortuitous heap of rubble are both evidence that there was a designer and are what makes it identifiable as a building to the observer. This example also illustrates the general Platonic principle at the heart of Cudworth's philosophy, that mind precedes the world, and that reality and true being belong to the metaphysical rather than the physical order of things. Cudworth expresses the relationship of true being to the created world, the world of sense, in classically Platonic terms of archtype and ectype, form and copy.

The view that mental or intellectual being is more real than material being is consistent with Descartes' assertion that the soul is more knowable than body. It does, of course, raise the question of the ontological status of the ideas, or 'conceptions of the mind'. Cudworth insists that they are not derived from body. Nor do they exist independently; rather, they are modifications of mind or intellect. He denies that they are merely figments of the human brain, and marshals a number of arguments, drawn chiefly from geometry, to demonstrate the independence of concepts from the physical world and sense experience. For example, he argues that it is possible to deduce the nature of a triangle without seeing one, by the application of Euclidean principles. Such conceptual entities are not the products of individual minds, but are the same in all minds. So absolute is their independence of the human mind and of the physical world, that they would be the same were the world to be destroyed and created anew. The mind of which conceptual entities may truly be said to be modifications is the divine mind, whence they derive their veracity, constancy, eternity and universality, and whence the human mind derives its capacity for knowledge. It is in this sense, therefore, that the human mind can be described as participating in the divine mind. And our knowledge of the external world entails a projection of ideas on to the world, leading Cudworth to the proto-Berkeleian formulation, that 'corporeal qualities' are nothing more than 'our own shadows, and the vital passive energies of our own souls' (p. 148). Furthermore, if conceptual entities belong to true being, every clear conception is true, and nothing which is false can be clearly conceived as existing. Thus the essence of truth is clear intelligibility. Although Cudworth in this way adopts the Cartesian principle of the clarity and distinctness of ideas as the criterion of certainty, he rejects as sceptical Descartes' supporting argument based on the truth of our faculties. It would, he argues be impossible even for God to construct the human mind so that it perceives falsity as true – just as it would be impossible for God to make contradictions true.

The ethical purpose of *A Treatise Concerning Eternal and Immutable Morality* resides in the fact that it supplies two major aspects of the theory of mind which underpin Cudworth's ethics. As he put it, 'the nature of morality cannot be understood without some knowledge of the nature of the soul' (p. 145). First of all, his metaphysical realism enables him to argue for a fundamental connection between the principles of morality and the principles of knowledge. If mind and intellect are 'first in the order of nature', conceptual entities must have more reality than material ones, and justice and morality, as modifications of mind, are more 'real and substantial things than the modifications of mere senseless matter'. Secondly, with regard to epistemology, Cudworth denies that the principles of morality can be deduced from sense knowledge. Accordingly he rejects the model of the mind as *tabula rasa*, and argues that only an innatist epistemology can provide knowledge of good and evil, just and unjust. There is a third, psychological, aspect of Cudworth's theory of mind, which is not dealt with in this work, but is treated in his writings on freewill. Cudworth prepares for this at the end of *A Treatise Concerning Eternal and Immutable Morality* when he asserts that moral principles are, like immutable ideas, 'anticipations', and that these are not 'mere intellectual forms', but derive from what he calls 'some other more inward and vital principle'. He does not elaborate on what this principle might be beyond describing it as 'a natural determination to do some things and avoid others' (p. 145). This is a formulation which corresponds to his concept of the will as *hegemonikon* in *A Treatise of Freewill*, where it is linked to the life-sustaining function of the soul. This underlines the continuity between both treatises, and confirms that *Eternal and Immutable Morality* is more of a prologue to a larger treatise on ethics than the discussion of ethics that the title implies.

A Treatise of Freewill

The three draft treatises on 'Liberty and Necessity' continue the same project as *Eternal and Immutable Morality* by taking the discussion forward to more obviously ethical questions. They all deal with the problem of moral responsibility, and with the psychology of autonomous action. They can be described as psychological both in the old sense of giving an account of the soul, and in the more modern sense of discussing mental factors which affect behaviour. For the will is the ruling principle which co-ordinates the functions of the soul and directs the actions of the individual being.

The only one of these treatises to be published, that printed here as *A Treatise of Freewill*, is the shortest of the three. As in the case of the other two, much of it is taken up with technical discussion, theological as well as philosophical. Chapters 18–27 deal with the objections of determinists to the freedom of the will, especially those of Hobbes but also of Pomponazzi and various unnamed others. And chapter 3 raises difficulties connected with a deterministic position – many of them drawn from Origen. In his concept of freewill as a power of the soul, combining the functions of intellect and volition, Cudworth dispenses with traditional faculty psychology, which divided the will from intellect as separate faculties of the soul. He is thus able to sidestep the two main opposing traditions concerning the relationship of reason and will in Western theology: the Thomist view, according to which the will follows the directives of the intellect, and the voluntarist position of Scotus and Ockham which subordinates intellect to will. In his critique of the doctrine of the indifference of the will he undoubtedly had Suarez and his followers in mind, although he does not name his theological opponents.

For Cudworth, moral behaviour is not shaped by external incentives and disincentives, but is founded on the principles of virtue innate to the soul. Cudworth conceives of the will as the self-determining power of the soul which predisposes it towards the good. This drive towards the good is the spring and motivation of all action. In *Freewill* it is described as a kind of premonition, 'a certain vaticination, presage, scent, and odour of one *summum bonum*, one supreme highest good transcending all others' (p. 174). In the manuscripts he also uses the term 'instinct'. This innate tendency towards goodness may be compared on the one hand to Henry More's concept of a 'boniform faculty' and to Shaftesbury's moral sense. It is this idea of the will as a bias towards the good which underlies his lengthy attack on those who argue that the freedom of the will is a 'liberty of indifference'. In Cudworth's view the liberty of the will is the prerequisite for moral responsibility. We cannot be blamed for what we do out of necessity any more than a watch can be blamed for not working properly. The fault in each case rests with the external cause, whatever forces us (in the first case), or the maker of the watch (in the second). The root concept of the treatise is that of the will as *hegemonikon*, or power of self-determination. Without power to direct our own actions, we would be little better than puppets, 'dead machines moved by gimmers and wires' (p. 195). The *hegemonikon* is not just the foundation of moral responsibility (that which earns us 'praise or blame'), but it is a principle of individuation: it is the freedom to act for oneself which also defines the self. It means that 'men have something in their own power, add something of their own, so that they can change themselves and determine themselves'

(p. 163). The *hegemonikon* individuates not only by differentiation from others, but by co-ordinating the functions of the soul. Cudworth conceives of the will as a unitive power of the soul. It is 'the soul as reduplicated upon itself, and self-comprehensive' (p. 185). As co-ordinator and director of the various appetites and functions of the soul, the will is the whole person. As he puts it in one of the manuscript treatises 'On Liberty and Necessity', it is the unifying soul which constitutes the self, 'denominates the whole man as such', and 'determines all ye passive capability of every man's nature, and makes every man such as he is' (Add. MS 4979, fol. 6). The will is especially identifiable with the individual person in the sense that it is the indelible mark of our humanity. Since it is that which predisposes the soul towards the good, it is therefore the means to improve the soul, to increase the perfection of the soul: it is 'a self-promoting, self-improving power' (p. 185). Although, for Cudworth, freewill is therefore a crowning attribute of human beings, as he argues in chapter 13, it is none the less a mark of human imperfection, since only imperfect beings require perfecting (see chapter 17). For this reason, since God is perfect, freewill cannot properly be ascribed to Him.

A Treatise of Freewill is the shortest of Cudworth's three writings on freewill. These elaborate a number of important elements that are only implicit here, in particular the practical and social aspects of his ethics. The unpublished manuscripts make clearer the practical dimension of Cudworth's moral theory, that it is 'Action that gives denomination to a Persone' (Add. MS 4981, fol. 16). In all three treatises the central element is goodness rather than duty. And goodness is a disposition of the whole person, 'ye inward dispositions of ye Mind & Will' (4980, fol. 10). The good as such is not defined here, that having been done in *The True Intellectual System*. There Cudworth writes unequivocally that the good is God. God is, he says referring to Plato, '*The very Idea or Essence of Good*' (*TIS*, p. 204). This is a definition that Cudworth repeats elsewhere, for example in the sermon he preached before the House of Commons in 1647, where he states 'That God is also God, because he is the highest and most perfect good', and that 'he is Essentially the most perfect *Good*'.[26] In identifying the good with God, Cudworth underlines the religious dimension of his philosophy. In

---

[26] Patrides, pp. 101–2.

religion as in morals, he advocated a *lived* goodness, not a theoretical goodness: 'the *Life* of divine truths is better expressed in Actions than in Words'.[27] The good conceived by Cudworth is not merely a metaphysical entity. Even when defined in terms of the deity, it unfolds into moral principles that entail the idea of practical action. This goodness, 'in which the Essence of the Deity principally consists', comprises on the one hand 'Benignity' and on the other hand the fountainhead of morality:

> it comprehends Eminently all *Vertue and Justice*, the *Divine Nature* being the *First Pattern* hereof; for which cause *Vertue* is defined to be, An *Assimilation to the Deity*. *Justice* and *Honesty* are no *Factitious* things, made by the Will and Command of the more Powerful to the Weaker, but they are *Nature* and *perfection*, and descend downward to us from the Deity. (*TIS*, p. 205)

Cudworth's emphasis on the primacy of goodness among the divine attributes, and his insistence on an ethics of action, a lived Christianity guided by the right disposition of heart and mind, place him firmly alongside the other Cambridge Platonists. Although he shares much with his Cambridge-Platonist colleagues, his philosophy is the fullest and most developed treatment of the outlook and ideas which they had in common.

Cudworth's philosophy is often treated as a historical curiosity, even among those who have taken the trouble to read him. It is tempting to argue that he had no appreciable impact, on the grounds that his *System* was never completed and his other writings were either never printed or were published posthumously. The argument that the content of *Eternal and Immutable Morality* and *Freewill* was not available to Cudworth's contemporaries or immediate successors might seem compelling until one acknowledges the possibility of manuscript circulation of Cudworth's writings, and also the fact that the basics of Cudworth's position in these treatises were available in the writings he published in his lifetime. Although Cudworth is prone to wordiness, he is a thoroughly self-consistent thinker, whose posthumously published writings develop themes and positions enunciated in earlier writings. In his *True Intellectual System* he anticipates the ethical position he elaborates in *Eternal and Immutable Morality* and gives an indication of the main

---

[27] ibid., p. 108.

points of his account of will. For example, in the *System* he asserts that 'the Differences of *Just* and *Unjust, Honest,* and *Dishonest,* are greater *Realities* in Nature than the *Differences* of *Hard* and *Soft, Hot* and *Cold, Moist* and *Dry*' (*TIS,* p. 858). His second sermon preached before the House of Commons attacks externalist accounts of moral obligation in terms which anticipate the phraseology of *Eternal and Immutable Morality,* 'as if *good* and *evil, just* and *unjust* (as some philosophers dreamed) were not φύσει but νόμῳ and δόξα only, had no reality in nature, but depend on certain laws, enforced by outward punishments or mere opinions'. In the last part of the *System,* Cudworth adumbrates the epistemology more fully stated in *Eternal and Immutable Morality*: that knowledge is eternal (*TIS,* p. 826) and that mind precedes things (p. 859). He talks in terms of *ectype* and *archtype* (p. 853) and denies that the mind is a *tabula rasa* (p. 861). He attacks 'a Modern Atheistick Pretender to Wit' (i.e. Hobbes) for reducing mental processes to local motion of corporeal particles, and refutes Protagoras' claim that man is the measure of all things, and that all knowledge is sense-knowledge (*TIS,* p. 852). Cudworth's account of the will is embryonic in the *System,* as compared with his manuscript writings on the subject, but he employs the same terminology for the same fundamental concepts that he describes in *Freewill.* He insists that there can be no system of morality without freewill (*TIS,* p. 869); conceives of freewill as a form of self-activity, using the term *autokinesis* (as opposed to *heterokinesis*) to express the idea of the soul's autonomy or 'self-active power'. Against the Hobbesian account that memory 'is nothing but *Fading* and *Decaying Sense,* and all our *Volitions* but Mechanick Motions caused from the *Actions* or [in]trusions of Bodies *upon us*', he denies that

> Mental *Conceptions* [can] be said to be the Action of *Bodies* without and the meer *Passion of the Thinker*; and least of all [are] *Volitions* such, there being plainly here, something ἐφ' ἡμῖν, *In our own Power,* by means whereof, we become a *Principle of Actions,* accordingly deserving *Commendation* or *Blame,* that is, something of *Self-Activity.* (*TIS,* p. 851)

Over forty years ago Passmore noted Cudworth's importance for Locke and more recently Stephen Darwall has re-opened the question of Cudworth's relationship to Kant, by noting parallels between the two. Cudworth certainly deserves attention for his possible impact on these and other philosophers. But he also deserves attention in his own right. By making important statements of his philosophy available in a readable modern edition, I hope to increase the likelihood of Cudworth being read on his own terms, as well as to lay the ground for a redrawing of the historical account in such a way as to re-integrate Cudworth into the philosophical developments of the early Enlightenment.

Chronology

1617 born in Aller, Somerset.
1632 enters the University of Cambridge as a student at Emmanuel College.
1635 graduates BA.
1637 Descartes, *Discours de la méthode*.
1639 graduates MA and is appointed to a fellowship at Emmanuel College.
1641 Descartes, *Méditations*.
1642 outbreak of Civil War.
1644 abolition of the Church of England.
   ejection of Cambridge dons who refused to subscribe to the covenant imposed by Parliament.
   Descartes, *Principia philosophiae*.
1647 appointed Master of Clare Hall and Regius Professor of Hebrew; preaches a sermon to the House of Commons.
1649 execution of Charles I.
1651 Cudworth becomes DD.
   Hobbes, *Leviathan*.
1652 Hobbes, *De corpore politico*.
1653 Oliver Cromwell becomes Lord Protector.
1654 appointed Master of Christ's College (a post he held until his death).
1655 advises Cromwell on the re-admission of the Jews to England. Meets Menasseh ben Israel.
1660 restoration of the monarchy, and re-establishment of the Church of England.
1667 Henry More, *Enchiridion ethicum*.
1670 Spinoza, *Tractatus theologico-politicus*.
1678 *The True Intellectual System of the Universe* published.
   Cudworth installed prebendary of Gloucester.
   'Popish Plot'.
1688 dies.

Further reading

(All items published in London, unless otherwise indicated)

A Treatise Concerning Eternal and Immutable Morality and *A Treatise of Freewill* were first printed posthumously. The former appeared in 1731, edited by Edward Chandler (facsimile reprint, New York, 1976). It was reprinted in the third volume of Harrison's edition of *The True Intellectual System of the Universe* (1845). A Latin translation, *De aeternis et immutabilibus iusti et honesti notionibus singularis*, by the German scholar J.L. Mosheim, was printed with his translation of Cudworth's *System* (see below). There is now a French translation by J.L. Bretau (Paris, 1995). The *Treatise* is the work of Cudworth most often reprinted in excerpt: L.A.S. Bigge, *British Moralists* (Oxford, 1897), G.R. Cragg (ed.), *The Cambridge Platonists* (New York, 1968), D.D. Raphael, *The British Moralists* (Oxford, 1969) and J.B. Schneewind's anthology, *Moral Philosophy from Montaigne to Kent* (Cambridge, 1990).

A Treatise of Freewill, ed. J. Allen (1838), is the shortest of three treatises on liberty and necessity in the British Library, London (Add. MSS 4978–82). There exists one other unpublished manuscript, Cudworth's 'Commentary on the Seventy Weeks of Daniel' (British Library, Add. MSS 4986–7). The original manuscripts of both the *System* and the *Treatise Concerning Eternal and Immutable Morality* are no longer extant.

In his own lifetime Cudworth published a number of sermons: *The Union of Christ and the Church* (1642), *A Discourse Concerning the True Notion of the Lord's Supper* (1642), *A Sermon Preached before the Honourable House of Commons* (1647), *A Sermon Preached before the Honourable Society of Lincolnes-Inne* (1647). He also published the thesis he defended when he graduated BD in 1644, *Dantur rationes boni et mali aeternae et indispensabiles* (1651). His major philosophical work, *The True Intellectual System of the Universe* (1678), was republished by Thomas Birch (1743, rpt. 1839) and by J. Harrison (1845) (with notes from Mosheim's translation). It was translated into Latin by J.L. Mosheim, *Radulphi Cudworthi systema intellectualis hujus universi* (Jena, 1733, repr. Leiden, 1773) and into Italian by Luigi Benedetti *Sistema intellettuale del mondo*, 5 vols. (Pavia, 1823). His *System* was reprinted in facsimile (Stuttgart-Bad Cannstatt, 1964), and in an abbreviated form by Thomas Wise, with the title *A Confutation of the Reason and Philosophy of Atheism being an Abridgement or an Improvement of what Dr Cudworth Offered in his 'True Intellectual System'* (1706, repr. 1732).

The most important modern study of Cudworth is J.A. Passmore, *Ralph Cudworth, an Interpretation* (Cambridge, 1951), which focuses on *A Treatise Concerning Eternal and Immutable Morality* and the three treatises on liberty and necessity. This has now been supplemented by Stephen Darwall's chapter on Cudworth in *The British Moralists and the Internal Ought* (Cambridge, 1992), chapter 5. *A Treatise Concerning Eternal and Immutable Morality* is discussed in J. Martineau, *Types of Ethical Theory*, 2 vols. (Oxford, 1885), L.A.S. Bigge, *British Moralists*, 2 vols. (Oxford, 1897), E.M. Austin, *The Ethics of the Cambridge Platonists* (Philadelphia, 1935), A.N. Prior, *Logic and the Basis of Ethics* (Oxford, 1949), D.D. Raphael, *British Moralists, 1650–1800*, 2 vols. (Oxford, 1969), J.B. Schneewind, *Moral Philosophy from Montaigne to Kant* (Cambridge, 1990).

For a survey of Cudworth's philosophy see S. Hutton, 'Edward, Lord Herbert of Cherbury and the Cambridge Platonists', in S. Brown (ed.), *British Philosophy and the Enlightenment, Routledge History of Philosophy*, vol. v (London, 1996). For bibliography prior to 1988, see G.A.J. Rogers, 'Die Cambridge Platoniker' and 'Ralph Cudworth', *Ueberwegs Grundriss der Geschichte der Philosophie: die Philosophie des 17. Jahrhunderts*, vol. 3.1 (Basle, 1988). See also G. Giglioni, 'Automata Compared: Boyle, Leibniz and the Debate on the Notion of Life and Mind', *British Journal for the History of Philosophy*, 3 (1995), 249–78; S. Hutton, 'Cudworth, Boethius and the Scale of Nature', in G.A.J. Rogers, J.-M. Vienne and Y.-C. Zarka (eds.), *The Cambridge Platonists* (Dordrecht, 1996); S. Hutton, 'Ralph Cudworth, God, Mind and Nature', in R. Crocker (ed.), *Reason, Religion and Nature* (forthcoming);

G. Musca, ' "Omne genus animalium". Antichità e Medioevo in una biblioteca privata inglese del Seicento', *Quaderni Medievali*, 25 (1988), 25–76 (on Cudworth's library); R.H. Popkin, 'Cudworth', in his *The Third Force in Seventeenth-century Philosophy* (Leiden, 1992) (on Cudworth and Scepticism); D. Scott, 'Platonic Recollection and Cambridge Platonism', *Hermathena*, 149 (1990), 73–97; L. Simonutti, 'Bayle and Le Clerc as Readers of Cudworth: Elements of the Debate on *Plastic Nature* in the Dutch Learned Journals', *Geschiedenis van de Wijsbegeerte in Nederland*, 4 (1993), 147–65 (which discusses Cudworth's *fortuna* in the Enlightenment); Udo Thiel, 'Cudworth and Seventeenth-Century Theories of Consciousness', in S. Gaukroger (ed.), *The Uses of Antiquity* (Dordrecht, Boston and London, 1991).

See also now

S. Hutton 'Classicism and Baroque: A note on Mosheim's footnotes to Cudworth's The True Intellectual System of the Universe in:

M. Mulsow et. al. (eds), Johann Lorenz Mosheim ... (Wiesbaden, 1997)

[cit J. Israel, Enlightenment Contested Bibl. p. 919]

A note on the text

My aim in preparing this edition is to make available Cudworth's philosophy in an accessible form. Re-appraisal of the philosophical canon plus increasing emphasis on a more historical approach to the philosophy of the past has resulted in more consideration being given, of late, to the less famous figures in the history of philosophy. Even in this more favourable climate, Cudworth is disadvantaged by the fact that, unlike those of his fellow-countrymen, Locke and Hobbes, his writings are not available in accessible modern editions. Both Cudworth's *Treatise Concerning Eternal and Immutable Morality* and *Treatise of Freewill* are relatively free of the weight of classical learning which encumbers *The True Intellectual System*, and for that reason, these writings are relatively more accessible to modern readers. In preparing this edition, I have attempted to provide enough notes to make the text comprehensible without over-burdening it with erudition. I have followed Chandler rather than Harrison in consigning original-language quotations to the footnotes, retaining only Cudworth's translations in the main text. This will, I hope, make reading easier in an age when a knowledge of classical languages can no longer be taken for granted. The exception to this practice is where Cudworth has not provided his own translations. In such cases I have kept the original in the text, and given a modern English translation in square brackets afterwards. The other exception is where Cudworth uses Greek and Latin terminology in apposition to the English terminology. These terms are taken from his classical sources but are not, strictly, quotations from Greek or Roman philosophy. Since the readability of the English is disrupted by repetition of such terms, and since Cudworth's habit of inserting Greek terms does not amount to a consistent philosophical vocabulary, I have normally retained such terms only on their first appearance in a particular passage and have deleted what seem to be otiose excess. On a few occasions I have inserted an English translation after a term not explained by Cudworth. Cudworth clearly observed a different standard in quotations from those normally observed today. I have tried to indicate in the notes the occasions where he has not been entirely faithful to the original Latin or Greek. This is sometimes explicable in terms of his sources, but often he makes wholesale adjustments to suit the grammatical flow of his argument. All such interpolations are placed in square brackets. I have based my edition of *Freewill* on the Allen edition of 1838, checked against the manuscript (BL, Add. MS 4978). In the case of *A Treatise Concerning Eternal and Immutable Morality* I have used the Chandler first edition. Unfortunately there is no extant manuscript against which to check it. Spelling and punctuation have been modernized throughout. Finally, in the interests of perspicuity, I have on occasion taken liberties with Cudworth's baroque sentences, subdividing the lengthier ones when this can be done without distorting his meaning.

A Treatise Concerning Eternal and Immutable Morality

Contents

Book I

superior to wisdom, which measures and determines his wisdom, as this does his will. A mystical or enigmatical representation of the nature of God.

Book II

CHAPTER I That, to avoid the force of what is above demonstrated, some philosophers have denied that there was any immutable nature or essence, affirming all being and knowledge to be fantastical and relative, of whom Protagoras, the Abderite, was the chief: whose intent in proposing it, and a consequence thereof was, the destroying of all morality, and to disapprove the absolute and immutable nature of good and evil, just and unjust. CHAPTER II The pretences or grounds for this opinion considered. That it was grounded on the Heraclitical philosophy, which introduced a moveable essence, affirming that nothing stood, but all things moved. Protagoras' inference from hence, who to the Heraclitical added the old atomical Phoenician philosophy, and by this mixture made up his own. CHAPTER III That the atomical or mechanical philosophy was known to Protagoras, who lived before Democritus. A brief account of it. That by the motion of particles all things are generated and corrupted is asserted by him, and that all sensible qualities are nothing without us, but only passions and sensations in us. CHAPTER IV That the atomical philosophy is more ancient than the Trojan war, and was invented by one Moschus, a Sidonian. That this Moschus, the Phoenician, is the same with Moschus the physiologer, who is the same with Moses, the Jewish lawgiver. That Plato and Aristotle were not unacquainted with this Phoenician philosophy, which was rejected by Plato, because abused to scepticism, as also by Aristotle; but revived by Epicurus, who so blended it with impiety and immorality, that it soon sunk again. It hath been successfully restored in the last age. CHAPTER V That the paradoxes Protagoras and others grounded on this atomical philosophy are absurd and contradictious, and inconsequent from it; and the assertion that nothing is absolutely true, but only relatively to him that thinks so, is no less absurd, and overturns itself. CHAPTER VI That these assertions of Protagoras, 'Knowledge is sense, and knowledge is but fantastical and relative', are effectually overturned by the atomical philosophy; of which the genuine result is, that sense alone is not the judge of what

4

does really and absolutely exist, but that there is another principle in us superior to sense.

Book III

CHAPTER I What sense is, and that it is not knowledge. How sensation is performed. The soul is passive in sensation, though not altogether so. Various kinds of sensations. CHAPTER II That sense is a confused perception obtruded on the soul from without, but knowledge the active energy of an unpassionate power in the soul, which is vitally united to the body. The difference betwixt sensitive and intellectual cogitation, and their different uses in general. CHAPTER III The difference between sense or sensation and intellection of knowledge, described more accurately in five particulars, with a further explication and demonstration from Plato. CHAPTER IV A further proof that sense is not science, illustrated by several instances. Sense is only a seeming or appearance of things corporeal existing, which may be though the things have not a real existence. Reasons of this. Phantasms and sensible ideas are really or materially the same things. Phantasms voluntary and involuntary. That Phantasms may become sensations, and *e contra*.

Book IV

CHAPTER I That knowledge is an inward active energy of the mind, not arising from things acting from without. Sense is not a mere passion, but a passive perception of the soul, having something of vital energy, and is a cogitation. The immediate objects of intellection not things without the mind, but the ideas of the mind itself, which is not weakened by the most radiant and illustrious truths, as the sense is by what is exceedingly sensible. Hath a criterion in itself whereby to know when it hath found what it sought. Two kinds of perceptive cogitations in the soul, the one passive, which are either αἰσθήματα, 'sensations', or φαντάσματα, 'imaginations'; the other kind are called νοήματα. That the νοήματα are not raised out of the *phantasmata* by the *intellectus agens*. CHAPTER II That some ideas of the mind proceed not from outward sensible objects, but arise from the inward activity of the mind itself. The cause of men's mistake herein. How far the passion of sense reaches, and where the mind's activity begins. Sense no competent

5

judge of the reality of relative ideas, which though they were mere notions of the mind or modes of conceiving, yet it follows not that they have no reality. They are not disagreeable to the reality of things, and so not false. The beauty, the strength, and ability of natural and corporeal things depend upon these relations and proportions. Instances proposed to illustrate this matter. All the ideas of things artificial have something in them that never came from sense. This true of plants and animals. No essential difference betwixt natural compounded and artificial things. Sense has no idea of the cogitative being joined to rational animals, nor of the universe as it is one corporeal frame, much less of the ideas or modes of thinking beings. CHAPTER III That even simple corporeal things, passively perceived by sense, are known or understood only by the active power of the mind. That sensation is not knowledge of these things, much less any secondary result from sense. Besides *aesthemata* and *phantasmata*, there must be *noemata* or intelligible ideas coming from the mind itself. This confirmed and illustrated by several instances and similitudes. That there is an intelligible idea of a triangle inwardly exerted from the mind, distinct from the phantasm or sensible idea; both [of] which may be in the mind together. Some sensible ideas not impressed on the soul by things without. That sense is a kind of speech of outward nature conversing with the mind. Two kinds of perceptive powers in the soul. Knowledge does not begin but end in individuals. A double error of vulgar philosophers. Immediate objects of all geometrical science are the intelligible and universal ideas of a triangle, &c. exerted from the mind, and comprehended in it. CHAPTER IV That individual material things cannot be the immediate objects of intellection and knowledge, besides which there must be some other kind of beings or entities, as the immediate objects of them, such things as do not flow, but remain immutably the same. The immutable entities, what they are, from whence, and where they exist. That there is an eternal mind, from which all created understandings are constantly furnished with ideas. Conclusion, that wisdom, knowledge, and understanding, are eternal and self-subsistent things, superior to matter, and all sensible things. CHAPTER V That the intelligible notions of things, though existing only in the mind, are not figments of the mind, but have an immutable nature. The criterion of truth. The opinion that nothing can be demonstrated to be true absolutely, but only hypothetically, refuted. Whatever is clearly intelligible, is absolutely true. Though men are often deceived, and think they clearly comprehend what they do not; it follows not that they can never be certain that they clearly comprehend any thing. The conclusion with Origen, that science and knowledge is the only firm thing in the world. CHAPTER VI In what sense the essences of things are eternal and immutable. Every thing is what it is, to science or knowledge whether absolutely or relatively, unchangeable by any mind. So that if moral good and evil, just and unjust, in things so denominated, as the actions or souls of men, they must have some certain natures unalterable by any will or opinion. That the soul is not a mere *rasa tabula*. That it is in order of nature before the body and matter, does not result out of it, but commands, governs, and rules it. The whole corporeal world a heap of dust and atoms. There can be no such thing as morality unless there be a God. The commendation of the atomical philosophy successfully revived by Cartesius. Epicurus taxed for his sottishness.

Book I

Chapter I

1. As the vulgar generally look no higher for the original of moral good and evil, just and unjust, than the codes and pandects, the tables and laws of their country and religion, so there have not wanted pretended philosophers in all ages who have asserted nothing to be good and evil, just and unjust, naturally and immutably (φύσει καὶ ἀκινήτως); but that all these things were positive, arbitrary, and factitious only (θετικὰ, νομιμὰ ψηφισματώδη). Such Plato mentions in his tenth book *De legibus* [*Laws*], who maintained,

> That nothing at all was naturally just but men changing their opinions concerning them perpetually, sometimes made one thing just, sometimes another; but whatsoever is decreed and constituted that for the time is valid, being made so by arts and laws, but not by any nature of its own.[1]

And again his *Theaetetus*:

> As to things just and unjust, holy and unholy, not only the Protagoreans (of whom we shall treat afterward), but many other philosophers also confidently affirm, that none of these things have in nature any essence of their own, but whatsoever is decreed by the authority of the city, that

---

[1] *Τὰ [δὲ] δίκαια οὐδ' εἶναι τὸ παράπαν φύσει, ἀλλ' ἀμφισβητοῦντας διατελεῖν ἀλλήλοις καὶ μετατιθεμένους ἀεὶ ταῦτα· ἃ δ' ἂν μετάθωνται καὶ ὅταν, τότε κύρια ἕκαστα εἶναι γιγνόμενα τέχνῃ καὶ τοῖς νόμοις, ἀλλ' οὐ δή τινι φύσει* (Plato, *Laws* 890A). The Loeb translation gives, 'as to things just they do not exist at all by nature, but men are constantly in dispute about them and continually altering them, and whatever alteration they make at any time is at that time authoritative; though it owes its exercise to art and the laws, and not in any way to nature' Plato, *Laws*, trans. R.G. Bury (London and New York, 1926).

is truly such whether it is so decreed, and for so long time, viz. just or unjust, holy or unholy.[2]

And Aristotle more than once takes notice of this opinion in his *Ethics*:

> Things honest and just, which politics are conversant about have so great a variety and uncertainty in them, that they seem to be only by law, and not by nature.[3]

And afterwards, Book 5, ch. 7, after he had divided that which is politically just (τὸ δίκαιον πολιτικόν) into natural (φυσικόν), '[that] which has everywhere the same force' (τὸ πανταχοῦ τὴν αὐτὴν ἔχον δύναμιν), and legal (νομικόν), 'which before there be a law made, is indifferent, but when once the law is made, is determined to be just or unjust':[4] which legal just and unjust (as he afterwards expresses it) are 'like to wine and wheat measures, as pints and bushels',[5] which are not everywhere of an equal bigness, being commonly lesser with those that sell and greater with those that buy: then he adds, 'some there are that think that there is no other just or unjust, but what is made by law and men, because that which is natural is immutable, and hath everywhere the same force, as fire burns alike here and in Persia; but they see that *jura* and *justa*, rights and just things are everywhere different'.[6]

2. The philosophers particularly noted for this opinion in Plato are Protagoras in his *Theaetetus*, Polus and Callicles in his *Gorgias*, Thrasymachus, and Glaucon in his *Politics*.[7] But Diogenes Laertius tells us some others, as of Archelaus, Socrates' master, that held 'that just

---

2 Ἐν τοῖς δικαίοις καὶ ἀδίκοις, καὶ ὁσίοις καὶ ἀνοσίοις, ἐθέλουσιν ἰσχυρίζεσθαι ὡς οὐκ ἐστὶ φύσει αὐτῶν οὐδὲν οὐσίαν ἑαυτοῦ ἔχον, ἀλλὰ τὸ κοινῇ δόξαν τοῦτο γίνεται ἀληθὲς τότε ὅταν δόξῃ καὶ ὅσον ἂν δοκῇ χρόνον· καὶ ὅσοι δὲ μὴ παντάπασι τὸν Πρωταγόρου λόγον λέγουσιν ὧδε πῶς τὴν σοφίαν ἄγουσι (Plato, *Theaetetus* 172B).

3 Τὰ δὲ καλὰ καὶ τὰ δίκαια περὶ ὧν ἡ Πολιτικὴ σκοπεῖται, τοσαύτην ἔχει διαφορὰν καὶ πλάνην ὥστε δοκεῖν νόμῳ μόνον εἶναι, φύσει δὲ μή (Aristotle, *Nicomachean Ethics* 1094b14–17).

4 ὃ ἐξ ἀρχῆς οὐδὲν διαφέρει οὕτως ἢ ἄλλως· ὅταν δὲ θῶνται διαφέρει (ibid. 1134b18–21). *EIM* (1731) refers to ch. 10.

5 ὅμοια[...]τοῖς μέτροις[...]οἰνηροῖς καὶ σιτηροῖς (Aristotle, *Nicomachean Ethics* 1135a1). The translation of the passages suggests the Greek original is a continuous passage, which it is not, in fact. *EIM* (1848) terminates the translation at 'bushels', but it should be as given here.

6 Δοκεῖ δὲ ἐνίοις πάντα εἶνα τοιαῦτα, ὅτι τὸ μὲν φύσει ἀκίνητον καὶ πανταχοῦ τὴν αὐτὴν ἔχει δύναμιν, ὥσπερ τὸ πῦρ καὶ ἐνθάδε καὶ ἐν Πέρσαις καίει. Τὰ δὲ δίκαια κινούμενα ὁρῶσιν (Aristotle, *Nicomachean Ethics* 1134b24–8. Loeb translation by H. Rackham (London, 1934): 'Some people think that all the rules of justice are merely conventional, because whereas a law of nature is immortal and has the same validity everywhere, as fire burns the same here and in Persia, rules of justice are seen to vary.')

7 Protagoras, Polus, Callicles, Thrasymachus, Glaucon are, respectively, the interlocutors of Socrates in the dialogues named.

and dishonest are not so by nature but by law';[8] and (as I conceive) Democritus,[9] for after he had set down his opinion concerning happiness, or the chief end, he adds this as part of the Democritical philosophy, ποιητὰ νομιμὰ εἶναι, which I understand thus, that things accounted just or unjust are all factitious or artificial things, not natural; nothing being real or natural but atoms and vacuum, as the following words are, φύσει δὲ ἄτομα καὶ κενόν.[10] The same is noted by Diogenes[11] also concerning Aristippus, Plato's contemporary, that he asserted 'that nothing was good or evil otherwise than by law or custom'.[12] And Plutarch in the *Life of Alexander*, tells us of Anaxarchus, that was Aristotle's equal, that when Alexander, repenting, sadly lamented the death of Clitus, whom he had rashly slain, he read this lecture in philosophy to him to comfort him, 'that whatsoever is done by the supreme power is *ipso facto* just'.[13] And Pyrrho, the Eliensic philosopher, and father of the Sceptics, that was Anaxarchus' scholar, seems to have been dogmatical in nothing else but this 'that there is nothing good or shameful, just or unjust, and so likewise as to all things, that there is nothing so in truth, but that men do all things according to law and custom'.[14]

3. After these succeeded Epicurus,[15] the reviver of the Democritical

---

[8] Τὸ δίκαιον εἶναι καὶ τὸ αἰσχρὸν οὐ φύσει ἀλλὰ νόμῳ (Diogenes Laertius, *Lives* II.16. Loeb translation by R.D. Hicks (London and Cambridge, Mass., 1934): 'that what is just and what is base depends not upon nature but upon convention'. Archelaus (fl. fifth century BC), was a pupil of Anaxagoras and is said to have taught Socrates.

[9] Democritus of Abdera (b. 460–457 BC) was a pupil of Leucippus and of Anaxagoras, and a proponent of an atomic theory of matter.

[10] Diogenes Laertius IX.45. Cudworth's two Greek quotations render Diogenes, 'ποιότητας δὲ νόμῳ εἶναι, φύσει δ'ἄτομα καί κενόν'. Loeb translation: 'The qualities of all things exist merely by convention; in nature there is nothing but atoms and void space.'

[11] Diogenes Laertius X.45.

[12] μηδὲν [τέ] εἶναι φύσει δίκαιον ἢ καλὸν ἢ αἰσχρὸν ἀλλὰ νόμῳ καὶ ἔθει (Diogenes Laertius II. 93). Aristippus of Cyrene, proponent of Epicureanism and founder of Cyrenaic school which taught that the immediate end of action is pleasure.

[13] πᾶν τὸ πραχθὲν ὑπὸ τοῦ κρατοῦντος, δίκαιον εἶναι (Plutarch, 'Alexander', in Plutarch, *Lives*, trans. B. Perrin (London and New York, 1919), vol. 7, 52.4. Original reads θεμιτὸν ἢ καὶ δίκαιον for δίκαιον εἶναι. Anaxarchus of Abdera (fl. fourth century BC), was a follower of Democritus and teacher of Pyrrho.

[14] οὔτε καλὸν οὔτε αἰσχρὸν, [οὔτε δίκαιον] οὔτε ἄδικον, καὶ ὁμοίως ἐπὶ πάντων μηδὲν εἶναι τῇ ἀληθείᾳ, νόμῳδὲ καὶ ἔθει πάντα τοὺς ἀνθρώπους πράττειν (Diogenes Laertius, IX.61). Loeb translation: '[He denied] that anything was honourable or dishonourable, just or unjust. And so universally, he held that there is nothing really existent, but custom and convention govern human action.' Pyrrho (c. 365/360–c.275/270 BC) was the father of Greek scepticism.

[15] Epicurus (c. 341–270 BC) was a proponent of Democritean atomism, whose philosophy, known in the Renaissance via Diogenes Laertius, was promoted by Justus Lipsius (1547–1606) and

philosophy, the frame of whose principles must needs lead him to deny justice and injustice to be natural things. And therefore he determines that they arise wholly from mutual pacts and covenants of men made for their own convenience and utility, and laws resulting from thence.

> Those living creatures that could not make mutual covenants together not to hurt, nor to be hurt by one another, could not for this cause have any such thing as just or unjust amongst them. And there is the same reason for those nations that either will not, or cannot make such mutual compacts not to hurt one another. For there is no such thing as justice by itself, but only in the mutual congresses of men, wheresoever they have entered together into covenant not to hurt one another.[16]

The late compiler of the Epicurean system expresses this philosopher's meaning after this manner:

> There are some that think that those things that are just [*justa*], are just according to their proper unvaried nature, and that the laws do not make them just, but only prescribe according to that nature which they have. But the thing is not so.[17]

After Epicurus, Carneades, the author of the New Academy as Lactantius testifieth, was also a zealous assertor of the same doctrine.[18]

4. And since in this latter age the physiological hypotheses of Democritus and Epicurus have been revived, and successfully applied to the solving of some of the phenomena of the visible world, there have not wanted those that have endeavoured to vent also those other paradoxes of the same philosophers, viz. 'That there is no incorporeal

---

Pierre Gassendi (1592–1655). Epicurus' denial of providence and his assertion that the world came about by chance rendered his philosophy suspect to Christians.

[16] Ὅσα τῶν ζῴων μὴ ἠδύνατο συνθήκας ποιεῖσθαι τὰς ὑπὲρ τοῦ μὴ βλάπτειν, ἀλλὰ μηδὲ βλάπτεσθαι, πρὸς ταῦτα οὐθέν ἐστι οὐδὲ δίκαιον οὐδὲ ἄδικον. ὡσαύτως δὲ καὶ τῶν ἐθνῶν ὅσα μὴ ἠδύνατο ἢ ἐβούλετο τὰς συνθήκας ποιεῖσθαι τὰς ὑπὲρ τοῦ μὴ βλάπτειν μηδὲ βλάπτεσθαι· οὐκ ἦν τι καθ' ἑαυτὸ δικαιοσύνη, ἀλλὰ ἐν ταῖς μετὰ ἀλλήλων συντροφαῖς, καθ' ὁπηλίκους δὴ ποτε ἀεὶ τόπους συνθήκη τις ὑπὲρ τοῦ μὴ βλάπτειν ἢ βλάπτεσθαι (Diogenes Laertius, x. 150, who here quotes from Epicurus Κύριαι Δόξαι, of 'Sovran Maxims', sects. 32 and 33).

[17] 'Ac sunt quidam, qui existimant ea, quae justa sunt, esse secundum propriam invariatamque naturam justa, et leges non ista justa facere sed duntaxat praescribere juxta eam quam habent naturam verum res non ita se habet' (Gassendi, *Philosophiae Epicuri syntagma continens canonicam, physicam et ethicam* (London, 1668), p. 267). Pierre Gassendi promoted a Christianized version of Epicurus' philosophy as an alternative to Aristotelianism.

[18] Lactantius, *Divinae institutiones* v.14. Carneades (214/213–129/128 BC) was a sceptical philosopher and founder, as Cudworth notes, of the New Academy. Lactantius (*c.* AD 240–320), was a Christian apologist.

substance, nor any natural difference of good and evil, just and unjust';[19] and to recommend the same under a show of wisdom, as the deep and profound mysteries of the atomical or corpuscular philosophy. As if senseless matter and atoms were the original of all things, according to that song of old Silenus in the poet:

> He sung the secret seeds of nature's frame;
> How seas, and earth, and air, and active flame,
> Fell through the mighty void, and in their fall
> Were blindly gathered in this goodly ball.[20]

Of this sort is that late writer of ethics and politics, who asserts,

> that there are no authentic doctrines concerning just and unjust, good and evil, except the laws which are established in every city: and that it concerns none to inquire whether an action shall be reputed just or unjust, good or evil, except such only whom the community have appointed to be the interpreters of their laws.[21]

And again, 'Even a Christian government hath power to determine what is righteous, and what is the transgression of it.'[22] And he gives the same over again in English 'In the state of nature nothing can be unjust; the notions of right and wrong, justice and injustice have no place; where there is no common power, there is no law; where no law, no transgression.' 'No law can be unjust'.[23] Nay, temperance is no more natural ($\phi\acute{v}\sigma\epsilon\iota$), according to this civil (or rather uncivil) philosopher, than justice. 'Sensuality in that sense in which it is condemned, hath no place till there be laws'.[24]

---

[19] Not a quotation, but a summary of the principles of all materialists and relativists. Mention of a denial of incorporeal substance alludes to Thomas Hobbes.

[20]
> Namque canebat uti magnum per inane coacta
> Semina terrarumque marisque fuissent,
> Et liquidi simul ignis; ut his exordia primis
> Omnia, et ipse tener mundi concreverit orbis.
>
> (Virgil, *Eclogue* VI)

[21] 'Doctrinas de justo et injusto, bono et malo, praeter leges in unaquaque civitate constitutas, authenticas esse nullas; et utrum aliqua actio justa vel injusta, bona vel mala futura sit, a nemine inquirendum esse, praeterquam ab iis, ad quos legum suarum interpretationem [civitas] demandaverit' (Hobbes, *Elementorum philosophiae sectio tertia, de cive*, in *Thomae Hobbes Malmesburiensis opera philosophica quae latine scripsit omnia,* ed. W. Molesworth, 5 vols. (London, 1839–45), vol. II, p. 145). Cudworth interpolates '*civitas*'.

[22] 'Ad civitatem pertinere etiam Christianam, quid sit justitia, quid injustitia, sive peccatum contra justitiam, determinare' (ibid., p. 387). See also *The English Works of Thomas Hobbes*, ed. W. Molesworth, 11 vols. (London, 1839–45), vol. III, p. 267.

[23] Hobbes, *Leviathan*, Book 1, ch. 13, in Hobbes, *English Works*, vol. III, p. 113.

[24] ibid., p. 42.

5. But whatsoever was the true meaning of these philosophers, that affirm justice and injustice to be only by law, and not by nature (of which I shall discourse afterwards),[25] certain it is that divers modern theologers do not only seriously, but zealously, contend in like manner, that there is nothing absolutely, intrinsically, and naturally good and evil, just and unjust, antecedently to any positive command or prohibition of God; but that the arbitrary will and pleasure of God (that is, an omnipotent Being devoid of all essential and natural justice), by its commands and prohibitions, is the first and only rule and measure thereof.[26] Whence it follows unavoidably that nothing can be imagined so grossly wicked, or so foully unjust or dishonest, but if it were supposed to be commanded by this omnipotent Deity, must needs upon that hypothesis forthwith become holy, just, and righteous. For though the ancient fathers of the Christian church were very abhorrent from this doctrine (as shall be showed hereafter),[27] yet it crept up afterward in the scholastic age, Ockham being among the first that maintained *nullum actum malum esse nisi quatenus a Deo prohibitum, et qui non possit fieri bonus, si a Deo praecipiatur; et e converso,* 'that there is no act evil but as it is prohibited by God, and which cannot be made good if it be commanded by God. And so on the other hand as to good.'[28] And herein Petrus Alliacus and Andreas de Novo Castro, with others, quickly followed him.[29]

But this doctrine hath been since chiefly promoted and advanced by such as think nothing so essential to the Deity as uncontrollable power and arbitrary will, and therefore that God could not be God if there should be anything evil in its own nature which he could not do; and who impute such dark counsels and dismal actions unto God, as cannot be justified otherwise than by saying that whatsoever God can be

---

[25] See below, Book II.   [26] Cf. *TIS*, Preface.
[27] Cudworth does not discuss the opinion of the Fathers in *EIM*. He does draw significantly on the opinions of Origen in *Freewill*. See below, pp. 155, 161–3, 175, 188.
[28] William of Ockham (*c.*1285–1347/9), Franciscan theologian, who, like Duns Scotus before him, stressed the primacy of the divine will and the absolute freedom of God. Positions such as those cited by Cudworth are to be found in his *Super quatuor libros sententiarum subtilissimae quaestiones*, e.g. I *Sent.*, d.43 q. 1 art. 4C, II *Sent.*, q. 19 art. 30. For Ockham see P. Boehner, *Ockham. Philosophical Writings* (Edinburgh and London, 1957).
[29] Petrus Alliacus (Pierre d'Ailly) (1350–1420/1), Andreas de Novo Castro (André de Neufchâteau) (fl. *c.*1360), Cudworth's mention of these figures and of Ockham supports the view that the early seventeenth century saw a revival of scholasticism in England. See C.B. Schmitt, *John Case and Aristotelianism in Renaissance England* (Kingston and Montreal, 1983), pp. 61–8.

supposed to do or will, will be for that reason good or just, because he wills it.

Now the necessary and unavoidable consequences of this opinion are such as these:

> That to love God is by nature an indifferent thing, and is morally good only, because it is commanded by God; that to prohibit the love of God, or command the hatred of God, is not inconsistent with the nature of God, but only with his free will; that it is not inconsistent with the natural equity of God to command blasphemy, perjury, lying, &c. That God may command what is contrary, as to all the precepts of the Decalogue, so especially to the first, second, third; that holiness is not a conformity with the nature of God; that God may oblige man to what is impossible; that God hath no natural inclination to the good of the creatures; that God can justly doom an innocent creature to eternal torment.[30]

All which propositions, with others of like kind, are word for word asserted by some late authors. Though I think not fit to mention the name of any of them in this place, excepting only one, Joannes Szydlovius, who in a book published at Franeker,[31] hath professedly avowed and maintained the grossest of them. And yet neither he, nor the rest, are to be thought any more blameworthy herein than many others, that holding the same premisses have either dissembled or disowned those conclusions which unavoidably follow therefrom: but rather to be commended for their openness, simplicity, and ingenuity, in representing their opinion nakedly to the world, such as indeed it is, without any veil or mask.

Wherefore since there are so many, both philosophers and theologers,

---

[30] 'Amare Deum φύσει esse ἀδιάφορον et moraliter bonum solummodo, quia a Deo jubetur: prohibere Dei amorem vel praecipere Dei odium, non pugnare cum Dei natura, sed tantum cum voluntate libera. Non repugnare juri divino naturali praecipere peccata. Deum posse imperare blasphemiam, perjurium, mendacium, &c. Deum posse praecipere contrarium, ut omnibus praeceptis decalogi, ita potissimum primo, secundo, tertio. Sanctitatem non esse conformitatem cum natura Dei; Deum posse hominem obligare ad impossibile; Deum nullam habere naturalem inclinationem in bonum creaturarum; Deum jure posse creaturam insontem aeternis cruciatibus damnare.' This is a summary of the positions argued in Szydlovius (see next note). There is further discussion of Divine will in Cudworth's manuscript treatises on free will.

[31] Jan Szydlowski (Joannes Szydlovius), *Vindiciae quaestionum aliquot difficilium et controversarum in theologia oppositae illustri cuidam...viro, tum et theologi cujusdam absurdae opinioni de Christo mediatore et potestate Dei in creaturas a Johanne Szydlovio* (Franeker, 1643). A Pole resident in the Netherlands, Szydlowski cites extreme predestinarians Johannes Maccovius, William Twisse and Piscator.

that seemingly and verbally acknowledge such things as moral good and evil, just and unjust, that contend notwithstanding that these are not by nature (φύσει), but institution (θέσει), and that there is nothing naturally or immutably just or unjust; I shall from hence fetch the rise of this ethical discourse or enquiry concerning things good and evil, just and unjust, laudable and shameful περὶ τῶν ἀγαθῶν καὶ κακῶν, δικαίων καὶ ἀδίκων (for so I find these words frequently used as synonymous in Plato and other ancient authors): demonstrating in the first place, that if there be anything at all good or evil, just or unjust, there must of necessity be something naturally and immutably good and just (δίκαιον φυσικὸν καὶ ἀκίνητον). And from thence I shall proceed afterward to show what this natural, immutable, and eternal justice is, δίκαιον φυσικὸν, ἀκίνητον, καὶ αἰώνιον, with the branches and species of it.

Chapter II

1. Wherefore in the first place, it is a thing which we shall very easily demonstrate, that moral good and evil, just and unjust, honest and dishonest (if they be not mere names without any signification, or names for nothing else but willed and commanded, but have a reality in respect of the persons obliged to do and avoid them) cannot possibly be arbitrary things, made by will without nature; because it is universally true, that things are what they are, not by will but by nature. As for example, things are white by whiteness, and black by blackness, triangular by triangularity, and round by rotundity, like by likeness, and equal by equality, that is, by such certain natures of their own. Neither can Omnipotence itself (to speak with reverence) by mere will make a thing white or black without whiteness or blackness; that is, without such certain natures, whether we consider them as qualities in the objects without us according to the Peripatetical philosophy, or as certain dispositions of parts in respect of magnitude, figure, site, and motion, which beget those sensations or phantasms of white and black in us.[32] Or, to instance in geometrical figures, omnipotence itself cannot by mere will make a body triangular without having the nature and

---

[32]   See, for example, Descartes, *Principia philosophiae* II. Also IV.190ff.

properties of a triangle in it; that is, without having three angles equal to two right ones nor circular without the nature of a circle; that is, without having a circumference equidistant every where from the centre or middle point. Or lastly, to instance in things relative only: omnipotent will cannot make things like or equal one to another, without the natures of likeness and equality. The reason whereof is plain, because all these things imply a manifest contradiction: that things should be what they are not. And this is a truth fundamentally necessary to all knowledge, that contradictories cannot be true; for otherwise nothing would be certainly true or false. Now things may as well be made white or black by mere will, without whiteness or blackness, equal and unequal, without equality and inequality, as morally good and evil, just and unjust, honest and dishonest (*debita* and *illicita*), by mere will, without any nature of goodness, justice, honesty. For though the will of God be the supreme efficient cause of all things, and can produce into being or existence, or reduce into nothing what it pleaseth, yet it is not the formal cause of any thing besides itself, as the schoolmen have determined, in these words, 'That God himself cannot supply the place of a formal cause' (*Deum ipsum non posse supplere locum causae formalis*); and therefore it cannot supply the formal cause, or nature of justice or injustice, honesty or dishonesty. Now all that we have hitherto said amounts to no more than this, that it is impossible any thing should be by will only, that is without a nature or entity, or that the nature and essence of any thing should be arbitrary.

2. And since a thing cannot be made any thing by mere will without a being or nature, every thing must be necessarily and immutably determined by its own nature, and the nature of things be that which it is, and nothing else. For though the will and power of God have an absolute, infinite, and unlimited command upon the existences of all created things to make them to be, or not to be at pleasure; yet when things exist, they are what they are, this or that, absolutely or relatively, not by will or arbitrary command, but by the necessity of their own nature. There is no such thing as an arbitrarious essence, mode, or relation, that may be made indifferently any thing at pleasure. For an arbitrarious essence is a being without a nature, a contradiction, and therefore a nonentity. Wherefore the natures of justice and injustice cannot be arbitrarious things, that may be applicable by will indifferently to any actions or dispositions whatsoever. For the modes of all

subsistent beings, and the relations of things to one another, are immutable and necessarily what they are, and not arbitrary, being not by will but by nature.

3. Now the necessary consequence of that which we have hitherto said is this, that it is so far from being true that all moral good and evil, just and unjust are mere arbitrary and factitious things, that are created wholly by will, that (if we should speak properly) we must needs say that nothing is morally good or evil, just or unjust by mere will without nature, because everything is what it is by nature, and not by will. For though it will be objected here, that when God, or civil powers command a thing to be done, that was not before obligatory or unlawful, (*debitum* or *illicitum*), the thing willed or commanded doth forthwith become obligatory (δέον or *debitum*), that which ought to be done by creatures and subjects respectively; in which the nature of moral good or evil is commonly conceived to consist. And therefore if all good and evil, just and unjust be not the creatures of mere will (as many assert) yet at least positive things must needs owe all their morality, their good and evil, to mere will without nature. Yet notwithstanding, if we well consider it, we shall find that even in positive commands themselves, mere will doth not make the thing commanded just or obligatory, or beget and create any obligation to obedience; but that it is natural justice or equity which gives to one the right or authority of commanding, and begets in another duty and obligation to obedience. Therefore it is observable, that laws and commands do not run thus to will that this or that thing shall become just or unjust, obligatory or unlawful, or that men shall be obliged or bound to obey; but only to require that something be done or not done, or otherwise to menace punishment to the transgressors thereof. For it was never heard of that any one founded all his authority of commanding others, and others' obligation or duty to obey his commands, in a law of his own making, that men should be required, obliged, or bound to obey him. Wherefore since the thing willed in all laws is not that we should be obliged to obey, this thing cannot be the product of the mere will of the commander, but it must proceed from something else, namely the right or authority of the commander, which is founded in natural justice and equity, and an antecedent obligation to obedience in the subjects. Which things are not made by laws, but presupposed before all laws to make them valid. And if it should be imagined that anyone should make a positive law to

require that others should be obliged or bound to obey him, everyone would think such a law ridiculous and absurd. For if they were obliged before, then this law would be in vain and to no purpose. And if they were not before obliged, then they could not be obliged by any positive law, because they were not previously bound to obey such a person's commands. So that obligation to obey all positive laws is older than all laws, and previous or antecedent to them. Neither is it a thing that is arbitrarily made by will, or can be the object of command, but that which either is or is not by nature. And if this were not morally good and just in its own nature before any positive command of God that God should be obeyed by his creatures, the bare will of God himself could not beget an obligation upon any to do what he willed and commanded, because the natures of things do not depend upon will, being not things that are arbitrarily made (γιγνόμενα) but things that are (ὄντα). To conclude therefore, even in positive laws and commands it is not mere will that obligeth, but the natures of good and evil, just and unjust, really existing in the world.

4. Wherefore that common distinction betwixt things naturally and positively good and evil, or (as others express it) betwixt things that are therefore commanded because they are good and just, and things that are therefore good and just,[33] because they are commanded, stands in need of a right explication, that we be not led into a mistake thereby, as if the obligation to do those thetical and positive things did arise wholly from will without nature. Whereas it is not the mere will and pleasure of him that commandeth that obligeth to do positive things commanded, but the intellectual nature of him that is commanded. Wherefore the difference of these things lies wholly in this, that there are some things which the intellectual nature obligeth to of itself (*per se*) and directly, absolutely, and perpetually, and these things are called naturally good and evil. Other things there are which the same intellectual nature obligeth to by accident only, and hypothetically, upon condition of some voluntary action either of our own or some other person's, by means whereof those things which were in their own nature indifferent, falling under something that is absolutely good or evil, and thereby acquiring a new relation to the intellectual nature, do for the time become such things as ought to be done or omitted (*debita or illicita*), being made

[33] This is the fundamental question posed in Plato's *Euthyphro* 10A. Cudworth poses the same question in his *Sermon Preached before the House of Commons* (1647). See *TIS* II, part 2, p. 48.

such not by will but by nature. As for example, to keep faith and perform covenants is that which natural justice obligeth to absolutely. Therefore, upon supposition (*ex hypothesi*) that any one maketh a promise, which is a voluntary act of his own, to do something which he was not before obliged to by natural justice, upon the intervention of this voluntary act of his own, that indifferent thing promised falling now under something absolutely good and becoming the matter of promise and covenant, standeth for the present in a new relation to the rational nature of the promiser, and becometh for the time a thing which ought to be done by him, or which he is obliged to do. Not as if the mere will or words and breath of him that covenanteth had any power to change the moral natures of things, or any ethical virtue of obliging, but because natural justice and equity obligeth to keep faith and perform covenants. In like manner natural justice, that is the rational or intellectual nature, obligeth not only to obey God, but also civil powers, that have lawful authority of commanding, and to observe political order amongst men. And therefore if God or civil powers command any thing to be done that is not unlawful in itself, upon the intervention of this voluntary act of theirs, those things that were before indifferent become by accident for the time obligatory, such things as ought to be done by us, not for their own sakes, but for the sake of that which natural justice absolutely obligeth to.

And these are the things that are commonly called *positively* good and evil, just or unjust, such as though they are adiaphorous or indifferent in themselves, yet natural justice obligeth to accidentally, on supposition (*ex hypothesi*) of the voluntary action of some other person rightly qualified in commanding, whereby they fall into something absolutely good. Which things are not made good or *due* by the mere will of the commander, but that natural justice which gives him right and authority of commanding, and obligeth others to obey him, without which natural justice, neither covenants nor commands, could possibly oblige any one. For the will of another doth no more oblige in commands, than our own will in promises and covenants. To conclude, therefore, things called naturally good and due are such things as the intellectual nature obliges to immediately, absolutely, and perpetually, and upon no condition of any voluntary action that may be done or omitted intervening. But those things that are called positively good and due are such as natural justice or the intellectual nature obligeth to accidentally and hypothetically, upon condition of some voluntary act of another person invested with lawful authority in commanding.

And that it is not the mere will of the commander that makes these positive things to oblige or become due but the nature of things appears evidently from hence because it is not the volition of every one that obligeth, but of a person rightly qualified and invested with lawful authority. And because the liberty of commanding is circumscribed within certain bounds and limits, so that if any commander go beyond the sphere and bounds that nature sets him, which are indifferent things, his commands will not at all oblige.

5. But if we would speak yet more accurately and precisely, we might rather say, that no positive commands whatsoever do make any thing morally good and evil, just and unjust, which nature had not made such before. For indifferent things commanded, considered materially in themselves, remain still what they were before in their own nature, that is indifferent, because, as Aristotle speaks, 'will cannot change nature' (τὸ φύσει ἀκίνητον). And those things that are by nature indifferent (φύσει ἀδιάφορα), must needs be as immutably so as those things that are by nature just or unjust (φύσει δίκαια or ἄδικα), honest or shameful (καλά or αἰσχρά). But all the moral goodness, justice, and virtue, that is exercised in obeying positive commands and doing such things as are *positive* only, and to be done for no other cause but because they are commanded, or in respect to political order, consisteth not in the materiality of the actions themselves, but in that formality of yielding obedience to the commands of lawful authority in them. Just as when a man covenanteth or promiseth to do an indifferent thing which by natural justice he was not bound to do, the virtue of doing it consisteth not in the materiality of the action promised, but in the formality of keeping faith and performing covenants. Wherefore in positive commands, the will of the commander doth not create any new moral entity, but only diversely modifies and determines that general duty or obligation of natural justice to obey lawful authority and keep oaths and covenants, as our own will in promising doth but produce several modifications of keeping faith. And therefore there are no new things just or due made by either of them, besides what was always by *nature* such, to keep our own promises, and obey the lawful commands of others.

6. We see then that it is so far from being true that all moral good and

evil, just and unjust (if they be any thing) are made by mere will and arbitrary commands (as many conceive), that it is not possible that any command of God or man should oblige otherwise than by virtue of that which is naturally just (φύσει δίκαιον). And though particular promises and commands be made by will yet it is not will but nature that obligeth to the doing of things promised and commanded, or makes them such things as ought to be done (*debita*). For mere will cannot change the moral nature of actions, nor the nature of intellectual beings. And therefore, if there were no natural justice, that is, if the rational or intellectual nature in itself were indetermined and unobliged to any thing, and so destitute of all morality, it were not possible that any thing should be made morally good or evil, obligatory or unlawful (*debitum* or *illicitum*), or that any moral obligation should be begotten by any will or command whatsoever.

Chapter III

1. But some there are that will still contend, that though it should be granted that moral good and evil, just and unjust, do not depend upon any created will, yet notwithstanding they must needs depend upon the arbitrary will of God, because the nature and essences of all things, and consequently all verities and falsities depend upon the same. For if the natures and essences of things should not depend upon the will of God, it would follow from hence that something that was not God was independent upon God.[34]

2. And this is plainly asserted by that ingenious philosopher Renatus Descartes, who in his answer to the Sixth Objector against his Metaphysical Meditations, writes thus:

> It is a contradiction to say that the will of God was not from eternity indifferent to all things which are or ever shall be done; because no good or evil, nothing to be believed, or done, or omitted, can be fixed upon, the idea whereof was in the divine intellect before that his will determined itself to effect that such a thing should be. Neither do I speak this concerning the priority of time, but even there was nothing prior in

---

[34] 'Independent upon', i.e. 'independent of'.

order or by nature, or by reason as they call it, so as that idea of good inclined God to choose one thing rather than another. As for example's sake he would therefore create the world in time, because that he saw that it would be better so than if he had created it from eternity; neither willed he that the three angles of a triangle should be equal to two right angles, because he knew that it could not be otherwise. But on the contrary, because he would create the world in time, therefore it is better than if he had created it from eternity; and because he would that the three angles of a triangle should necessarily be equal to two right angles, therefore this is true and no otherwise; [...] and so of other things. And thus the greatest indifference in God is the greatest argument of his omnipotence.[35]

And again afterward:

To him that considers the immensity of God it is manifest that there can be nothing at all which doth not depend upon him, not only nothing subsisting, but also no order, no law, no reason of truth and goodness.[36]

And when he was again urged by the Sixth Objector,

Could not God cause that the nature of a triangle should not be such and how, I pray thee, could he from eternity cause that it should not be true, that twice four are eight?[37]

He confesseth ingenuously that those things were not intelligible to us;

[35] 'Repugnat Dei voluntatem non fuisse ab aeterno indifferentem ad omnia, quae facta sunt aut unquam fient, quia nullum bonum vel verum, nullum credendum vel faciendum vel omittendum fingi potest, cujus idea in intellectu divino prius fuerit, quam ejus voluntas se determinarit ad efficiendum ut id tale esset. Neque hic loquor de prioritate temporis, sed ne quidem prius fuit ordine, vel natura, vel ratione ratiocinata ut vocant, ita scilicet ut ista boni idea impulerit Deum ad unum potius quam aliud eligendum. Nempe exempli causa, non ideo voluit creare mundum in tempore, quia vidit sic melius fore, quam si creasset ab aeterno, nec voluit tres angulos trianguli aequales esse duobus rectis, quia cognovit aliter fieri non posse, &c. Sed contra, quia voluit mundum creare in tempore, ideo sic melius est, quam si creatus fuisset ab aeterno; et quia voluit tres angulos trianguli necessario aequales esse duobus rectis, idcirco jam hoc verum est, et fieri aliter non potest; atque ita de reliquis [...] Et ita summa indifferentia in Deo summum est ejus omnipotentiae argumentum' (Descartes, *Meditationes de prima philosophia...hic adjunctae sunt variae objectiones...cum responsionibus auctoris* (Amsterdam, 1678), sect. 6, p. 291. *AT* vii, 431–2). For a modern English translation, see CSM ii, 291ff. The sixth set of Objections to Descartes' *Meditationes de prima philosophia* (*Meditations on First Philosophy*) came from various anonymous hands and were compiled by Marin Mersenne.

[36] 'Attendenti ad Dei immensitatem manifestum est, nihil omnino esse posse, quod ab ipso non pendeat, non modo nihil subsistens, sed etiam nullum ordinem, nullam legem, nullamve rationem veri et boni' (Descartes, *Meditations*, sect. 8, *AT* vii, 435. CSM ii, 281).

[37] 'Numquid ergo [Deus] potuit efficere, ut natura trianguli non fuerit? Et qua ratione, amabo, potuisset ab aeterno facere, ut non fuisset verum bis quatuor esse octo?' (Descartes, *Meditations, Sixth Set of Replies, AT* vii, 418. CSM ii, 294).

but notwithstanding they must be so because, 'Nothing in any sort of being can be, which doth not depend upon God.'[38] Which doctrine of Cartesius is greedily swallowed down by some servile followers of his that have lately written of the old philosophy (*de prima philosophia*).[39]

3. Perhaps some may make a question for all this, whether Cartesius were any more in earnest in this, than when he elsewhere goes about to defend the doctrine of transubstantiation by the principles of his new philosophy because, in his Meditations upon the old philosophy [*Meditations*] (where it is probable he would set down the genuine sense of his own mind more undisguisedly, before he was assaulted by these objectors, and thereby forced to turn himself into several shapes) he affirmeth that the essences of things were eternal and immutable. But afterward urged by Gassendus with this inconvenience, that then something would be eternal and immutable besides God, and so independent upon God, he doth in a manner unsay it again, and betakes himself to this pitiful evasion,

> As the poets feign that the fates were indeed fixed by Jupiter, but that when they were fixed, he had obliged himself to the preserving of them, so I do not think that the essences of things, and those mathematical truths which can be known of them, are independent on God. But I think nevertheless, that because God so willed and so ordered, therefore they are immutable and eternal.[40]

Which is plainly to make them in their own nature mutable. But whether Cartesius were in jest or earnest in this business, it matters not, for his bare authority ought to be no more valued by us than the

---

[38] 'Nihil in ullo genere entis esse potest, quod a Deo non pendeat' (Descartes, *Meditations AT* vii, 436. CSM, ii, 261). The objections by Pierre Gassendi were printed as the fifth set of Objections in 1647. After reading Descartes' reply, Gassendi composed a further set of criticisms which were published with his original set of objections in *Disquisitio metaphysica sive dubitationes et instantiae* (Amsterdam, 1644).

[39] 'De prima philosophia', in the title of the *Meditations*, is normally given in modern editions as *Meditations on First Philosophy*, metaphysics being the 'first' philosophy, in the sense of the fundamentals of philosophy. Cudworth, however, translates 'prima' as 'old', i.e. 'original' philosophy. This is consistent with his view that the essentials of philosophy are contained in a *philosophia perennis* or perennial philosophy, dating back to earliest times. Cudworth regarded Cartesianism as reviving theories originally enunciated in ancient times. See below, pp. 38 and 151.

[40] 'Quemadmodum poetae fingunt a Jove quidem fata fuisse condita, sed postquam condita fuere ipsum se iis servandis obstrinxisse; ita ego non puto essentias rerum, mathematicasque illas veritates, quae de ipsis cognosci possunt, esse independentes a Deo; sed puto nihilominus, quia Deus sic voluit, quia sic disposuit, ipsas esse immutabiles et aeternas' (*AT* vii, 380). CSM ii, 261.

authority of Aristotle and other ancient philosophers was by him, whom he so freely dissents from.

4. For though the names of things may be changed by any one at pleasure, as that a square may be called a circle, or a cube a sphere, yet that the nature of a square should not be necessarily what it is, but be arbitrarily convertible into the nature of a circle, and so the essence of a circle into the essence of a sphere, or that the self same body, which is perfectly cubical without any physical alteration made in it, should by this metaphysical way of transformation of essences, by mere will and command be made spherical or cylindrical; this doth most plainly imply a contradiction, and the compossibility of contradictions destroys all knowledge and the definite natures (*rationes*) or notions of things. Nay, that which implies a contradiction is a nonentity and therefore cannot be the object of divine power. And the reason is the same for all other things, as just and unjust; for every thing is what it is immutably by the necessity of its own nature. Neither is it any derogation at all from the power of God to say, that he cannot make a thing to be that which it is not. Then there might be no such thing as knowledge in God himself. God might will that there should be no such thing as knowledge.

5. And as to the being or not being of particular essences, as that God might, if he pleased, have willed that there should be no such thing as a triangle or circle, and therefore nothing demonstrable or knowable of either of them. Which is likewise asserted by Cartesius, and those that make the essences of things dependent upon an arbitrary will in God. This is all one as if one should say that God could have willed, if he had pleased, that neither his own power nor knowledge should be infinite.

6. Now it is certain that if the natures and essences of all things, as to their being such or such, do depend upon a will of God that is essentially arbitrary, there can be no such thing as science or demonstration, nor the truth of any mathematical or metaphysical proposition be known by any otherwise, than by a certain enthusiastic or fanatic faith and persuasion thereupon, that God would have such a thing to be true or false at such a time or for so long. And so nothing would be true or false naturally (φύσει), but positively (θέσει) only, all truth and science being mere arbitrarious things. Truth and falsehood would be only names. Neither would there be any more certainty in the knowledge of God himself, since it must wholly depend upon the mutability of a will in him essentially indifferent and undetermined. And if we would speak

properly according to this hypothesis, God himself would not know or be wise by knowledge or by wisdom, but by will.[41]

7. Wherefore as for that argument, that unless the essences of things and all verities and falsities depend upon the arbitrary will of God, there would be something that was not God, independent upon God. If it will be well considered, it will prove a mere mormo, bugbear, and nothing so terrible and formidable as Cartesius seemed to think it.[42] For there is no other genuine consequence deducible from this assertion, that the essences and verities of things are independent upon the will of God, but that there is an eternal and immutable wisdom in the mind of God, and thence participated by created beings independent upon the will of God. Now the wisdom of God is as much God as the will of God. And whether[43] of these two things in God, that is, will or wisdom, should depend upon the other, will be best determined from the several natures of them. For wisdom in itself hath the nature of a rule and measure, it being a most determinate and inflexible thing. But will being not only a blind and dark thing as considered in itself, but also indefinite and indeterminate, hath therefore the nature of a thing regulable and measurable. Wherefore it is the perfection of will, as such, to be guided and determined by wisdom and truth. But to make wisdom, knowledge, and truth to be arbitrarily determined by will, and to be regulated by such a plumbean and flexible rule ($\kappa\alpha\nu\grave{\omega}\nu$ $\mu o\lambda\acute{\upsilon}\beta\delta\iota\nu o\varsigma$) as that is, is quite to destroy the nature of it. For science or knowledge is the comprehension of that which necessarily is ($\kappa\alpha\tau\acute{\alpha}\lambda\eta\psi\iota\varsigma$ $\tau o\tilde{\upsilon}$ $\check{o}\nu\tau o\varsigma$), and there can be nothing more contradictious than truth and falsehood arbitrary. Now all the knowledge and wisdom that is in creatures, whether angels or men, is nothing else but a participation of that one eternal, immutable, and increated wisdom of God, or several signatures of that one archetypal seal, or like so many multiplied reflections of one and the same face, made in several glasses, whereof some are clearer, some obscurer, some standing nearer, some further off.

8. Moreover, it was the opinion of the wisest philosophers (as we shall show afterward) that there is also in the scale of being a nature of goodness superior to wisdom, which therefore measures and determines the wisdom of God, as his wisdom measures and determines his will, and which the ancient cabalists were wont to call כתר crown, as being

---

[41] Compare *TIS*, p. 646.   [42] *AT* VII, 380; CSM II, 261. Cf. CSM III, 23.
[43] i.e. which.

the top or crown of the Deity, of which more afterward. Wherefore although some novelists[44] make a contracted idea of God consisting of nothing else but will and power, yet his nature is better expressed by some in this mystical or enigmatical representation of an infinite circle, whose inmost centre is simple goodness, the radii [or] rays and expanded area (plat) thereof all comprehending and immutable wisdom, the exterior periphery or interminate circumference, omnipotent will or activity by which every thing without God is brought forth into existence. Wherefore the will and power of God having no command inwardly (*imperium ad intra*) either upon the wisdom and knowledge of God, or upon the ethical and moral disposition of his nature which is his essential goodness, but the sphere of its activity is without God (*extra Deum*), where it hath an absolute command upon the existences of things, and is always free, though not always indifferent, since it is its greatest perfection to be determined by infinite wisdom and infinite goodness. But this is to anticipate what according to the laws of method should follow afterward in another place.

[44] i.e. innovators or recent writers.

Book II

Chapter I

1. Now the demonstrative strength of our cause lying plainly is this, that it is not possible that anything should be without a nature, and the natures or essences of all things being immutable, therefore upon supposition that there is any thing really just or unjust, due or unlawful (*debitum* or *illicitum*), there must of necessity be something so both naturally and immutably, which no law, decree, will, nor custom can alter. There have not wanted some among the old philosophers that rather than they would acknowledge any thing immutably just or unjust, would not stick to shake the very foundations of all things, and to deny that there was any immutable nature or essence of any thing, and by consequence any absolute certainty of truth or knowledge, maintaining this strange paradox, that both all being and knowledge was fantastical and relative only, and therefore that nothing was good or evil, just or unjust, true or false, white or black, absolutely and immutably, but relatively to every private person's humour or opinion.

2. The principal assertor of this extravagant opinion was Protagoras the Abderite, who, as Plato instructs us in his *Theaetetus*, held

> that nothing was any thing in itself absolutely, but was always made so to some thing else, and essence or being was to be removed from every thing.[1]

---

[1] οὐδὲν εἶναι ἓν αὐτὸ καθ' αὑτό, ἀλλά τινὶ ἀεὶ γίγνεσθαι τὸ δ' εἶναι πανταχόθεν ἐξαιρετέον (Plato, *Theaetetus* trans. H.N. Fowler (London and New York, 1928), 157A). In this and the following quotations Cudworth translates γίγνεσθαι as 'be made' (Loeb 'become'). Protagoras (b. *c.* 485 BC) was one of the earliest Sophists.

In which position of his there seems to be these two things asserted: first that all things were in perpetual motion and nothing had any being (*esse*) but a possibility to be (*fieri*), which the said Protagoras thus expressed:

> All things are made by motion and mixture of things together, and therefore are not rightly said to be. For nothing is but every thing is always made.[2]

Secondly, that nothing is made absolutely, but only relatively to something else,

> If any one say that any thing either is or is made, he must say that it is so to something, or in respect of some body for we cannot affirm that any thing either is or is made absolutely in itself but relatively to something else.[3]

3. Now from hence proceeded those known aphorisms of his, recorded both in Plato and Aristotle, 'that those things which appear to every one, are to him to whom they appear'. And again, 'that every fancy or opinion of every body was true'.[4] And again, 'That man is the measure of all things whether existing or not existing.'[5] Which sentence seemed so pretty and argute to him that he placed it in the very front of his book, as Plato tells us.[6] And indeed it comprises in it all the singularity of his philosophy, the true meaning thereof being this: not only that man taken generally is the measure of all things (which in some sense might be affirmed that our own human faculties are the measure of all things unto us), but also that 'every individual man is the measure of all being and truth' respectively to himself. For so the following words in Plato explain it:

> Your meaning (saith Socrates) is this, that as every thing appears to me, such it is to me. And as it appears to you, such it is to you, both of us being alike men.[7]

---

[2] Ἐκ δὲ δὴ φορᾶς τε καὶ κινήσεως καὶ κράσεως πρὸς ἄλληλα γίγνεται, ἃ δή φαμὲν εἶναι οὐκ ὀρθῶς προσαγορεύοντες (ibid., 152D).

[3] Εἴτε τις εἶναί τι ὀνομάζει, τινὶ εἶναι, ἢ τινὸς, ἢ πρός τι, ῥητέον αὐτῷ, εἴτε γίγνεσθαι· αὐτὸ δὲ ἐφ' αὑτοῦ τι ἢ ὂν ἢ γιγνόμενον, οὔτε αὐτῷ λεκτέον οὔτ' ἄλλου λέγοντος ἀποδεκτέον (ibid., 160B).

[4] τὰ φαινόμενα ἑκάστῳ ταῦτα καὶ εἶναι τούτῳ ᾧ φαίνεται (ibid., 158A). Compare 152A and C. πᾶσα φαντασία ἐστιν ἀληθής (Sextus Empiricus, *Against the Mathematicians* VII.390).

[5] πάντων χρημάτων μέτρον ἄνθρωπον εἶναι, τῶν μὲν ὄντων ὡς ἔστι, τῶν δὲ μὴ ὄντων ὡς οὐκ ἔστιν (*Theaetetus*, 152A).

[6] ibid., 161C.

[7] Οὐκοῦν οὕτως πως λέγεις, ὡς οἷα μὲν ἕκαστα ἐμοὶ φαίνεται, τοιαῦτα μὲν ἐστιν ἐμοί· οἷα δὲ σοὶ, τοιαῦτα ἂν σοί· ἄνθρωπος δὲ σύ τε κἀγώ (ibid., 152A).

Wherefore it is elsewhere expressed after this manner, 'that every man is the measure of what is and is not, that is to himself', and 'that every one is the measure of his own wisdom to himself'.[8] Sextus Empiricus gives a short account of this Protagorean philosophy in a few words thus, 'He asserts that which seems to every one to be, and so makes all things relative.'[9] Now this was a higher strain of madness than the Pyrrhonian scepticism, which was not so extravagant as to affirm that all things were fantastical and relative only, but that we could not affirm what things absolutely were in their own nature, but only what they seemed to us.

4. But that all this was intended chiefly as a battery or assault against morality, and principally levelled by Protagoras against the absolute and immutable natures of good and evil, just and unjust, appeareth also from sundry passages of that learned dialogue called *Theaetetus*,

> Tell me therefore, dost thou in good earnest think that nothing is good or honest, but is always made so?[10]

And afterwards Protagoras affirms,

> that whatsoever things seem to be good and just to every city or commonwealth, the same are so to that city or commonwealth so long as they seem so.[11]

Again,

> Whatsoever things any city thinking doth decree to be honest or dishonest, just or unjust, holy or unholy, those things are really or truly such to that city. And in such things as these no one private person or city is wiser than another.

Because,

> None of these things have any nature or essence of their own, being merely fantastical and relative.[12]

---

[8] μέτρον ἕκαστον ἡμῶν εἶναι τῶν τε ὄντων καὶ μή· μέτρον εἶναι αὐτῷ ἕκαστον αὐτοῦ σοφίας (ibid., 166D).

[9] τίθησι τὰ φαινόμενα ἑκάστῳ [νόμα], καὶ οὕτως εἰσάγει τὸ πρὸς τι (Sextus Empiricus, 'Outlines of Pyrrhonism', 1.216, in *Sextus Empiricus*, with an English translation by R.G. Bury, 3 vols. (London and New York, 1933), vol. 1.

[10] Λέγε τοίνυν πάλιν, εἰ σοὶ ἀρέσκει τὸ μή τι εἶναι, ἀλλὰ γίγνεσθαι αἰεὶ ἀγαθὸν καὶ καλόν (Plato, *Theaetetus*, 157D). Loeb: 'Then say once more whether the doctrine pleases you that nothing is, but is always becoming – good or beautiful or any of the other qualities.'

[11] οἷά γ' ἂν ἑκάστῃ πόλει δίκαια καὶ καλὰ δοκῇ, ταῦτα καὶ εἶναι αὐτῇ, ἕως ἂν αὐτὰ νομίζῃ (ibid., 167C).

[12] Καλὰ μὲν καὶ αἰσχρὰ, [καὶ] δίκαια καὶ ἄδικα, καὶ ὅσια καὶ μὴ, οἷα ἂν ἑκάστη πόλις οἰηθεῖσα

Lastly, to name no more places,

> The thing that we were about to show was this that they which made the
> natures and essences of all things, flowing and mutable, and which held
> that what seemed to every body, was that to whom it so seemed, as they
> do maintain this concerning all other things, so concerning nothing more
> than just and unjust, as being unquestionably true of these, that
> whatsoever any city thinks to be good and just and decrees them such,
> these things are so to that city, so long as they are so decreed.[13]

Chapter II

1. Wherefore, since in order to the taking away of the immutable
natures of good and evil, just and unjust, and the moral differences of
humane actions, there was so strange an attempt made by these
philosophers to overthrow the absolute essences and truths of all things,
let us in the next place consider what pretences or grounds they could
possibly have for maintaining so wild a paradox as this.

First, therefore, it is evident from Plato's writings that Protagoras laid
his foundation in the Heraclitical philosophy, at that time in great vogue
and request in the world, which did, as that philosopher writes, 'bring
in a floating and moveable essence', and maintained, 'that nothing stood,
but all things moved and flowed'.[14] An opinion which most of the
ancients were inclining to, as appears from the poets, who made 'all
things to be the offspring of flux and motion',[15] in so much that Homer
himself (as Plato observes) deriving the pedigree of the gods, made the
ocean their father and Tethys their mother.[16]

And there were not any philosophers of note besides Parmenides and

---

θῆται νόμιμα ἑαυτῇ, ταῦτα καὶ εἶναι τῇ ἀληθείᾳ ἑκάστῃ καὶ ἐν τούτοις μὲν οὐδὲν σοφώτερον
οὔτε ἰδιώτην ἰδιώτου οὔτε πόλιν πόλεως εἶναι (ibid., 172A). οὐκ ἔστι φύσει αὐτῶν οὐδὲν
οὐσίαν ἑαυτοῦ ἔχον (ibid., 172B).

13 Οὐκοῦν ἐνταῦθά που ἦμεν τοῦ λόγου ἐν ᾧ ἔφαμεν τοὺς τὴν φερομένην οὐσίαν λέγοντας, καὶ
τὸ ἀεὶ δοκοῦν ἑκάστῳ, τοῦτο καὶ εἶναι τούτῳ ᾧ δοκεῖ, ἐν μὲν τοῖς ἄλλοις ἐθέλειν δὴ
διϊσχυρίζεσθαι, καὶ οὐχ ἥκιστα περὶ τὰ δίκαια ὡς παντὸς μᾶλλον ἃ ἂν θῆται πόλις δόξαντα
αὐτῇ, ταῦτα καὶ ἔστι δίκαια τιθεμένη ἕωσπερ ἂν κέηται (ibid., 177C–D).

14 φερομενα οὐσίαν εἰσάγειν. οὐδὲν ἑστάναι πάντα δὲ κινεῖσθαι (ibid., 168B).

15 πάντα ἔκγονα ῥοῆς [εἴρηκεν] τε καὶ κινήσεως (ibid., 152E).

16 Ὠκεανόν τε θεῶν γένεσιν, καὶ μητέρα Τήθυν 'Oceanus the origin of the gods, and Tethys their
mother' (ibid., 152E; Loeb translation). A quotation of *Iliad* XIV, 201.

Melissus, that opposed it, who also ran into another extreme.[17] And therefore the former of these Plato facetiously calls 'the flowing philosophers' (τοὺς ῥέοντας) and the latter, the 'standers' (στασιώτας).[18] Now the true meaning of this Heraclitical philosophy was plainly this, that there is no other being in the world besides individual body or matter, and no such thing as standing intelligible forms (εἴδη), that is no intellectual being. Which matter or corporeal being as it is liable to motion and mutation because of its divisibility, every part of it being separable from another, so by the mutation that we find in all corporeal things, we may reasonably conclude that it is throughout perpetually moved and agitated by streams and subtle matter passing the pores of all bodies. Whence it was that they affirmed 'that all things flowed like a stream',[19] and that there was no stability either of essence or knowledge any where to be found. For that Cratylus and Heraclitus endeavoured to destroy the certainty of all science from this principle is evident in that they maintained that contradictories might be true concerning the same thing, and at the same time. And indeed if there were no other being in the world but individual matter, and all knowledge proceeded from the impresses of that matter, that being always agitated, it is not conceivable how there could be any stability of knowledge any more than of essence found in this rapid whirlpool of corporeal things. Nay, nor how there should be any such thing as knowledge at all. Wherefore according to this Heraclitical philosophy, Protagoras in the first place concluded, 'that knowledge is nothing else but sense'.[20] For as Plato writes, 'These two assertions come all to one, that all things flow like a stream, and that knowledge and sense are one and the self same thing.'[21]

2. But Protagoras went further, and made a superstructure upon this Heraclitical philosophy out of the old atomical or Phoenician philo-

---

[17] ibid., 180E, Sextus, *Outlines* III.65 and *Against the Physicists* II.46.

[18] *Theaetetus*, 181A and Sextus, *Against the Physicists* II.46. Compare *TIS*, p. 22: 'there was a great controversy amongst Philosophers before *Plato's time*, between such as held all things to Flow, namely *Heraclitus* and *Cratylus*; and others who asserted that some things did Stand, and that there was ἀκίνητος οὐσία, *a certain Immutable Nature*, to wit, an Eternal Mind, together with Eternal and Immutable Truths (amongst which were *Parmenides* and Melissus).'

[19] οἶον ῥεύματα κινεῖσθαι τὰ πάντα (*Theaetetus*, 160D).

[20] ὅτι ἐπιστήμη οὐκ ἄλλο τι ἐστὶν ἢ αἴσθησις (ibid.). Aristotle attributes to Heraclitus and Cratylus the view that all things are in motion. *Metaphysics* 1010a.

[21] εἰς ταὐτὸν συμπέπτωκε[ν] [...] οἶον ῥεύματα κινεῖσθαι τὰ πάντα [...] καὶ αἴσθησιν ἐπιστήμην γίγνεσθαι (*Theaetetus*, 160D).

sophy, which clearly asserted that all those sensible qualities, as they are called, of heat and cold, light and colours, sounds, odours and sapors, formally considered are not things really and absolutely existing without us, but only passions, sensations, and phantasms in us, occasioned by certain local motions made upon the organs of sense from the objects without us, and so indeed, but relative and fantastical things. And thus Protagoras made up his business complete from this mixture of the Heraclitical and atomical philosophy together. For taking it for granted according to Heraclitus' doctrine, that knowledge is nothing else but sense, and according to the Phoenician or atomical philosophy, that the sensible qualities are not things really and absolutely existing without us, but appearances or sensations in us, he concluded, 'all sensible and intelligible things' not to be absolute essences, but things merely relative, fantastical, and imaginary.[22]

Chapter III

1. Now that this atomical, corpuscular, or mechanical philosophy, that solves all the phenomena of the corporeal world by those intelligible principles of magnitude, figure, site, and motion, and thereby makes sensible things intelligible, banishing away those unintelligible corporeal forms and sensible qualities,[23] was known to Protagoras, who lived not only before Plato and Aristotle, but also before Democritus himself, as Plutarch testifies (though he abused it in grounding so strange a paradox upon it), I shall make it undeniably evident from several testimonies out of Plato's *Theaetetus*. For besides that passage afore mentioned, 'That all things are made by local motion and mixture with one another'[24] and what follows after, 'That motion is that which makes every thing to seem to be, or to be generated',[25] he plainly describes the nature of colours according to this hypothesis, the sense whereof is this,

---

[22] πάντα τὰ νοητὰ καὶ αἰσθητά. Compare *TIS*, Preface and pp. 10–11, for a summary of Protagoras' position that uses the examples given here and in the next chapter.

[23] Compare *TIS*, pp. 7–8.

[24] Ἐκ δὲ δὴ φορᾶς τε κινήσεως καὶ κράσεως πρὸς ἄλληλα γίγνεται πάντα (*Theaetetus* 152D). The page references in the 1731 edition are to the Serranus/Stephanus edition, *Platonis opera quae extant omnia* (Geneva, 1578).

[25] τὸ μὲν εἶναι δοκοῦν καὶ τὸ γίγνεσθαι κίνησις παρέχει (*Theaetetus* 153A).

Let us begin first with the eyes or sight. That which is called a white colour is not any real quality existing either without the eyes or in the eyes; for then it would not consist only in motion and generation. But taking it for granted that no sensible thing is such absolutely in itself, we must say that a white and black colour, and every other colour is generated by certain motions made and impressed upon the eye, and every colour is neither that which makes the impression nor that which receiveth it (that is, neither any thing in the eye nor in the object absolutely), but a certain middle thing between them both.[26]

Which can be nothing else but a passion or sensation in us. Elsewhere in that dialogue he proves this assertion, that colours and the like sensible things are no real and absolute qualities either in the sentient or in the object because the same object seems to have different qualities to different persons as,

The same wind blowing seems cold to one and warm to another. And the same wine which to one in health seems sweet, will to the same person appear bitter and distasteful if he be sick.[27]

Whence he concluded that heat and cold, sweet and bitter, were not things really and absolutely existing in the objects without, but relative things, being passions or sensations that may be diversified by the different tempers and complexions of the body.

2. Afterward, we have the sum of this atomical or mechanical philosophy, more copiously set down after this manner,

The beginning upon which all things depend is this, that the whole world is motion and nothing else besides. Now of motion there are two kinds, each of which containeth innumerable branches under it. But the power of one is action, of the other passion. From the mutual congress and contrition of both which together, are begotten innumerable offsprings which may all be reduced to these two general heads, whereof the one [is] the sensible, the other sense, which is always joined together with the

---

[26] ΣΩ. ὑπόλαβε τοίνυν, ὦ ἄριστε, οὑτωσὶ κατὰ τὰ ὄμματα πρῶτον ὃ δὴ καλεῖς χρῶμα λευκὸν, μὴ εἶναι αὐτὸ ἕτερόν τι ἔξω τῶν σῶν ὀμμάτων, μηδ' ἐν τοῖς ὄμμασι μηδέ τιν' αὐτῷ χώραν ἀποτάξῃς· ἤδη γὰρ ἂν [εἴη τε δήπου ἐν τάξει καὶ] μένοι, καὶ οὐκ ἂν ἐν τῇ γενέσει γίγνοιτο. Θέαιτ. Ἀλλὰ πῶς; Σω. Ἑπώμεθα τῷ ἄρτι λόγῳ, μηδὲν αὐτὸ καθ' αὑτὸ ἓν ὂν τιθέντες, καὶ ἡμῖν οὕτω μέλανβτε καὶ λευκὸν καὶ ὁτιοῦν ἄλλο χρῶμα ἐκ τῆς προσβολῆς τῶν ὀμμάτων πρὸς τὴν προσήκουσαν φορὰν φανεῖται γεγεννημένον. καὶ ὃ δὴ ἕκαστον εἶναί φαμεν χρῶμα, οὔτε τὸ προσβάλλον, οὔτε τὸ προσβαλλόμενόν ἐστ[α]ι, ἀλλὰ μεταξύ τι ἑκάστῳ ἴδιον γεγονός (ibid., 153E).

[27] Πνέοντος ἀνέμου τοῦ αὐτοῦ ὁ μὲν ἡμῶν ῥιγοῖ, ὁ δ' οὔ· καὶ ὁ μὲν ἠρέμα, ὁ δὲ σφόδρα (ibid.,152B).

sensible. The senses have such names as these, sight, hearing, tasting, touching, pleasures, pains, desires, fears, and others innumerable without names, but many that have names. The sensible kind doth answer and correspond to every one of these. To the sight all manner of colours, to the hearing sounds, and to the other senses other sensibles, that are of kin to them ... When therefore the eye, and some other thing analogous to it, meet together, they beget whiteness, and a certain sense proportionable thereunto, neither of which would have been made, if either of these had not met with the other. Then these things being carried respectively, sight to the eyes, and whiteness to the object, which did actively beget it, the eye becomes full of sight, and sees, and is not made sight in the abstract, but an eye seeing. And that which did congenerate the colour is fitted with whiteness, and is made not whiteness in the abstract but a thing white, whether wood or stone. The same is to be conceived of all other sensible things, as hard and hot, and the like, that nothing is by itself absolutely any of these things, but they are all made from a mutual congress of the outward object and the sense, by means of motion.[28]

3. Here we see it plainly asserted, that the whole world is made by nothing else but the motion of particles, by means of which all things are generated and corrupted. Neither did Protagoras acknowledge any other motion but local, as is plainly intimated. And that all sensible qualities which we take notice of by the several senses, as colours, sounds, sapors, odours and the like, are not things really existing without us, but passions or sensations in us, caused by several local

---

[28] Ἀρχὴ δὲ ἐξ ἧς καὶ ἃ νῦν δὴ ἐλέγομεν πάντα ἤρτηται, ἥδε αὐτῶν. Ὡς τὸ πᾶν κίνησις ἦν, καὶ ἄλλο παρὰ τοῦτο οὐδέν. Ἔστι δὲ κινήσεως δύο εἴδη, πλήθει μὲν ἄπειρον ἑκάτερον, δύναμιν δὲ τὸ μὲν ποιεῖν ἔχον, τὸ δὲ πάσχειν. Ἐκ δὲ τῆς τούτων ὁμιλίας τε καὶ τρίψεως πρὸς ἄλληλα, γίγνεται ἔκγονα, πλήθει μὲν ἄπειρα, δίδυμα δέ. τὸ μὲν αἰσθητόν, τὸ δὲ αἴσθησις, ἀεὶ συνεκπίπτουσα καὶ γεννωμένη μετὰ τοῦ αἰσθητοῦ. Αἱ μὲν οὖν αἰσθήσεις τὰ τοιάδε ἡμῖν ἔχουσιν ὀνόματα, ὄψεις τε καὶ ἀκοαὶ καὶ ὀσφρήσεις, καὶ ψύξεις τε καὶ καύσεις, καὶ ἡδοναί γε δὲ καὶ λῦπαι καὶ ἐπιθυμίαι καὶ φόβοι κεκλημέναι. Καὶ ἄλλαι ἀπέραντοι μὲν αἱ ἀνώνυμαι, παμπληθεῖς δὲ αἱ ὠνομασμέναι. Τὸ δὲ αὖ αἰσθητὸν γένος τούτων ἑκάσταις ὁμόγονον. Ὄψεσι μὲν παντοδαπαῖς χρώματα παντοδαπά· ἀκοαῖς δὲ ὡσαύτως φωναί, καὶ ταῖς ἄλλαις αἰσθήσεσι τὰ ἄλλα αἰσθητὰ ξυγγενῆ γιγνόμενα.... ἐν φορᾷ αὐτῶν ἡ κίνησις πέφυκεν. Ἐπειδὰν οὖν ὄμμα καὶ ἄλλο τι τῶν τούτῳ συμμέτρων πλησιάσαν γεννήσῃ τὴν λευκότητά τε καὶ αἴσθησιν αὐτῇ ξύμφυτον, ἃ οὐκ ἂν ποτὲ ἐγένετο, ἑκατέρου ἐκείνων πρὸς ἄλλο ἐλθόντος, τότε δὴ μεταξὺ φερομένων [τῆς μὲν ὄψεως πρὸς τῶν ὀφθαλμῶν, τῆς δὲ λευκότητος πρὸς τοῦ συναποτίκτοντος τὸ χρῶμα] ὁ μὲν ὀφθαλμὸς ἄρα ὄψεως ἔμπλεως ἐγένετο, καὶ ὁρᾷ δὴ τότε, καὶ ἐγένετο οὔτι ὄψις, ἀλλὰ ὀφθαλμὸς ὁρῶν. τὸ δὲ συγγεννῆσαν τὸ χρῶμα, λευκότητος περιεπλήσθη, καὶ ἐγένετο οὐ λευκότης αὖ, ἀλλὰ λευκόν, εἴτε ξύλον εἴτε λίθος εἴτε ὁτιοῦν συνέβη χρῆμα χρωσθῆναι τῷ τοιούτῳ χρώματι. Καὶ τἆλλα δὴ οὕτω σκληρὸν καὶ θερμὸν, καὶ πάντα τὸν αὐτὸν τρόπον ὑποληπτέον, αὐτὸ μὲν καθ' αὑτὸ μηδὲν εἶναι, ὃ δὴ καὶ τότε ἐλέγομεν, ἐν δὲ τῇ πρὸς ἄλληλα ὁμιλίᾳ πάντα γίγνεσθαι καὶ παντοῖα ἀπὸ τῆς κινήσεως (ibid., 156A–D).

motions upon the organs of sense. Which if that be not sufficient that I have already alleged, is yet more plainly expressed after this manner:

> Nothing is absolutely any one thing by itself, neither the agent nor the patient, but from both of these meeting together, are generated at once both the senses and the sensible things.[29]

4. These passages which I have cited are so clear and evident, that they cannot possibly be capable of any other sense, than what I have expressed. And therefore those two Latin interpreters, Ficinus and Serranus,[30] that lived before the restitution of this mechanical philosophy, and therefore understood it not, yet expound them after the same manner. The first thus:

> Colour is neither the sight of the eyes, nor the motion of bodies, but a certain middle thing resulting from the sight and motion, that is such a passion about the eyes.[31]

The other in this manner,

> That from the different disposition of the beholder, and so the different affection of the intermediate sensible organ, the various colours are both made and seen, but so as that they are all fantastical, nor have any subsistence but in the mind, are varied by the different congress of motion, which is to be concluded concerning all the senses.[32]

Only Protagoras, in order to his sceptical design, made these sensible things not only relative to animals in general, but also to individuals, because it is impossible to demonstrate, as he urges, that all brute beasts, nay, that any two men have the very same phantasms or ideas of

---

[29] Μέμνησαι γὰρ [...] ὅτι οὕτως ἐλέγομεν, ἓν μηδὲν αὐτὸ καθ᾽ αὑτὸ εἶναι, μηδ᾽ αὐτὸ ποιοῦν ἢ πάσχον, ἀλλὰ ἐξ ἀμφοτέρων πρὸς ἄλληλα συγγιγνομένων ταῖς αἰσθήσεσι, καὶ τὰ αἰσθητὰ ἀποτικτόντων, τὰ μὲν ποιὰ ἄττα γίγνεσθαι, τὰ δὲ αἰσθανόμενα (ibid., 182B).

[30] Marsilio Ficino (1433–99), Florentine philosopher and translator of Plato. Jean de Serres, French translator of Plato, who dedicated his *Platonis opera quae extant omnia* (Geneva, 1578) to Elizabeth I. Cudworth makes the same point, *TIS*, p. 11.

[31] 'Color neque oculorum aspectus est, neque corporum motus, sed ex aspectu motu medium quiddam resultans: id est, talis circa oculos passio' (Ficino, 'Epitome Marsilii Ficini in Theaetum, vel de scientia', *Divini Platonis opera omnia quae exstant Marsilio Ficino interprete* (Frankfurt 1602), p. 101. (Cudworth has 'Color neque' for Ficino's 'albedo, et quisque color nec').) The first edition of Ficino's translation (1590) does not include this part of the epitome. Ficino's own *Opera omnia* (Basel, 1576) does, but misprints 'color' as 'calor'.

[32] 'Ex varia aspicientis *diathesei*, variaque adeo intermedii sensilis schesi*, colores varios et videri et fieri, ita tamen ut omnia sint *phantastika*, nec nisi in animo subsistant, vario autem motus congressu varientur; quod de omnibus sensibus constituendum est' (*Theaetetus* 156D, in margin in Plato, ed. Serranus. (*Original in Greek.)).

red or green, these being idiopathies, and because experience shows, that not only the gratefulness and ungratefulness of tastes and smells, but also that heat and cold are relative to individuals.

Chapter IV

[see summary on p. 4]

1. Wherefore we have made it evident that that very mechanical or atomical philosophy that hath been lately restored by Cartesius and Gassendus, as to the main substance of it, was not only elder than Epicurus, but also than Plato and Aristotle, nay than Democritus and Leucippus also, the commonly reputed fathers of it. And therefore we have no reason to discredit the report of Posidonius the Stoic, who, as Strabo tells us, affirmed this atomical philosophy to have been ancienter than the times of the Trojan war, and first to have been brought into Greece out of Phoenicia.

> If we may believe Posidonius the Stoic, the doctrine of atoms is ancienter than the times of the Trojan war and was first invented and delivered by one Moschus a Sidonian.[33]

Or rather Phoenician, as Sextus Empiricus cites the testimony of Posidonius:

> Democritus and Epicurus invented the doctrine of atoms, unless we make that physiology to be ancienter, and derive it, as Posidonius the Stoic doth, from one Moschus, a Phoenician.[34]

And since it is certain from what we have shown, that neither Epicurus nor yet Democritus were the first inventors of this physiology, this testimony of Posidonius the Stoic ought in reason to be admitted by us.

2. Now what can be more probable than that this Moschus the Phoenecian, that Posidonius speaks of, is the very same person with

---

[33] Εἰ δεῖ πιστεῦσαι τῷ Ποσειδωνίῳ, τὸ περὶ τῶν ἀτόμων δόγμα παλαιὸν ἐστὶν, ἀνδρὸς Σιδονίου Μόσχου πρὸ τῶν Τρωϊκῶν χρόνων γεγονότος (Strabo, XVI.2.24). See *Strabo*, trans. H. Lloyd Jones, 8 vols. (London and New York, 1917–32) vol. VII, p. 271. Cudworth's Greek accords with that in Isaac Casaubon's edition: *Strabonis rerum geographicarum libri xvii Isaacus Casaubonus recensuit* (Geneva, 1587), p. 521.

[34] Δημόκριτος δὲ καὶ Ἐπίκουρος ἀτόμους, εἰ μήτι ἀρχαιοτέραν ταύτην θητέον τὴν δόξαν, καὶ ὡς ἔλεγεν ὁ Στωϊκὸς Ποσειδώνιος, ἀπὸ Μόσχου τινὸς ἀνδρὸς Φοίνικος καταγομένην (Sextus Empiricus, *Against the Physicists*, 1.363).

that Moschus the physiologer, that Iamblichus mentions in the Life of Pythagoras, where he affirms that Pythagoras, living some time at Sidon in Phoenecia, conversed with the prophets that were the successors of Mochus Physiologer, and was instructed by them. 'He conversed with the Prophets that were the successors of Mochus and other Phoenician priests.'[35] And what can be more certain than that both Mochus and Moschus the Phoenician and philosopher was no other than Moses, the Jewish lawgiver, as Arcerius rightly guesses: 'It seems that it ought to be read Moschus, unless they had rather read it Mochus or Moses.'[36] Wherefore according to the ancient tradition, Moschus or Moses the Phoenician being the first author of the atomical philosophy, it ought to be called neither Epicurian nor Democritical, but Moschical or Mosaical.

3. It must be acknowledged that neither of these two famous and renowned philosophers, Plato and Aristotle, had the good hap to be rightly and thoroughly instructed in this ancient Phoenician and Moschical or Mosaical philosophy. Protagoras so much abusing it to scepticism and the taking away of the natural discrimination of good and evil, might probably beget a prejudice in Plato against it, though he doth not confute the physiological part of it in all his *Theaetetus*, where good occasion was offered him. And yet in his *Timaeus* he hath a little smattering of it,[37] where he endeavours to resolve the differences of the four elements, fire, air, water, earth, into the different geometrical figures of their insensible parts, making the small particles of the earth to be cubical, by reason of their solidity and mobility, but the fire, pyramidal, 'It is reasonable that that figure which hath the smallest basis, should be attributed to that body which is most moving, cutting and piercing'.[38] And that he doth not mean mystically in this but physically, appears from his own explication of it concerning the insensible parts, 'These cubes and pyramids in the earth and the fire can only be perceived by the mind and understanding, since the single

---

[35] Τοῖς τε Μώχου τοῦ φυσιολόγου προφήταις ἀπογόνοις καὶ τοῖς ἄλλοις καὶ φοινικικοῖς ἱεροθύταις (Iamblichus, *On the Pythagorean Life*, trans. Gillian Clark (Liverpool 1989), p. 6).

[36] 'Arcerius Μόσχου legendum videtur, nisi quis Μόχου vel Μοσέως legere malit'. In *TIS*, p. 12, Cudworth says of Arcerius, 'the first publisher of Iamblichus', that Selden approved of this view that Moschus was to be identified as Moses.

[37] *Timaeus* 55E.

[38] Τὸ [μὲν] ἔχον ὀλιγίστας βάσεις εὐκινητότατον ἀνάγκη πεφυκέναι, τμητικώτατόν τε ὀξύτατον ὂν πάντῃ πάντων (ibid., 56A).

particles alone are not sensible, but only the aggregation of many of them together.'[39]

4. But Aristotle plainly rejects it. Jacobus Carpentarius, in his notes upon Alcinous, treating of the nature of universals writes thus,

> Some do not altogether deny universals, but will have it that they only are when they are understood, but that there is nothing in nature which answers to the motion of the mind. Which to me indeed is the same thing as if they should say that colours are not in their nature actually anything, but are made such when they are in very deed seen, which opinion also hath its assertors, but is condemned by Aristotle.[40]

This opinion that colours are not actually existent according to those very ideas that we have of them before vision, is the mystery (*arcanum*) of the old atomical or Mosaical philosophy which Carpentarius understood not. Which makes them not qualities absolutely existing without us, but passions and sensations in us. And indeed this philosophy is condemned by Aristotle in his third book *De anima* [*On the Soul*], ch. 2, and that as the received doctrine of the ancient physiologists before his time:

> The former physiologists (saith he), were, generally, mistaken in this, in that they thought blackness and whiteness were no absolute qualities without the sight nor sweet and sour without the taste.[41]

Again, he endeavours to confute the same philosophy which resolves

---

[39] Πάντα οὖν δεῖ ταῦτα διανοεῖσθαι σμικρὰ οὕτως ὡς καθ' ἓν ἕκαστον μὲν τοῦ γένους ἑκάστου διὰ σμικρότητα οὐδὲν ὁρώμενον ὑφ' ἡμῶν, συναθροισθέντων δὲ πολλῶν τοὺς ὄγκους αὐτῶν ὁρᾶσθαι (ibid., 56c).

[40] 'Qui[dam] universalia non omnino quidem tollunt, sed ea tantum esse volunt, quando intelliguntur, nihil vero haberi in natura quod mentis notioni respondeat [...] quod mihi sane perinde est, ac si ille dicerent colores* nihil actu esse, sed tales effici, quando reipsa videntur. Quae etiam opinio suos habuit assertores, sed ab Aristotele est damnata' ('De comparatione Platonis et Aristotelis in quaestione de ideis et universalibus, Iacobi Carpentarii disputatio', in *Platonis cum Aristotele in universa philosophia comparatio. Quae hoc commentario, in Alcinoi Institutionem ad eiusdem Platonis doctrinam, explicatur, authore Iac. Carpentario* (Paris, 1573), p. 209. (*Original has 'colores ille diceret' for 'dicerent colores')). Jacobus Carpentarius (Jacques Charpentier; 1521–74) was an anti-Ramist French philosopher. Alcinous was a Platonist philosopher, of the second or third century AD. He was author of the *Epitome* or *Didaskalikos*, to which Cudworth refers, but nothing more is known about him. Recently John Dillon has challenged Freudenthal's identification of Alcinous with Albinus. See his translation of Alcinous, *The Handbook of Platonism* (Oxford, 1993). An English edition of this work by John Fell was printed in 1667. Thomas Stanley included an English translation of it in his *History of Philosophy* (1656; 2nd edn, London, 1687), pp. 180–96.

[41] Οἱ πρότεροι φυσιολόγοι τοῦτο οὐ καλῶς ἔλεγον, οὐδὲν οἰόμενοι οὔτε λευκὸν οὔτε μέλαν ἄνευ ὄψεως, οὐδὲ χυμὸν ἄνευ γεύσεως (Aristotle, *De anima* 426a21).

those sensible qualities into figures, site and motion of particles, not only attributing it to Democritus, but also making it the most generally received physiology before his time:

> Democritus and most of the Physiologers commit a great absurdity in this, in that they make all sense to be touch, which is a thing at first sight plainly impossible. Moreover, they do not distinguish betwixt the objects common to all the senses and those which are proper and peculiar to the several senses apart. For magnitude and figure, roughness and smoothness, sharpness and bluntness, which belong to bulk, are common to all the senses, or if not to all, yet to sight and touch. Whereas our sense is deceived concerning these common objects, but it is not deceived about colours, nor the hearing about sounds. But most of the ancient physiologists refer these proper objects to the common *sensilia*, as Democritus, who as for white and black, makes one of them to consist in roughness and ruggedness (*scabrities*), the other in smoothness and evenness of parts. He also reduceth sapors to figures, though it belong chiefly to sight to take cognizance of figures and magnitude, and the like. Whereas according to this philosophy, the sense of touch would be the most critical of them.[42]

Aristotle there concludes this discourse with two general arguments against that philosophy (that made the sensible qualities to be properly sensations in us, and nothing else in the objects without us but magnitude, figure, site of parts and motion) in this manner:

> That there is contrariety in qualities, but not in figures, and that the variety of figures being infinite, tastes, colours and the rest would be so likewise.[43]

Which arguments, though they be handsome and ingenious (that is

---

[42] Δημόκριτος καὶ οἱ πλεῖστοι τῶν φυσιολόγων [...] ἀτοπώτατόν τι ποιοῦσι· πάντα γὰρ τὰ αἰσθητὰ ἁπτὰ ποιοῦσι. [...] Καίτοι εἰ καὶ τοῦτο οὕτως ἔχει, δῆλον ὅτι καὶ τῶν ἄλλων αἰσθήσεων ἑκάστη ἁφή τίς ἐστι· τοῦτο δὲ ὅτι ἔστι ἀδύνατον, οὐ χαλεπὸν συνιδεῖν· Ἔτι δὲ τοῖς κοινοῖς τῶν αἰσθήσεων πασῶν χρῶνται ὡς ἰδίοις. Μέγεθος γὰρ καὶ σχῆμα, καὶ τὸ τραχὺ καὶ τὸ λεῖον, ἔτι δὲ τὸ ὀξὺ καὶ τὸ ἀμβλὺ τὸ ἐν τοῖς ὄγκοις κοινὰ τῶν αἰσθήσεων ἐστι εἰ δὲ μὴ πασῶν, ἀλλὰ ὄψεώς γε καὶ ἁφῆς. [...] οἱ δὲ τὰ ἴδια ἐνταῦθα ἀνάγουσιν ὥσπερ Δημόκριτος. Τὸ γὰρ λευκὸν καὶ τὸ μέλαν, τὸ μὲν τραχὺ φησὶν εἶναι, τὸ δὲ λεῖον. Εἰς δὲ τὰ σχήματα ἀνάγει τοὺς χυμούς, καίτοι ἢ οὐδεμιᾶς ἢ μᾶλλον τῆς ὄψεως τὰ κοινὰ γνωρίζειν (Aristotle, *De sensu* 442a30 f.). See also *TIS*, I, p. 6. Apart from the gaps (here marked) there are minor variations of Cudworth's Greek from Aristotle.

[43] Ἔτι τὰ μὲν αἰσθητὰ πάντα ἔχει ἐναντίωσιν, οἷον ἐν χρώματι τῷ μέλανι τὸ λευκὸν, καὶ ἐν χυμοῖς τὸ γλυκὺ τῷ πικρῷ, σχῆμα δὲ σχήματι οὐ δοκεῖ εἶναι ἐναντίον. τίνι γὰρ τῶν πολυγώνων τὸ περιφερὲς ἐναντίον; Ἔτι ἀπείρων ὄντων τῶν σχημάτων, ἀναγκαῖον καὶ τοὺς χυμοὺς εἶναι ἀπείρους (Aristotle, *De sensu* 442b15–20).

41

Aristotelical) to prove that there are such entities as qualities visible, tangible, tasteable and the like, really existing in the objects without us. Yet as they will not counterbalance the weight of those other arguments that militate on the contrary side, so that they will without any difficulty be answered by the assertors of this Novantique philosophy.

5. But after Plato's and Aristotle's time, this old physiology was again revived by Epicurus, but so blended with immorality and impiety as that it soon sunk again, there being nothing left of all those voluminous treatises of Epicurus concerning it, saving what is preserved in Diogenes Laertius,[44] nor no other system thereof transmitted to posterity but what is comprised in the poem of Lucretius Carus.[45] So that the world was generally seized with a deep and profound oblivion of this physiology, there being only some obscure footsteps and dark intimations of it now and then found in the writings of some learned authors. As when Sextus tells us that some of the Stoics held 'that sensitive things were relative to animals and depended upon our sensation' and 'that not the things themselves were comprehended by sense, but only our passions from them';[46] and when the Pyrrhonian Sceptics themselves affirmed, 'that all things are relative, that is, to that which judges of them, and everything appears to be according to sense'.[47]

And when Plotinus makes a doubt whether sensible things did really exist in the objects without us, or were only passions within us,

> it may be well doubted concerning sensible things themselves, that we seem to have the greatest assurance of, whether they really exist in the objects without us, or whether they be passions in us.[48]

6. But in this last age it hath been so successfully restored by the writings of some learned authors, and the truth thereof so convincingly evidenced by many other experiments besides that of the glassy prism

---

[44] Diogenes Laertius, *Lives*, IX.150, which contains Epicurus' 'Sovran Maxims'. See above pp. 11 and 12, nn. 15 and 16.

[45] Lucretius, *De rerum natura*.

[46] Τὰ αἰσθητὰ εἶναι πρός τι, and τὰ πάθη μόνα καταλαμβάνεσθαί. Sextus, *Against the Logicians*, 1.191.

[47] πάντα εἶναι πρός τι, τουτέστι πρὸς τὸ κρῖνον, ὅτι πρὸς τόδε τὸ ζῷον καὶ τόνδε τὸν ἄνθρωπον, καὶ τήνδε τὴν αἴσθησιν ἕκαστον φαίνεται. This appears to be a rendition of Sextus, *Outlines*, 1.135 and 136.

[48] Ἐπεὶ καὶ τὰ ἐπὶ τῆς αἰσθήσεως, ἃ δὲ δοκεῖ πίστιν ἔχειν ἐναργεστάτην, ἀπιστεῖται μήποτε οὐκ ἐν τοῖς ὑποκριμένοις, ἀλλ᾽ ἐν τοῖς πάθεσιν ἔχῃ τὴν δοκοῦσαν ὑπόστασιν, καὶ νοῦ δεῖ ἢ διανοίας τῶν κρινόντων (Plotinus, *Enneads* v.5.1, 13–16).

and rainbow, that there is little doubt left concerning it.[49] And indeed unless this philosophy be acknowledged to be true, we must of necessity affirm, that the sensible and corporeal world is altogether unintelligible. For as Timaeus Locrus long ago observed, that sensible things (τὰ αἰσθητά) could not be apprehended any other way than 'by sense and a certain kind of spurious reason',[50] so it is most certainly true that we cannot possibly have any clear and intelligible ideas of heat and cold, light and colours as such qualities really existing in the objects of sense without us, but as passions and sensations in ourselves we may. Wherefore unless we will assert that these lower sensible things are utterly incomprehensible (ἀκατάληπτα) to our understanding, whilst it is able clearly to comprehend things of a higher nature, we must conclude this old atomical, Moschical or Mosaical philosophy to be true.

Chapter V

1. But though this old atomical philosophy be most solidly and substantially true, the paradoxes that Protagoras and others endeavoured to ground upon it, are not only ridiculously absurd and contradictious in themselves, but also altogether inconsequent from the same.

For as for those assertions, that whatever seems is, and that every fancy is true, though they seem ridiculously absurd, yet those two learned philosophers, Plato and Aristotle, vouchsafe them a serious confutation. Plato from hence in his *Theaetetus*, because that the fancies of them that dream would be as true and real as the sensations of those that are awake, and that all men would be alike wise, and the opinions of the most illiterate idiots in geometry as true as any geometrical theorems, and all predictions of future things alike true, and that in the actions of human life it would be indifferent what any man did in order to any end, and so all deliberation and consultation cease.

But Aristotle, in his metaphysics, with some mixture of facetiousness

[49] Probably a reference to Descartes, *Dioptrics*, especially Discourses 2 and 8, and *Meteors*, Discourse 8. See also R. Hall, *The Revolution in Science, 1500–1700* (London, 1983), pp. 264–72. Descartes' theory of sensation underlies Cudworth's whole discussion of ancient opinion on the senses.

[50] αἰσθήσει καὶ νόθῳ λογισμῷ. Compare *Timaeus*, 51D.

also writes after this manner: 'To those that put their finger under their sight or between their eyes, it will be both two and one'.[51] But Sextus Empiricus bestows more subtlety upon it than either of them,

> If every fancy be true, then when one fancies that every fancy is not true, that must be true also, and so then this proposition that every fancy is true, will be false.[52]

2. Whereas the meaning of these assertions, that whatever seems is, and every fancy is true, was no other than this, that nothing was absolutely true at all, but that all truth and knowledge were but seeming, fantastical and relative things. And because one seeming or appearance is as true as another, therefore they were all equally true, that is to say, none of them true at all. This Aristotle elsewhere rightly apprehended, 'He that saith that all things that appear are true, makes all beings to be relative.'[53]

But if nothing be absolutely true, but only relatively to him that thinks so, then this very opinion of Protagoras, that nothing was absolutely true, and that man was the measure of all things, was not itself absolutely true, but only seemingly and relatively to Protagoras. Whereas this is asserted for an absolute truth by him, that nothing is absolutely true.

And what a ridiculous folly was this in one that would be accounted a philosopher, to take a great deal of pains in writing a large volume, and to endeavour industriously to convince the world, that nothing was absolutely, but only relatively and fantastically true. Since it must needs follow from thence that this very thing itself was not absolutely true, but only relatively to those that thought so, and the contrary altogether as true to those that thought otherwise. For it would no more concern the world to know that this was relatively and fantastically true to Protagoras that nothing was absolutely true, than to know what Protagoras dreamt of the last night. For since according to him,

51 Τοῖς ὑπὸ τὴν ὄψιν ὑποβάλλουσι τὸν δάκτυλον καὶ ποιοῦσιν ἐκ τοῦ ἑνὸς φαίνεσθαι δύο, δύο [δεῖν] εἶναι διὰ τὸ φαίνεσθαι ταῦτα, καὶ πάλιν ἓν τοῖς γὰρ μὴ κινοῦσι τὴν ὄψιν ἓν φαίνεται τὸ ἕν. (τοσαῦτα not ταῦτα). (Aristotle, *Metaphysics* 1063a7–10). Aristotle makes a similar point in *Metaphysics*, 1011a25.
52 Εἰ [γὰρ] πᾶσα φαντασία ἐστὶν ἀληθής, καὶ τὸ μὴ πᾶσαν φαντασίαν εἶναι ἀληθῆ, κατὰ φαντασίαν ὑφιστάμενον ἔσται ἀληθές· καὶ οὕτω τὸ πᾶσαν φαντασίαν εἶναι ἀληθῆ γενήσεται ψεῦδος (Sextus, *Against the Logicians* 1.390).
53 Ὁ λέγεν ἅπαντα τὰ φαινόμενα εἶναι ἀληθῆ, ἅπαντα ποιεῖ τὰ ὄντα πρός τι (Aristotle, *Metaphysics* 1011a19–20).

'that every man does but think'[54] his own truths, it cannot concern any man to know another's opinions any more than his dreams. And therefore Protagoras had done more wisely if he had spared his pains and kept those private relative truths of his own, that is his dream or imagination, wholly to himself.

But by this industrious endeavouring to convince the world of this, that nothing was absolutely true, but only relatively, he plainly confuted his own doctrine in asserting that this was absolutely true, that nothing was absolutely true, which is a manifest contradiction. There need be the less pains taken in confuting scepticism and fantasticism, since it always too easily confutes itself.

3. For if nothing be absolutely true, then not so much as this could be absolutely true, that it seemed to Protagoras that nothing was absolutely true. And it could only seem to be true. Nay, it could not be absolutely true that Protagoras, to whom all truth seemed to be relative, had any real existence, much less that there are any objects without from whence the impressions or motions are made upon our senses; or that there is any such thing as magnitude, motion, figure and site of parts, or 'that matter is floating' and that 'the reasons of all appearances are founded therein'.[55] Which things, as Plato and Sextus tell us, were dogmatically affirmed by Protagoras.

Chapter VI

1. Again, as this scepticism or fantasticism of Protagoras is most absurd and contradictious in itself, so there is not any foundation for it at all in the old atomical philosophy, but contrariwise, nothing doth more effectually and demonstratively overthrow both these assertions, that knowledge is sense, and that all truth and knowledge is but fantastical and relative, than this atomical philosophy doth.

For first, since no sense can judge of itself, or its own appearances, much less make any judgements of the appearances belonging to another sense for,

---

[54] αὐτὸς τὰ αὑτοῦ ἕκαστος μόνα δοξάζει. Compare *Theaetetus* 170–1C.
[55] τὴν ὕλην ῥευστὴν εἶναι. καὶ τοὺς λόγους τῶν φαινομένων πάντων ὑποκεῖσθαι ἐν αὐτῇ (Sextus, *Outlines*, 1.216 and 217).

those things which are perceived by one of our powers, it is impossible to perceive them by another, as the objects of hearing by sight, or the objects of sight by hearing and the like.[56]

The sight cannot judge of sounds which belong to the hearing nor the hearing of light and colours. Wherefore that which judges of all the senses and their several objects, cannot be itself any sense, but something of a superior nature.

2. Moreover, that which judges that appearances of all the senses have something fantastical in them, cannot possibly be itself fantastical, but it must be something which hath a power of judging what really and absolutely is or is not. This being not a relative, but an absolute truth, that sensible appearances have something fantastical in them. Neither could Protagoras ever have arrived to the knowledge of this truth if he had not had some faculty in him superior to sense, that judgeth of what is and is not absolutely.

Now this same rational faculty, that discovers, according to the atomical philosophy, that there is something in our sensations that is merely fantastical and relative, doth assure us also not only that there are absolutely and really such passions, affections, and seemings in us, but that they that do perceive (*sentire*), have an absolute and real entity. For though it should be supposed that our senses did deceive us in all their representations, and that there were no sun, no moon, no earth, that we had no hands, no feet, no body, as by sense we seem to have, yet reason tells us that of necessity that must be something, to whom these things seem to be, because nothing can seem to that that is not. This being an absolute and immutable truth 'that of nothing there is not any either action or passion whatsoever' (*nihil nullam esse neque actionem neque passionem*), but also that when we are awake and use our senses, there are corporeal objects really existing without us, which make those sensible impressions upon us, and that those corporeal objects have absolutely and really as many correspondent varieties in them in respect of magnitude, figure, site, and motion, as there are varieties in sensible ideas and phantasms that we take notice of by them. For Protagoras himself, according to the old atomical philosophy, acknowledges that local motion, magnitude, figure, and site of parts, absolutely are in

---

[56] ἃ δι᾽ ἑτέρας δυνάμεως αἰσθάνει, ἀδύνατον [εἶναι] δι᾽ ἄλλης τούτων αἰσθέσθαι, οἷον ἃ δι᾽ ἀκοῆς, δι᾽ ὄψεως· ἢ ἃ δι᾽ ὄψεως, δι᾽ ἀκοῆς (Plato, *Theaetetus* 185A).

corporeal things themselves, only that colour and such other things are relative. Therefore all being and truth according to Protagoras himself, is not fantastical and relative, but there is some absolute.

3. Wherefore, the proper and genuine result of this old atomical philosophy, which is the triumph of reason over sense, is nothing else but this, that sense alone is not the criterion or judge of what does really and absolutely exist without us, but that there is a higher and superior intellectual faculty in us that judges of our senses, which discovers what is fallacious and fantastical in them, and pronounces what absolutely is and is not. And Democritus, who did more thoroughly and perfectly understand this atomical philosophy than Protagoras, makes this to be the proper result and consequence of it, the invalidating the judgement of sense concerning bodies themselves, and the asserting a higher faculty of reason in us to determine what is absolutely true and false, which is worth noting. For so Sextus, the philosopher, writes concerning Democritus,

> Democritus doth discredit sense, attributing not truth to it but only appearance and that really nothing exists in the corporeal world but atoms and vacuum.[57]

And Democritus' own words concerning it are these,

> Sweet and bitter, hot and cold, colours and the like, are by law and opinion, atoms and vacuum really. That which is supposed and fancied to be are sensibles. But these are not according to truth, only atoms and vacuum.[58]

Sextus Empiricus likewise in another place writes thus concerning Democritus,

> Democritus in his canons saith, that there are two kinds of knowledge, the one by the senses, the other by the mind, of which that by the mind he calls knowledge, accounting it that which may be trusted for the judgement of truth. That by the senses he calleth dark and obscure, denying it to have any certainty as to the knowledge of truth. His own words are these: 'Of knowledge there are two kinds, the one genuine, the

[57] Δημόκριτος [ότε μεν] δὲ ἀναιρεῖ τὰ φαινόμενα ταῖς αἰσθήσεσιν, καὶ τούτων λέγει μηδὲν φαίνεσθαι κατὰ ἀλήθειαν, ἀλλὰ μόνον κατὰ δόξαν ἀληθὲς δὲ ἐν τοῖς οὖσιν ὑπάρχειν τὸ ἀτόμους εἶναι καὶ κενόν (Sextus Empiricus, *Against the Logicians*, 1.135).
[58] Νόμῳ [...] γλυκὺ καὶ νόμῳ πικρὸν, νόμῳ θερμὸν καὶ νόμῳ ψυχρὸν, νόμῳ χροιά· ἐτεῇ δὲ ἄτομα καὶ κενόν (ibid.).

other dark and obscure. To the dark kind of knowledge are referred seeing, hearing, smelling, tasting, touching. But the genuine knowledge is more hidden and recondite than this.'[59]

Now, this concerning Democritus I note the rather more carefully, because Epicurus afterward dotingly fumbling about the same philosophy, made senses to be the only criterion of truth and falsehood, and consequently abused this old atomical philosophy to atheism and immorality. Whereas, if rightly understood, it is the most impregnable bulwark against both. For this philosophy, discovering that the ideas of sense are fantastical, must needs suppose another principle in us superior to sense, which judges what is absolutely and not fantastically or relatively only true or false.

[59] Ἐν δὲ τοῖς κανόσι δύο φησὶν εἶναι γνώσεις, τὴν μὲν διὰ τῶν αἰσθήσεων, τὴν δὲ διὰ τῆς διανοίας, ὧν τὴν μὲν διὰ τῆς διανοίας γνῶσιν κατάγει προσμαρτυρῶν αὐτῇ τὸ πιστὸν εἰς ἀληθείας κρίσιν, τὴν δὲ διὰ τῶν αἰσθήσεων σκοτίην ὀνομάζει, ἀφαιρούμενος αὐτῆς τὸ πρὸς διάγνωσιν τοῦ ἀληθοῦς ἀπλανές· λέγει δὲ κατὰ λέξιν. Γνώμης δὲ δύο εἰσὶν Ἰδέαι, ἡ μὲν γνησίη, ἡ δὲ σκοτίη. Καὶ σκοτίης μὲν τὰ δὲ σύμπαντα Ὄψις, Ἀκοή, Ὀδμή, Γεῦσις, Ψαῦσις· ἡ δὲ γνησίη ἀποκεκρυμμένη δὲ ταύτης (ibid., 1.138).

Book III

Chapter I

1. Now, although what I have already said may possibly seem a sufficient confutation of Protagoras' objections against the immutable and absolute natures or essences of all things, from that very atomical physiology which he appeals to, which, if rightly understood is the most compliable with true metaphysics and the most subservient to it of any; yet notwithstanding, I think it very proper to the business which I have in hand, to launch out further into this argument, to show the different natures of sense and intellection, or knowledge, not only that I may thereby the more fully confute this scepticism, or rather fantasticism of Protagoras, and also assert the immutable natures or essences of things, but also for other purposes, which I shall give an account of in the close of this discourse, and I hope then to make it appear that this was no impertinent digression.

2. I shall begin with sense, to show what it is, and that it is not knowledge.

First therefore it is acknowledged by all, that sense is passion. And there is in all sensation without dispute, first a passion in the body of the sentient, which bodily passion is nothing else but local motion impressed upon the nerves from the objects without, and thence propagated and communicated to the brain, where all sensation is made. For there is no other action of one body upon another, nor other change or mutation of bodies conceivable or intelligible besides local motion. Which motion in that body which moves another, is called action, in that which is moved by another, passion. And therefore, when a corporeal object very remotely distant is perceived by us, since it is by some passion made upon our body, there must of necessity be a continued propagation of some local motion or pressure from thence unto the organs of our sense, or nerves, and so unto the brain. As when we see many fixed stars sparkling in a clear night, though they be all of them so many thousand semi-diameters of the earth distant from us, yet it must of necessity be granted, that there are local motions or pressures from them, which we call the light of them, propagated continuedly or uninterruptedly through the fluid heavens unto our optic nerves, or else we could not see them. And that motion or pressure by which we see all other opaque bodies, is nothing but the pushing (ἀντέρεισμα) against each other of the ethereal globulous particles (*globula*) striving to move outward from the centre of the vortices resisted or rejected from the solid superficies of them. In the same manner as we feel things at a distance in the dark by the resistancy which they make upon the further end of the staff that we hold in our hands.[1] And when we hear the sound of a bell or cannon a great way off, the tremulous vibrations of the air, like the circlings of the water when a stone is flung into it, are from thence continually propagated to our ears or acoustic nerves, the undulations still growing the wider and weaker, the further they go.

3. But forasmuch as sense is not mere local motion impressed from one body upon another, or a body's bare reaction or resistance to that motion of another body, as some have fondly conceited, but a cogitation, recognition, or vital perception and consciousness of these motions or passions of the body, therefore, there must of necessity be another kind of passion also in the soul or principle of life, which is vitally united to the body, to make up sensation. Which passion notwithstanding is of a different kind or species from the former. For the soul, that is a cogitative being, is supposed to be such a thing as can penetrate a body, and therefore cannot be conceived to be moved by the local motion of the body. For we see that light which pervades the air, though it be a corporeal motion, yet it is not moved or shaken by the agitations of the air, because it is not a body far more subtle than the air, that runs through the spongy pores of it. Wherefore the soul, though it be conceived to be an extended substance, yet being penetrative of body,

---

[1] Descartes uses the analogy of finding one's way in the dark by the aid of a stick in his *Optics*, Discourse I. See *AT* VI, 84; CSM I, 153.

not by filling up the pores of it, but co-existing in the same place with it, cannot be locally moved by the motions of it.

Neither is this passion of the soul in sensation a mere naked passion or suffering, because it is a cogitation or perception which hath something of active vigour in it. For those ideas of heat, light, and colours, and other sensible things, being not qualities really existing in the bodies without us, as the atomical philosophy instructs us, and therefore not passively stamped or imprinted upon the soul from without in the same manner that a signature is upon a piece of wax, must needs arise partly from some inward vital energy of the soul itself, being phantasms of the soul, or several modes of cogitation or perception in it. For which cause some of the Platonists would not allow sensations to be passions in the soul, but only active knowledges of the passions of the body ($\pi\alpha\theta\tilde{\omega}\nu$ $\gamma\nu\dot{\omega}\sigma\epsilon\iota\varsigma$).

4. But as I said before, sense is a passion of the soul also, viz., such a passion as a vital and cogitative being is capable of, because we find by experience that it is not elicited from the soul itself, but obtruded upon it from without. So that the soul cannot choose but have such sensations, cogitations, or affections in it when such or such external objects are presented to the outward senses. The soul receiving its information from without by sympathizing with the passions of its own body concerning what individual bodies exist round about it, and the general modes of them; which no innate reason of its own could possibly discover to it. And therefore the soul being necessarily determined to exert such cogitations within itself when such local motions are impressed upon the body which she is vitally united to, these sensations are certain kinds of passive energies of the soul. For the soul and body, by reason of that vital union which is betwixt them making up one compound (*compositum*) or animal, do of necessity mutually suffer from each other, the body being variously moved by the soul, and the soul again variously affected from the body, or the motions which are made upon it. Neither doth the soul suffer indifferently from any body, but all sense arises from that natural sympathy or compassion which the soul hath with that individual body with which it is vitally united. And had not the soul such a passive principle in it, it could not possibly be vitally united to any body, neither could there be any such thing as an animal or living creature.

Moreover these sensitive cogitations, as we shall show afterward, do plainly differ, in the mode of them, from those pure cogitations that are the actions of the soul itself; there being a vast difference between the senses of hunger and thirst, and mere volitions in the soul to eat and drink, likewise betwixt that grief and sadness that arises from some ill tidings told and understood by the mind (though there be something of corporeal passion consequent or concomitant here also) and betwixt a sense of pain when the body is hurt. And in like manner in those other sensations of light and colours, heat and cold, the soul doth not merely know or understand the figure and motions of those corporeal particles, but hath certain confused affections and phantasms within itself by reason of them. From whence it is evident, that these sensitive cogitations are not pure actions springing from the soul itself, but compassions with the body. And therefore that opinion of the Platonists is no way to be admitted, that sensations are not passions, but knowledges of the passions (παθῶν γνώσεις), actions of the soul, or released and unpassionate knowledges in it of the passions of the body.

5. Wherefore sensations formally considered are certain passions or affections in the soul fatally connected with some local motions in the body, whereby the soul perceiveth something else besides those immediate corporeal motions in the nerves, spirits, or brain. For though the soul do only sympathize with the motions of its own body, yet by sense it doth not take immediate cognizance of those very motions themselves, in the brain, spirits, and nerves, perceiving them as they are in themselves, but it is secretly instructed by nature to take notice of some other things thereby that may concern the body.

For first the soul is sometimes so affected by reason of those local motions of the blood and heart communicated by the nerves unto the brain, as that it perceives something within itself, viz., certain passions (*pathemata*) of joy or pleasantness, dullness or sadness, or contristation, irascible and concupiscible inclinations, when we know no rational cause for them within ourselves, and therefore they could not spring from the soul itself.

Again, the soul is sometimes so affected by motions communicated from the nerves that belong to the stomach and windpipe (*oesophagus*), thirst in those parts of the body, and the like may be said of the other pains or pleasures, pruriences and titillations of the body, which the soul perceives as things existing in some certain parts of the body itself; when the nerves are in a certain way moved.

Lastly, the soul is frequently so affected by the motions of those five other conjugations of nerves, as that by natural instinct it takes notice of some corporeal things existing without our bodies, whence that motion upon the nerves comes, as light, colours, sound, heat and cold, hardness, softness, gravity, levity, odours, sapors. The objects being many times remotely distant from us; though it does not perceive them in the same manner as they absolutely exist without us.

Now though all these three kinds mentioned be equally passions and sensations in the soul, yet the use of speech hath appropriated the denomination of passions only to the former, and styled the two latter by the name of sensations, the first of them being commonly called internal corporeal senses, the second external. Wherefore corporeal senses in general may be thus defined, to be affections in the soul caused by certain local motions made upon some parts of the body, by reason of the vital sympathy betwixt the soul and body, whereby the soul seems to perceive corporeal things existing without itself, either in its own body, or else at a distance from it.

Chapter II

1. Wherefore, sense being a passion in the soul, or a compassion with its own body, which it is vitally united to, that is diversified according to the difference both of local motions and of bodily organs through which those motions are conveyed. There being a necessary and fatal connection between certain motions in some parts of the enlivened body, and certain affections or sympathies of the soul, which Democritus seems to intimate in those words, 'By law a thing is cold, or by law hot',[2] that hot and cold, and the like were passions or phantasms fatally connected with certain local motions in the body. Sense is a kind of dull, confused, and stupid perception obtruded upon the soul from without, whereby it perceives the alterations and motions within its own body, and takes cognizance of individual bodies existing round about it, but doth not clearly comprehend what they are, nor penetrate into the nature of them, it being intended by nature πρὸς χρείαν, οὐ πρὸς γνῶσιν as

---

[2] Νόμῳ ψυχρὸν νόμῳ θερμόν (Sextus Empiricus, *Against the Logicians* 1.135).

Plotinus speaks,[3] not so properly for knowledge as for the use of the body. For the soul suffering under that which it perceives by way of passion, cannot master or conquer it, that is to say, know or understand it. For so Anaxagoras in Aristotle very fitly expresses the nature of knowledge and intellection under the notion of conquering (κρατεῖν).

> Wherefore it is necessary, since the mind understands all things, that it should be free from mixture and passion, for this end, as Anaxagoras speaks, that it may be able to master and conquer its objects, that is to say, to know or understand them.[4]

In like manner, Plotinus, in his book of Sense and Memory, makes 'to suffer' (πάσχειν) and 'to be conquered' (κρατεῖσθαι) all one, as also 'to know and to conquer' (γιγνώσκειν καὶ κρατεῖν) for which cause he concludes that that which suffers doth not know: 'That which we make to suffer', *eo nomine*, 'in saying so', 'we make it not to know, because to know is to conquer, and not to be mastered or conquered'.[5] Sense, that suffers from external objects, lies as it were prostrate under them, and is overcome by them: wherefore no sense judges either of its own passion, or of the passion of any other sense, but judgement or knowledge is the active energy of an unpassionate power in the soul.

2. And for this cause Aristotle himself tells us, that the soul is a heterogeneous thing, and hath several parts (μόρια) in it of a very different nature from one another.[6] First, a higher and active part, which he calls τὸ χωριστὸν καὶ ἀπαθές, that which acts separately from the matter, and is impassible, and this is τὸ νοητικόν, that which knows or understands. The other [is] a lower, passive, or sympathetical part which suffers from without and acts in conjunction with the body, and this is τὸ αἰσθητικόν, that to which sensation belongs. So that knowledge and intellection are the clear, serene, and unpassionate perceptions of that higher part of the soul which acts alone, by and from itself. Sensations are the energies of that lower, passive, and sympathetical part, whereby the soul is vitally united to the body, and cleaving to it,

---

[3]   Plotinus, *Enneads* IV.iv.24. Not a quotation.

[4]   'Ανάγκη ἄρα, ἐπεὶ πάντα νοεῖ, ἀμιγῆ εἶναι τὸν νοῦν, ὥσπερ φησὶν 'Αναξαγόρας, ἵνα κρατῇ, τοῦτο δ' ἐστιν ἵνα γνωρίζῃ (Aristotle *De anima* 429a17–19). (Interpolated from previous sentence.)

[5]   Πάσχειν ἀλλ' οὐ γινώσκειν τὸ ἐγγὺς ποιοῦμεν, ὅτι κρατεῖν δέδοται, ἀλλ' οὐ κρατεῖσθαι (Plotinus, *Enneads* IV.vi.2.8–9).

[6]   Aristotle, *De anima* 430a18. Also 432a25ff., where he distinguishes among the rational, sensitive and nutritive functions of the soul.

54

makes up one animal with it. Or else they may be said to be the cogitations of the whole compound (*compositum*) or animal which is the reason they are so cloudy and confounded, because they arise from the very mixture (*crasis*) and confusion of the soul and body as it were blended together.

3. For though the soul be a distinct substance, and of a different nature from the body, yet notwithstanding in every animal it is intimately conjoined with the body, and cleaves to it in such a manner, as that both together compound and make up one thing. And therefore it is not present with it only as a mariner with a ship, that is merely locally, or knowingly and unpassionately present, they still continuing two distinct things; but it is vitally united to it, and passionately present with it. And therefore when the body is hurt, the soul doth not unpassionately know or understand it, as when a mariner knows that a ship hath sprung a leak, or when a man is informed that his neighbour's house is set on fire. But it feels a strong and vehement pain, and hath a dolorous sense or perception of it, as being one thing with it. So in like manner when the body wants either meat or drink, the soul doth not unpassionately know this as an indifferent by-stander, and therefore rationally only will or desire meat and drink for it, but it feels a passionate sense of hunger and thirst in itself, as being intimately concerned in the business. Now the same is true also in those other sensations in which the animal seems to be less concerned, as of light and colour, heat and cold, sounds and odours, that they are not simple knowledges or intellections of that part of the soul which acts alone by itself, but they are the perceptions of that which is vitally united with the body, and sympathizing with the motions and passions of it makes up one compound (*compositum*) with it. Wherefore though all cogitations of the soul, as of the mixed (τò μικτόν) or both together (συναμφότερον), as Plotinus calls it, the compound of soul and body, or as that philosopher will have it, of the 'body and a certain vivificating light imparted from the soul to it'. And therefore, as he observeth out of Aristotle, 'As it is absurd to say the soul weaves'[7] (or indeed the body either, weaving being a mixed action of the man and weaving instruments) so it is absurd to say that the soul alone doth covet, grieve,

---

[7] Ὥσπερ ἄτοπον τὴν ψυχὴν ὑφαίνειν. Not an exact quotation. Plotinus, *Enneads* IV.iv.25. Compare Aristotle *De anima* 408b13.

or perceive (*concupiscere*, *dolere*, or *sentire*), these things proceeding from the compound or the coalescence of soul and body together, being not pure mental, but corporeal cogitations of the soul, as it vitally informs the body and is passionately united to it.

4. Sense therefore is a certain kind of drowsy and somnolent perception of that passive part of the soul, which is as it were asleep in the body, and acts concretely with it. So Plotinus expresses it 'Sense is of that part of the soul that sleeps, for that of the soul that is immersed into the body, is as it were asleep.'[8] It is an energy arising from the body, and a certain kind of drowsy or sleeping life of the soul blended together with it. The perceptions of which compound (*compositum*) or of the soul as it were half asleep and half awake (*animae semisomnis*) are confused, indistinct, turbid, and encumbered cogitations, very different from the energies of the noetical part that acts alone, without sympathy with the body, which are free, clear, serene, satisfactory, and awakened cogitations, that is to say knowledges.

And that these cogitations of the passive part of the soul called sensations are not knowledges or intellections, is evident by experience also, not only in the senses of hunger and thirst, pain and corporeal titillation, but also in all those other perceptions of light and colours, heat and cold, sounds, odours, and sapors. For if they were knowledges or intellections, then all men would rest satisfied in the sensible ideas or phantasms of them, and never enquire any further, at least when the stroke or impression made upon sense were strong and vigorous, as when we see the clear light of the meridian sun, or hear the loud noise of thunder, whereas the one doth but dazzle our eyes, the other deafens our ears, but neither enlighten nor inform our understandings. Whereas, on the contrary, the minds of men are restlessly inquisitive after some further intellectual comprehension of all these things that we perceive by our several senses. Neither is it true of the vulgar only, but it is very observable that the most acute philosophers in all ages have complained of their ignorance of these things, and indeed have confessed themselves more puzzled and at a loss about these sensible things, than those abstract immaterial things which are remote from bodily sense. 'The essences of light and colours', saith Scaliger, 'are as dark to the understanding as they

---

[8] τὸ τῆς αἰσθήσεως ψυχῆς ἐστιν εὐδούσης· ὅσον γὰρ ἐν σώματι ψυχῆς, τοῦτο εὕδει (Plotinus, *Enneads* III.vi.6.70).

themselves are to the sight."[9] Nay, undoubtedly so long as we consider these things no otherwise than sense represents them, that is as really existing in the objects without us, they are and must needs be eternally unintelligible. Now when all men naturally enquire what these things are, what is light, and what are colours, the meaning hereof is nothing else but this, that men would fain know or comprehend them by something of their own which is native and domestic, not foreign to them, some active exertion or anticipation of their own minds, as I shall show afterwards.

Wherefore though sense be adequate and sufficient for that end which nature hath designed it to, viz. to give advertisement of corporeal things existing without us, and their motions for the use and concernment of the body, and such general intimations of the modes of them, as may give the understanding sufficient hints by its own sagacity to find out their natures, and invent intelligible hypotheses to solve those appearances by (for otherwise reason alone without sense could not acquaint us with individual existent things without us, or assure us of the existence of any thing besides God, who is the only necessarily existent being). Yet notwithstanding sense, as sense, is not knowledge or intellection. Which I shall still make further appear by these following more particular considerations.

Chapter III

1. For first, sense only suffering and receiving from without, and having no active principle of its own, to take acquaintance with what it receives, it must needs be a stranger to that which is altogether adventitious to it, and therefore cannot know or understand it. For to know and understand a thing is nothing else but by some inward anticipation of the mind, that is native and domestic, and so familiar to it, to take acquaintance with it; of which I shall speak more afterward.

2. Sense is but the offering or presenting of some object to the mind

---

[9] Julius Caesar Scaliger, *Exotericarum exercitationum liber quintus decimus de subtilitate ad Hieronymum Cardanum* (Paris, 1557, first published 1540), no. 325, section 1, p. 435v. Cudworth's translation follows the Latin of the 1665 Frankfurt edition, p. 1025: 'luminis et colorum essentiae sunt intellectui tam obscurae, quam sunt ipsa visui manifesta'.

to give it an occasion to exercise its own inward activity upon. Which two things being many times nearly conjoined together in time, though they be very different in nature from one another, yet they are vulgarly mistaken for one and the same thing, as if it were all nothing but mere sensation or passion from the body. Whereas sense itself is but the passive perception of some individual material forms, but to know or understand, is actively to comprehend a thing by some abstract, free, and universal reasonings (*rationes*) from when the mind, 'as it were looking down', as Boethius expresseth it, 'upon the individuals below it, views and understands them'.[10] But sense which lies flat and grovelling in the individuals, and is stupidly fixed in the material form, is not able to rise up or ascend to an abstract universal notion. For which cause it never affirms or denies any thing of its object, because (as Aristotle observes) in all affirmation and negation at least, the predicate is always universal. The eye which is placed in a level with the sea, and touches the surface of it, cannot take any large prospect upon the sea, much less see the whole amplitude of it. But an eye elevated to a higher station, and from thence looking down, may comprehensively view the whole sea at once, or at least so much of it as is within our horizon. The abstract universal reasons (*rationes*) are that higher station of the mind from whence looking down upon individual things, it hath a commanding view of them, and as it were *a priori* comprehends or knows them.

But sense which either lies in the same level with that particular material object which it perceives, or rather under it and beneath it, cannot emerge to any knowledge or truth concerning it.

3. Sense is but a slight and superficial perception of the outside and accidentals of a corporeal substance, it doth not penetrate into the profundity or inward essence of it. For a body may be changed as to all the several senses, and remain really the same that it was before. Wherefore, though men are commonly said to know things when they

---

[10] 'quasi desuper spectans concepta forma quae subsunt dijudicat', Boethius, *De consolatione philosophiae* v, pr. iv. The English part of the quotation is longer than the Latin. Harrison terminates it prematurely at 'understands them', but it is clear from the source that Cudworth's English renders several more lines of Boethius. Loeb translation (by S.J. Tester), v, pr. iv lines 97–100: 'the intelligence, as it were looking down from above, by conceiving Form distinguishes all the things subject to that Form, but only because of the way it comprehends the Form itself'. Original Latin: 'sed intelligentia quasi desuper spectans concepta forma quae subsunt etiam cuncta diiudicat, sed eo modo quo formam ipsam, quae nulli alii nota esse poterat, comprehendit'. Cudworth refers to the same passage again, below, pp. 73 and 88.

see and feel them, yet in truth by their bodily senses they perceive
nothing but their outsides and external induments. Just as when a man
looking down out of a window into the streets, is said to see men
walking in the streets, when indeed he perceives nothing but hats and
clothes, under which, for aught he knows, there may be Daedalean
statues walking up and down.[11] Neither is this spoken only in respect of
that defect of sight (to omit the other senses) which is a little relieved by
microscopical glasses, yet it cannot perceive the figures and contextures
of those minute particles out of which bodies are compounded, nor
penetrate beyond the superficies into their corporeal profundity. For
though our sight were so much more than Lyncean, that it could
discover the very pores in glass through which the light passes, as
Aristotle complains it cannot, nay though it could discern the particular
globulous particles (*globuli*) in the motion of which light consisteth, and
the triangular spaces between them through which the smallest and
most subtle striated matter passes, yet notwithstanding it would not
reach to the essential profundity either of body or sphericalness, or
triangularity, which nothing but the subtle sharpness (*acies*) of the mind
can penetrate into, so as to comprehend the immutable reason (*ratio*) of
any of them. And therefore it is rightly pronounced by that excellent
restorer of the old atomical and Moschical philosophy,

> That even bodies themselves are not properly perceived by the senses or
> by the imagination, but by the understanding alone; nor are therefore
> perceived because they are touched or seen but only because they are
> understood.[12]

Descartes Meditations (handwritten margin note)

4. The essence of nothing is reached unto by the senses looking
outward, but by the mind's looking inward into itself. That which
wholly looks abroad outward upon its object is not one with that which
it perceives, but is at a distance from it, and therefore cannot know and
comprehend it. But knowledge and intellection doth not merely look
out (*prospicere*) upon a thing at a distance, but makes an inward

[11] Daedalus, mythical Greek inventor, reputed to have made life-like automata. This passage is
closely modelled on Descartes, *Meditation*, II. *AT*, IX, 25; CSM, II, 21. 'But then if I look out of
the window and see men crossing the square, as I just happen to have done, I normally say that
I see the men themselves ... Yet do I see any more than hats and coats which could conceal
automatons? I *judge* that they are men.'
[12] 'Ipsamet corpora non proprie a sensibus vel ab imaginandi facultate, sed a solo intellectu
percipi, ne ex eo percipi, quod tangantur aut videantur, sed tantum ex eo, quod intelligantur'
(Descartes, *Meditations*, II). *AT*, VII, 34. CSM, II, 22.

reflection upon the thing it knows, and according to the etymon of the word, the intellect (*intellectus*) doth read inward characters written within itself (*in interioribus legere*), and intellectually comprehend its object within itself, and is the same with it. For though this may be conceived to be true of individual things known (although the mind understands them also under abstract notions of its own) yet at least in Aristotle's sense, it is unquestionably true, 'In abstract things themselves', which are the primary objects of science, 'the intellect and the thing known are really one and the same'.[13] For those ideas or objects of intellection are nothing else but the modifications of the mind itself. But sense is that which is without (αἴσθησις τοῦ ἔξω), sense wholly gazes and gads abroad, and therefore doth not know and comprehend its object, because it is different from it. 'Sense is a line, the mind is a circle.'[14] Sense is like a line which is the flux of a point running out from itself, but intellect like a circle that keeps within itself.

5. Sense apprehends individual bodies without by something derived from them and so *a posteriori*, 'The senses being last are the images of the things'.[15] The sensible ideas of things are but umbratile and evanid images of the sensible things like shadows projected from them; but knowledge is a comprehension of a thing proleptically, and as it were, *a priori*. But now, to lay aside metaphysics, and speak plainly, all that which comes from the individual object of sense from without (as we have already declared) is nothing at all but local motion or pressure, when an enlivened body is jogged or thrust upon by some other body without. But to receive or feel a jog, knock, or thrust from without made upon the body which the soul is united to, this is not to know, no not so much as what local motion is, much less to know all other things. For knowledge is not a knock or thrust from without, but it consisteth in the awakening and exciting of the inward active powers of the mind.

6. This point which I have hitherto insisted upon concerning the shallowness, dullness, and bluntness of sense, in that it cannot penetrate to the essences of things, is very ingeniously and philosophically handled by Plato, in his *Theaetetus*, where he demonstrates against Protagoras, that science is not sense, but that there is another power in

---

[13] Ἐπὶ [μὲν γὰρ] τῶν ἄνευ ὕλης τὸ αὐτό ἐστι τὸ νοοῦν καὶ τὸ νοούμενον (Aristotle, *De anima* 430a5).
[14] Αἴσθησις γραμμὴ νοῦς κύκλος. Compare Plotinus, *Enneads*, iv.i.7.8 and v.vii.6.10.
[15] Ὕστεραι οὖσαι αἰσθήσεις εἰκόνες εἰσι. Compare *Enneads* v.v.1.17–18.

the soul besides that of sense or passion, to which science, knowledge, and intellection is to be referred after this manner. First, Socrates obtains this from *Theaetetus*, that sense is when the soul, by or through several organs of the body, takes cognizance of corporeal things without. And secondly, that one sense or organical perception cannot take cognizance of the object of another, as sight cannot see sounds, nor the hearing hear light and colours. And therefore, where we think of the objects of several senses comparing them together, and considering of some things common to them all, this cannot be sense or organical perception, because one sense cannot consider the object of another sense, 'If any thing concerns both, it cannot perceive it by either organ.'[16] As when we consider sound and colour together at once, and attribute several things to them in common, as, first of all essence, and then that in each of them is identity with itself, and diversity to the other, that both of them are two and each of them one; that they are not like but unlike to one another. What sense or organ is there by which the soul perceives all these things, viz. essence and non-essence, identity, diversity, unity, duality, similitude, dissimilitude, things common both to sound and colour? Surely it cannot be neither by the senses of sight or of hearing, because these cannot consider one another's objects. Neither can we find any other organ in the body by which the soul may passively take cognizance of all these things, and consider the objects of both those other senses of sight and hearing. Whereby he makes Theaetetus confess that these things the soul doth not organically perceive by any sense, but by itself alone without any bodily organ. And therefore, 'Some things the soul perceives by itself, or by its own active power',[17] as essence, similitude, dissimilitude, identity, alterity, good and evil, honest and dishonest. Other things it perceives by and through the organs of the body: as for example, by the sense of touch the soul perceives nothing but the hardness of that which is hard, and the softness of that which is soft, and the like. But essence, and what hardness and softness is, and their contrariety to one another, and again, the essence of contrariety itself, the soul alone by itself discoursing endeavours to judge of. Wherefore there is this difference

---

[16] *Εἴ τι ἄρα περὶ ἀμφοτέρων διανοῇ, οὐκ ἂν διά γε τοῦ ἑτέρου ὀργάνου αἰσθάνοι ἄν* (Plato, *Theaetetus* 185A).

[17] *Τὰ μὲν αὐτὴν δι᾽ αὐτῆς [τὴν] ψυχὴν ἐπισκοπεῖν, τα δὲ τῶν τοῦ σώματος δυνάμεων* (Plato, *Theaetetus* 185E).

between those things that come into the soul by the passions of the body, and those things that arise from the ratiocinative power of the soul itself.

> That both men and beasts do naturally perceive as soon as they be born those things that come into the soul by the passions of the body. But ratiocinations concerning these things as to the natures and essences of them, and their utilities, are slowly by labour and help of institution attained unto.[18]

Now, that which doth not reach to the essence of anything, cannot reach truth or knowledge. Wherefore, he concludes that

> there is no knowledge or science in passions but in the discourse of the mind upon them. For in this latter way it is possible to reach to the essence and truth of things, but impossible in the former.

And that we ought not

> to seek knowledge any more in sense, but in that of the soul, whatsoever it be called, which doth alone by itself contemplate things that are.[19]

Chapter IV

1. But I have still something more to add concerning this argument before I dismiss it. Wherefore in the next place, I shall make it further appear, that sense is not science or intellection, because the soul by sense doth not perceive the things themselves, or the absolute natures of them, but only her own passions from them. This Sextus the philosopher took notice of: 'The senses do not reach to the objects that are placed without but to their own passions alone.'[20] And this is that which

---

[18] Τὰ μὲν εὐθὺ γενομένοις πάρεστι φύσει αἰσθάνεσθαι ἀνθρώποις τε καὶ θηρίοις, ὅσα διὰ τοῦ σώματος παθήματα ἐπὶ τὴν ψυχὴν τείνει· τὰ δὲ περὶ τούτων ἀναλογίσματα πρός τε οὐσίαν καὶ ὠφέλειαν μόγις καὶ ἐν χρόνῳ διὰ πολλῶν πραγμάτων καὶ παιδείας παραγίγνεται, οἷς ἂν καὶ παραγίγνηται (ibid., 186c).

[19] Ἐν μὲν ἄρα τοῖς παθήμασιν οὐκ ἔστιν ἐπιστήμη, ἐν δὲ τῷ περὶ ἐκείνων συλλογισμῷ· οὐσίας γὰρ καὶ ἀληθείας ἐνταῦθα μὲν ὡς ἔοικε δυνατὸν ἅψασθαι, ἐκεῖ δὲ ἀδύνατον (ibid., 186D). Original has ἐνι for ἔστιν. Ζητεῖν [ἐπιστήμην] ἐν αἰσθήσει τὸ παράπαν, ἀλλ' ἐν ἐκείνῳ τῷ ὀνόματι ὅτι ποτ' ἔχει ἡ ψυχή, ὅταν αὐτὴ καθ' αὑτὴν πραγματεύηται περὶ τὰ ὄντα, (ibid., 187A).

[20] Αἴ [δὲ] αἰσθήσεις τὰ ἐκτὸς ὑποκείμενα οὐ καταλαμβάνουσιν, μόνα δὲ εἰ ἄρα τὰ ἑαυτῶν πάθη (Sextus, *Outlines of Pyrrhonism*, II.7.72).

Protagoras so much insisted on, that all our sensible ideas (τὰ αἰσθητά) of light and colours, sounds, odours, sapors, heat and cold, and the like, are not absolute but relative things. For neither is sensation (αἴσθησις) any thing of the soul considered absolutely in itself, it being no pure and sincere cogitation of the soul alone, neither is the sensible idea (τὸ αἰσθητόν) any absolute quality of the object without, but both these (viz. sense and sensible) are certain middle things begotten betwixt the agent and the patient, and resulting from the activity of the object without and the passion of the mind within and severally respecting each of them. Or, as he expressed it,

> From the congress or collision of these two together are generated at once both sense and the sensible. For the sensible (formally considered, according to that idea that we have of it) hath no existence before sensation, but is begotten with it.[21]

And therefore, 'Colour and the rest is neither anything in the soul itself, but a middle thing betwixt both',[22] that is a passion. Which is the very same with that which Aristotle imputes to the ancient physiologers as a paradox, that black and white were not without the sight.

The truth of which is so evident in some instances, that none can possibly gainsay it. For when the body is either pricked with a needle or wounded with a sword, no man can imagine that those pains that result from thence were such real and absolute qualities existing in the needle or sword before our sensation, but that they are our own passions, and so relative things to us, or perceptions of the motions of the needle or sword relatively to the enlivened body, and as they are hurtful to it. And the same is vulgarly acknowledged in those colours that are therefore called fantastical, as in the rainbow (*iris*) and the prism, whereas in reality all colours are as fantastical as the colours of the rainbow, and the colours of the rainbow as real as any other. And it is likewise true of the other proper objects of the several senses. For as Sextus the philosopher observes, 'Honey is not the same thing with my being sweetened, nor wormwood the same with my having sense of bitterness.'[23] That which

---

21 Ἐκ [δὲ] τῆς τούτων ὁμιλίας τε καὶ τρίψεως πρὸς ἄλληλα γίγνεται [...] τὸ μὲν αἰσθητὸν, ἡ δὲ αἴσθησις, ἀεὶ συνεκπίπτουσα καὶ γεννωμένη μετὰ τοῦ αἰσθητοῦ (*Theaetetus* 156A).

22 Ὃ δὴ ἕκαστον εἶναί φαμεν χρῶμα οὔτε τὸ προσβάλλον οὔτε τὸ προσβαλλόμενόν ἐστι, ἀλλὰ μεταξύ τι (*Theaetetus* 154A). Loeb translation: 'that which we call colour will be in each instance neither that which impinges, nor that which is impinged upon, but something in between'.

23 Οὐ [γὰρ] τὸ αὐτὸ ἔστι τὸ μέλι τῷ γλυκάζεσθαί με, καὶ τὸ ἀψίνθιον τῷ πικράζεσθαι (Sextus Empiricus, *Outlines of Pyrrhonism*, II.7.72).

we know by sense concerning honey and wormwood, is only that our taste is so affected from them. But what absolute mode or disposition of parts in them [which] causes these different sensations in us, belongs to some other faculty of the soul to discover. And hence it comes to pass, that though the natures or essences of things be simple, yet one and the same thing perceived by our several senses begets several passions and phantasms in us. Flame, which is nothing but a violent agitation of the small particles of a body by the rapid subtle matter; the same motion communicated to the eye or optic nerves begets one kind of sensible idea or phantasm called light, but to the nerves of touch another quite different from it called heat. Therefore neither light nor heat, according to those sensible ideas that we have of them, are really and absolutely in the flame without, which is but one kind of motion or agitation of matter, but only fantastically and relatively, the one to our sight, the other to our touch. And hence it proceeds also that sensations are diversified from the same thing to several individuals of the same kind, and to the same individual at several times, by reason of some difference in the idiosyncrasy or proper temperament of the body, as (to omit the instance of those that are icterical) appears plainly in the degrees of heat and cold, the gratefulness or ungratefulness of several tastes and odours to several individuals, or to the same considered both in sickness and in health. Which things could not be if all sensible ideas were absolute qualities in the thing itself, and so taken notice of by sense. And it is worth the while to see how Protagoras philosophized about this latter instance, improving it to this purpose,

> When I drink wine, being in health, it appears pleasant and sweet. For the agent and the patient betwixt them beget both sense and sweetness, severally respecting the agent and the patient. For sense respecting the patient, makes and denominates the tongue sentient, and sweetness respecting the agent (that is, the wine) makes and denominates that sweet, not absolutely but respectively to the tongue of one that is in health. But when the patient is altered by sickness, and becomes different from what it was, then it receives quite another taste than formerly, for it comes to a very different patient. Quite different things are produced by the person and the drinking of the wine. Respecting the tongue a sense of bitterness, and as to the wine its being made and denominated bitter.[24]

---

[24] Ὅταν [δὴ] οἶνον πίνω ὑγιαίνων, ἡδύς μοι [φαίνεται] καὶ γλυκὺς. [...] Ἐγέννησε γὰρ δὴ [...] τό τε ποιοῦν καὶ τὸ πάσχον γλυκύτητά τε καὶ αἴσθησιν ἅμα φερόμενα ἀμφότερα. Καὶ ἡ μὲν

Wherefore since by sense the soul doth not perceive corporeal objects as they are truly, really, and absolutely in themselves, but under some fantastical representations and disguises, sense cannot be knowledge, which comprehends a thing as it is. And indeed if the soul had no other power in it but only this of passion or sensation (as Protagoras supposed), then there could be no such thing at all as any absolute truth or knowledge. But that hypothesis of his, as we have already showed, plainly contradicts and confutes itself. For that which pronounces that our sensible ideas of things are fantastical and relative, must needs be something in us superior to sense, that is, not relative or fantastical, but that judges what really and absolutely is and is not.

2. But to strike this business home, I shall in the last place further observe that sense cannot be knowledge, nor the certainty of all things ultimately resolvable into sense, as many men beside Protagoras conceive, for this reason, because the nature of sense consists in nothing else but mere seeming or appearance. This was intimated before in that definition that we gave of sense, that is a passion or affection (ἐν τῷ δοκεῖν or ἐν τῷ φαίνεσθαι) in the soul whereby it seems to perceive some corporeal things existing. That is, sense is when the soul is so affected as if there were such a corporeal thing existing. So that all the reality that is necessarily required to sense is only this, that there be really a passion in the soul, or that the soul be really so affected as if there were such a thing. That is, that it have really such a seeming or appearance, but not that the thing really be, as it appears. For as to a thing's being such or such, its having such a mode or quality, we have already demonstrated by reason, that in this respect most of our sensible ideas are fantastical things. And the same may be evinced and made evident also by sense itself. For it is as true and real a sensation when a man looking upon a staff that is partly in the air, and partly in the water, sees it crooked (though it be really straight), as when he looks upon it all in the air, and sees it straight as really it is. For we are as really affected

αἴσθησις πρὸς τοῦ πάσχοντος οὖσα αἰσθανομένην τὴν γλῶσσαν ἀπειργάσατο. Ἡ δὲ γλυκύτης πρὸς τοῦ οἴνου περὶ αὐτὸν φερομένη γλυκὺν τὸν οἴνον τῇ ὑγιαινούσῃ γλώσσῃ [ἐποίησεν] καὶ εἶναι καὶ φαίνεσθαι. [...] Ὅταν δὲ ἀσθενοῦντα ἄλλο τι ἢ πρῶτον μὲν τῇ ἀληθείᾳ οὐ τὸν αὐτὸν ἔλαβεν, ἀνομοίῳ γὰρ δὴ προσῆλθε[ν]. [...] Ἕτερα δὴ αὖ ἐγεννησάτην ὅ τε τοιοῦτος καὶ ἡ τοῦ οἴνου πόσις περὶ μὲν τὴν γλῶτταν αἴσθησιν πικρότατος, περὶ δὲ τὸν οἴνον γιγνομένην καὶ φερομένην πικρότητα (*Theaetetus* 159D). It is not Protagoras but Socrates who is speaking at the opening of this quotation. Cudworth also omits the responses of Theaetetus. He does not indicate this either in the English or the Greek. As a result a passage of dialogue appears as a monologue.

and there is as much a seeming in one as in the other. And innumerable instances might be given in this kind, to prove that as to things being such or such, there is no other truth or reality necessarily required in sensation, but only that of appearance.

But this is not all, for I shall observe in the next place that there is not so much as the reality of being or existence of the object necessarily required to sensation, but there may be a true sensation, though there be no object at all really existing without the soul. A known and approved instance whereof we have in those that, after they had their arms and legs cut off, have been sensible, when they were awake, of a strong violent pain in their fingers and toes, though really they had no such members. And we have all constant experience of the same in our dreams, which are as true sensations, as those which we have when we are awake, and when the objects are really existent without us. Because the soul is as really affected, and hath as lively images, ideas, and phantasms of sensible things as existent [things] then, as when we are awake, and many times is really sensible of violent and exquisite pain, which is a real sense, though it be but a fantastical thing, and immediately vanishes away upon our awakening. Because there was nothing really in the body, that by the motions of the nerves could beget a real pain.

3. Now the reason of this, that the soul may be passively affected in this manner, when there is no object at all really existing without it, is from hence: because by sense the soul doth not suffer immediately from the objects themselves, but only from its own body, by reason of that natural and vital sympathy which it hath with it, neither doth it suffer from its own body in every part of it, or from the outward organs of sense immediately – as from the eye when we see, the tongue when we taste, or the exterior parts of the body when we feel, but only in the brain, or from the motions of the spirits there.[25] But so as that it doth not take immediate cognizance of those very motions immediately as they are in themselves, but by the secret instinct of nature doth by means of them take cognizance of those corporeal things existing without us, from whence the original of the motion comes: as for example of the stars that are so vastly distant when we look upon the heavens. Whence it comes to pass that if that body from which the soul immediately suffers, and that is the spirits in the brain, be so moved as

---

[25] Compare Descartes, *Principia philosophiae*, Part 4, sections 189ff. (CSM 1, 279ff.). By 'suffer' Cudworth does not mean 'to feel pain', but 'to be acted upon'.

it would be moved by the nerves when any outward objects make their several impressions upon the organs of sense, the soul must needs have the same passions, affections, and sensations in it, as if the objects were really existing without. Now this may come to pass either by the fortuitous motions or agitations of the spirits themselves, casually falling into the same figurations, that the motions of the nerves would impress upon them from some outward objects, or else by the spirits rushing against certain prints, traces, or marks in the brain made by former sensations when we were awake, whereby their motions are determined. Or, lastly, by the fantastical power of the soul itself, which as it suffers from the body, so it can likewise act upon it, and according to our customary actions or inward affections, inclinations, or desires may move the spirits variously, and beget divers phantasms in us.

And that dreams are many times thus begotten or excited by the fantastical power of the soul in itself, is evident from the orderly connection and coherence of imaginations, which many times are continued in a long chain or series; with the fiction of interlocutory discourses and dialogues consisting of apt answers and replies made interchangeably to one another, and contain such things as never were before printed upon the brain in such a series or order. Which therefore could not proceed either from the fortuitous dancings or subsultations of the spirits, or from the determination of their motion, by antecedent prints or traces made by former sensations in the substance of the brain.

4. And the dreams that we have in our sleep are really the same kind of things with those imaginations that we have many times when we are awake, when the fancy, being not commanded or determined by the will, roves and wanders and runs at random, and spins out a long thread or concatenated series of imaginations or phantasms of corporeal things, quite different from those things which our outward senses at the same time take notice of. And some persons there are to whom these waking dreams are very ordinary and familiar.

And there is little doubt to be made but if a man should suddenly fall asleep in the midst of one of these waking dreams when his fancy is roving and spinning out such a long series of imaginations, those very imaginations and phantasms would of course, *ipso facto*, become dreams, and run on, and appear not as phantasms or imaginations only of things feigned or non-existent, but as perceptions of things really existent, that is as sensations.

Whereas these imaginations that we have of individual corporeal things when we are awake, and our outward senses employed upon their several objects, do not seem to be sensations of things really existing and present as our dreams do, but to be certain faint, evanid, shadowy, and umbratile things in comparison of those sensations which we have at the same time with then when we are awake, that is, not as things existent without us, but as our own cogitations. The reason whereof is, because though they be both of the same kind, yet those motions of the spirits which are caused by the nerves, from the objects without when we are awake, being more vigorous, durable, constant, and prevalent, do naturally obscure or extinguish those other weaker phantasms or imaginations which we have at the same time. And reason interposing, brings in its verdict for those stronger phantasms also whose objects are durable and permanent, by means whereof the latter only seem to be real sensations, the former counterfeit and fictitious imaginations or mere picture and landscape in the soul. And this Aristotle long ago observed in this manner:

> In the day they are shut out and disappear, the senses and understanding working as the lesser fire is made to disappear by the greater, and small griefs and pleasures by great ones. But when we are at rest in our beds, the least phantasms make impressions upon us.[26]

In the day-time when we are awake, those more fleeting fancies and imaginations which proceed not from the motions of the nerves caused by the objects without must needs yield and give place, as being baffled and confuted by those stronger, more durable and lasting motions that come from the nerves, caused by permanent objects, reason also carrying it clearly for the latter, by means whereof the former cannot appear as real things or sensations. But when we are asleep, the same phantasms and imaginations are more strong, vivid, and lively, because the nerves are relaxated, there are often no motions transmitted by them from the outward objects into the brain, to confound those motions of the spirits within, and distract the soul's attention to them. Just as the same loudness of a voice in a still evening will be heard a great deal further and clearer, than in the day-time when the air is agitated with

---

[26] Μεθ' ἡμέραν ἐκκρούονται, ἐνεργουσῶν τῶν αἰσθήσεων καὶ τῆς διανοίας, καὶ ἀφανίζονται ὥσπερ παρὰ πολὺ πῦρ ἔλαττον, καὶ λῦπαι καὶ ἡδοναὶ μικραὶ παρὰ μεγάλας, παυσαμένων δὲ ἐπιπολάζει καὶ τὰ μικρά (Aristotle, *On Dreams*, 461a1–5).

many contrary motions crossing and confounding one another. But now there are no other motions of the spirits besides these which cause dreams to compare with them, and disgrace them, or put them out of countenance, and, as it were, by their louder noise and clamours, so to possess the animadversive part of the soul, that the weaker murmurs of the other cannot obtain to be heard, as it is when we are awake, or in the day-time. And therefore in sleep the mind naturally admits these phantasms as sensations, there appearing none other to contradict that verdict.

5. Wherefore, phantasms and sensible ideas are really or materially the same thing, which Aristotle intimates, affirming that fancy is a weak kind of sense ($\phi a \nu \tau a \sigma i a$ is $a \ddot{\iota} \sigma \theta \eta \sigma i \varsigma$ $\tau \iota \varsigma$ $\dot{a} \sigma \theta \epsilon \nu \dot{\eta} \varsigma$) and that phantasms are as sensations ($\phi a \nu \tau \acute{a} \sigma \mu a \tau a$ are $o \tilde{\iota} a$ $a \dot{\iota} \sigma \theta \acute{\eta} \mu a \tau a$).[27] For both phantasms and sensations are passions or sufferings in the soul from the body. And yet notwithstanding every phantasm doth not seem to be a corporeal thing really existing without the soul, as a sensation ($a \ddot{\iota} \sigma \theta \eta \mu a$) doth. Wherefore there are two cases in which a phantasm doth not seem to be a sensation. First when a phantasm is raised or excited purposely and voluntarily, by the mere imperium, command, or empire of our own will, as by experience we find it often is. For it is in our power to fancy what corporeal thing or person (formerly known to us) we please, though it be absent from us. Nay, and to compound such things as we never saw before, as a golden mountain, a centaur, a chimera. Now in this case, when the soul is conscious to itself, that these phantasms are arbitrarily raised by it, or by its own activity, it cannot look upon them as sensations, or things really existing without itself, but only as evanid images, pictures and adumbrations of things within itself. And such phantasms as these do usually accompany most of our other cogitations. Wherefore phantasms (*phantasmata*) do not seem to be sensations or perceptions of things as really existing without the soul, when they are voluntary, or when the soul is inwardly conscious that they are raised up by its own activity.

Secondly, neither doth every involuntary phantasm, or such as the soul is not conscious to itself to have purposely excited or raised up within itself, seem to be a sensation or perception of the thing as existing without us. For there may be straggling phantasms which come into the

---

[27] Aristotle, *Rhetoric* I.XI.6. See also *De anima* III.iii. 2.4.

mind we know not how and bubble up of themselves, which yet the soul may distinguish from sensations or perceptions of things as existing really without it, because of some other phantasms the same time in the soul, whose vigours and lustre do cloud and eclipse them. For when there are phantasms of several kinds at the same time in the soul, or such as arise from different motions of the spirits, the soul silently comparing both together naturally looks upon the more vigorous, strong, and permanent of those phantasms only as real existences, but the more faint, flitting, and transitory, as imaginary things. Now there are two kinds of involuntary phantasms, as I have already intimated, in the soul when we are awake. One that proceeds from such motions of the spirits as are caused by the nerves moved from the objects without. Another that proceeds from the spirits of the brain, otherwise moved than by the nerves. And therefore *in vigilia*, when we are awake, and have phantasms that arise from the motions of the nerves caused by the objects without, appearing very different from those other phantasms that arise from the spirits otherwise moved than by the nerves, both in respect of their vigour and constancy, do therefore to all such persons, as are not distempered either in body or in mind, naturally seem to be real, or things existing without the soul, but the latter imaginary. Whereas in sleep, when the nerves being relaxed, communicate no motion to the spirits, the very same phantasms (there being now no other and stronger to compare with them and discredit or disgrace them) do naturally appear to the soul as sensations of things really existing without the soul.

6. Now the truth of this matter doth evidently appear from hence, in that by reason of some disease either of body or mind, men's spirits may be so furiously, violently, and strongly agitated that those phantoms which do not arise from the motion of the nerves, being most prevalent and predominant, even when they are awake, may become sensations and appearances of things as really existing without the soul; that men may confidently believe they hear, see, and feel those things that are not, and be imposed upon in all their senses. Which is a thing that frequently happens, not only in phrenetical, maniac, and hypochondriacal persons, of which there are many instances recorded, but also in others possessed with strong passions of fear, love and the like. Wherefore as sense, that is the phantasms that arise from the motion communicated to the spirits of the brain by the nerves, do ordinarily

baffle and confute imaginations and fancy, that is, those phantasms that arise from the spirits otherwise moved than by the nerves, so likewise imaginations growing wild, rampant, and exorbitant, may in the same manner baffle and confute all our senses.

7. Which exorbitancy of fancy or imagination prevailing over sense, or those phantasms which arise form the motion communicated to the brain from the objects without by the nerves, may either proceed originally from some disease in the body, whereby the animal spirits being furiously heated and agitated may be carried with so great a force and career, as that the motions caused from the objects by the nerves being weakened, may yield and give place to them, and their phantasms be in a manner silent vanquished and obliterated by them. Those stronger phantasms that arise from the agitation of the spirits themselves, possessing the place of them, the affection or animadversion of the soul being always won by those phantasms that make the loudest noise, or have the greatest vigour. Or else the same thing may proceed originally from some disease or distemper in the soul itself. When the lower, irrational, and passive part of the soul (in which concupiscible and irascible affections are seated), and so by consequence, the fantastic power of the soul (the same power that begets in us those waking dreams before-mentioned) grows excessively and exorbitantly predominant, insomuch that it doth not only weaken and extinguish the noetical powers, which are always proportionably debilitated as this is invigorated, but also prevent the power of the soul itself, the immoderate activity of the fancy not permitting the soul to suffer from, or be passive to the action of the objects upon it, nor quietly to receive the impressions of them, without ruffling and confounding them. And this is that sad and lamentable condition that the soul of man is liable and obnoxious to, by its overmuch indulgence to that passive and irrational and corporeal part in which the affections, appetites, and desires are seated – a condition which, if it continue always, is worse than death itself, or perfect annihilation. To have not only reason degraded and dethroned, but even sense itself perverted or extinguished, and in the room thereof boisterous phantasms protruded from the irrational appetites, passions, and affections (now grown monstrous and enormous) to become the very sensations of it, by means whereof it is easy to conceive that the divine vengeance (nemesis) may make the soul its own tormentor, though there were no other hell without it, not only by

71

representing most loathsome and affrightful, dismal, and tragical scenes of things to itself, but also by cruciating itself with exquisite and sensible pains. And the serious consideration hereof should make us very careful how we let the reins loose to that passive irrational part of our soul which knows no bounds nor measures, lest thereby we unawares precipitate and plunge ourselves headlong into the most sad and deplorable condition that is imaginable.

8. I shall not discourse here of that power also which evil spirits (*genii*) may possibly have upon those that have either mancipated themselves into them, or otherwise forfeited that ordinary protection which divine providence commonly affordeth to all, by acting immediately upon the spirits of the brain, and thereby endeavour to give an account of those phenomena of wizards and witches vulgarly talked of, their seeming transportations in the air, nocturnal conventicles and junketings, and other such like things, as seem plainly contradictious and irreconcilable to philosophy.[28] But we have already said enough to prove that sense is nothing but seeming appearance. And therefore we can have no certainty by sense alone either concerning the absolute natures of individual corporeal things without us, nor indeed of their existence. But all the assurance that we have thereof arises from reason and intellect judging of the phantasms of appearances of sense, and determining in which of them there is an absolute reality, and which of them are but merely relative or fantastical.

[28] He means that these phenomena, not the belief in witches etc., seem to contradict philosophy. This was a view shared by his friend and colleague, Henry More, who adduces stories of witchcraft and the appearance of ghosts to corroborate his arguments in his *Immortality of the Soul* (London, 1659) and his *Antidote against Atheism* (London, 1653). Joseph Glanvill does the same in his *Sadducismus Triumphatus, or Full and Plain Evidence Concerning Witches and Apparitions* (London, 1681).

Book IV

Chapter I

1. Having hitherto showed that sense or passion from corporeal things existent without the soul is not intellection or knowledge, so that bodies themselves are not known or understood by sense, it must needs follow from hence that knowledge is an inward and active energy of the mind itself, and the displaying of its own innate vigour from within, whereby it doth conquer (κρατεῖν), master, and command its objects, and so begets a clear, serene, victorious, and satisfactory sense within itself.

Wherefore though it be vulgarly conceived that knowledge arises from the force of the thing known acting upon that which knows from without, yet contrariwise it is most certain, to use Boethius' expression,

> that intellection and knowledge do not arise from the force and activity of the thing known from without, upon that which knows, but from the inward power, vigour and activity of the mind that knows actively. Comprehending the object within itself, and subduing and prevailing over it.[1]

So that knowledge is not a passion from anything without the mind, but an active exertion of the inward strength, vigour, and power of the

---

[1] 'Id quod scitur, non ex sua vi, sed ex comprehendentis vi et facultate sciri vel cognosci' (Boethius, *De consolatione philosophiae* V, pr. iv, lines 75–7). The Latin quotation is not exact and the translation does not really fit the Latin as given. The original reads, 'Omne enim quod cognoscitur non secundum sui vim sed secundum cognoscentium potius comprehenditur facultatem.' Loeb translation: 'For everything which is known is grasped not according to its own power but rather according to the capability of those who know it.' See below p. 88 and *TIS*, p. 731.

mind, displaying itself from within, and the intelligible forms by which things are understood or known are not stamps or impressions passively printed upon the soul from without, but ideas vitally protended or actively exerted from within itself.

2. A thing which is merely passive from without, and [which] doth only receive foreign and adventitious forms, cannot possibly know, understand, or judge of that which it receives but must needs be a stranger to it, having nothing within itself to know it by. The mind cannot know anything, but by something of its own, that is native, domestic, and familiar to it. When in a great throng or crowd of people, a man looking round about, meets with innumerable strange faces that he never saw before in all his life and at last chances to espy the face of one old friend or acquaintance, which he had not seen or thought of many years before, he would be said in this case to have known that one, and only that one face in all that company, because he had no inward previous or anticipated form of any other face, that he looked upon in his mind. But as soon as ever he beheld that one face, immediately there revived and started forth a former anticipated form or idea of it treasured up in his mind, that, as it were taking acquaintance with that newly received form, made him know it or remember it. So when foreign, strange, and adventitious forms are exhibited to the mind by sense, the soul cannot otherwise know or understand them, but by something domestic of its own, some active anticipation or prolepsis within itself, that occasionally reviving and meeting with it, makes it know it or take acquaintance with it. And this is the only true and allowable sense of that old assertion, that knowledge is reminiscence,[2] not that it is the remembrance of something which the soul had some time before actually known in a pre-existent state, but because it is the mind's comprehending of things by some inward anticipations of its own, something native and domestic to it, or something actively exerted from within itself. And thus Plotinus, when he endeavours to prove that the immediate objects of knowledge and intellection are not things

---

[2] This refers to Plato's theory of *anamnesis*, the theory of knowledge as reminiscence or recollection, discussed in *Meno* 81A f. and *Phaedo* 72E f. In refusing to link *anamnesis* to the theory of the pre-existence of souls, Cudworth is closer to Nathaniel Culverwell than to Henry More. Culverwell's *Elegant and Learned Discourse on the Light of Nature* (London, 1652; modern edition by R.A. Greene and H. McCallum, Toronto, 1971) criticizes this doctrine. Henry More, by contrast, retained it as a hypothesis, in spite of the fact that, from a religious point of view, it was (and is) heterodox.

without the mind acting upon it at a distance, but contained and comprehended within the mind itself,

> Otherwise how should the mind know or judge when it had really apprehended any thing that is good, that is honest or just, these things being all strangers to the mind, and coming into it from without. So that the mind could not have any principles of judgement within itself in this case, but these would be without it, and then the truth must needs be without it also.[3]

3. If intellection and knowledge were mere passion from without, or the bare reception of extraneous and adventitious forms, then no reason could be given at all why a mirror or looking-glass should not understand, whereas it cannot so much as sensibly perceive those images which it receives and reflects to us. And therefore sense of itself, as was before intimated, is not a mere passion, but a passive perception of the soul, which hath something of vital energy in it, because it is a cogitation. To which vital energy of the soul those sensible ideas of light, colours, heat, and the like, owe all their entity. Much less therefore can intellection be a pure passion. But if intellection and knowledge were a mere passive perception of the soul from without and nothing but sense, or the result of it, then what reason could be given why brute animals that have all the same senses that men have, and some of them more acute, should not have intellection also, and be as capable of logic, mathematics, and metaphysics, and have the same notions of morality, of a deity and religion that men have? Wherefore it must of necessity be granted, that besides passion from corporeal things, or the passive perception of sense, there is in the souls of men another more active principle or an innate cognoscitive power (*vis cognoscendarum rerum innata*), whereby they are enabled to understand or judge of what is received from without by sense. And some, that would otherwise make the soul as naked a thing as is possible, are forced to acknowledge thus much. And hereby they grant all that we contend for and they deny though considering not in the mean time what they say. For this innate cognoscitive power in the soul can be nothing else but a power of raising intelligible ideas and conceptions of things from within itself. For it is not possible that any knowledge should be without an

---

[3] Πῶς δὲ καὶ γνώσεται ὅτι ἀντελάβετο ὄντως, πῶς δὲ ὅτι ἀγαθὸν τοῦτο, ἢ ὅτι καλὸν ἢ δίκαιον; Ἕκαστον γὰρ τούτων ἄλλο αὐτοῦ, καὶ οὐκ ἐν αὐτῷ αἱ τῆς κρίσεως ἀρχαὶ αἷς πιστεύσει, ἀλλὰ καὶ αὐταὶ ἔξω καὶ ἡ ἀλήθεια ἐκεῖ (Plotinus, *Enneads* v.v.1.29–33).

objective idea or conception of something known included in it, or that the intellection (νόησις) should be in one faculty, and the conception (νόημα) in another, one in the intellect, and the other in the fancy. That knowledge should be actively produced from within, and the conception or objective idea passively received from without, that the mind should exert an act of knowledge or intellection without an object, or upon an object without itself, and not comprehended by it, that the idea of the thing known should not be comprehended in the knowledge of it. Whereas, as Aristotle himself hath observed, 'Actual knowledge is in reality the same with the thing known, or the idea of it',[4] and therefore inseparable from it. It being nothing but the mind's being conscious of some intelligible idea within itself.

4. And therefore, whereas the only objects of sense are individual corporeal things existing without the mind, which the soul perceives by looking out from itself upon that from which it suffers, not actively comprehended within itself; the primary and immediate objects of intellection and knowledge, are not things existing without the mind, but ideas of the mind itself actively exerted, that is the intelligible reasons (*rationes*) of things. 'The intellection is not of what is without, as sense is.' And 'the immediate objects of intellection are not without the mind that understands'.[5] They are assertions that Plotinus at large demonstrates. And Aristotle frequently asserts the same: 'In abstracted things that which understands and that which is understood are the same',[6] for the theoretical science and the knowable (*scibile*) or object of knowledge are all one.[7] And 'the mind altogether is that which understands things'.[8] These being all but several modifications of intellect. For as hard and soft, hot and cold, and the like corporeal qualities are but several modifications of matter, so the several objective ideas of the mind in scientifical speculation are but several modifications of the mind knowing. Wherefore individual things existing without the soul, are but the secondary objects of knowledge and intellection, which the mind understands not by looking out from itself as sense doth, but by

---

4   *Τὸ [δ'] αὐτὸ ἔσ τιν ἡ κατ' ἐνέργειαν ἐπιστήμη τῷ πράγματι* (Aristotle, *De anima* 431a. Also 430a20).
5   *Νόησις οὐ τοῦ ἔξω, ὥσπερ ἡ αἴσθησις.* (Plotinus, *Enneads* v.v.1.26). And, *ὅτι οὐκ ἔξ τοῦ νοῦ τὰ νοητά.* This is the first part of the title of *Ennead* v.
6   *Ἐπὶ [μὲν γὰρ] τῶν ἄνευ ὕλης τὸ αὐτό ἐστι τὸ νοοῦν καὶ τὸ νοούμενον· ἡ γὰρ ἐπιστήμη ἡ θεωρητικὴ καὶ τὸ ἐπιστητὸν τὸ αὐτό ἐστι* (Aristotle, *De anima* 430a3–6).
7   Ibid., 431a1.
8   *ὅλως ὁ νοῦς [ἐστιν] ὁ κατ' ἐνέργειαν τὰ πράγματα νοῶν* (ibid., 431b18).

reflecting inwardly upon itself and comprehending them under those intelligible ideas or reasonings (*rationes*) of its own, which it protrudes from within itself. So that the mind or intellect may well be called (though in another sense than Protagoras meant it) 'the measure of all things' (τὸ μέτρον πάντων).

5. For the soul having an innate cognoscitive power universally (which is nothing else but a power of raising objective ideas within itself, and intelligible reasons of any thing) it must needs be granted that it hath a potential omniformity in it. Which is not only asserted by the Platonists, that the soul is 'all things intellectually' (πάντα νοερῶς), but also by Aristotle himself, 'That the soul is in a manner all things.'[9] The mind being a kind of notional or representative world, as it were a diaphanous and crystalline sphere, in which the ideas and images of all things existing in the real universe may be reflected or represented. For as the mind of God, which is the archetypal intellect, is that whereby he always actually comprehends himself, and his own fecundity, or the extent of his own infinite goodness and power – that is the possibility of all things – so all created intellects being certain ectypal models, or derivative compendiums of the same. Although they have not the actual ideas of all things, much less are the images or sculptures of all the several species of existent things fixed and engraven in a dead manner upon them, yet they have them all virtually and potentially comprehended in that one cognoscitive power (*vix cognitrix*) of the soul, which is a potential omniformity whereby it is enabled as occasion serves and outward objects invite, gradually and successively to unfold and display itself in a vital manner, by framing intelligible ideas or conceptions within itself of whatsoever hath any entity or cogitability. As the spermatic or plastic power doth virtually contain within itself, the forms of all the several organical parts of animals, and displays them gradually and successively, framing an eye here and an ear there.

6. Now because intellection and knowledge are not passion[s] from without, but an active exertion of the mind from within itself, hence it comes to pass, as Aristotle hath observed, that the mind by knowing that which is exceedingly intelligible (σφόδρα νοητόν), the most radiant and illustrious truths, is not debilitated thereby or overpowered, as

---

[9] τὴν ψυχὴν εἶναι τὰ ὄντα πως πάντα (*De anima* 431b20). (Original reads, ἡ ψυχὴ τὰ ὄντα τώς ἐστι πάντα.) (Loeb: 'that in a sense the soul is all the existing universe'. Compare *De anima* 430a15, where Aristotle talks of mind (νοῦς) rather than soul (ψυχή).)

sense is in perceiving that which is exceedingly sensible (σφόδρα
αἰσθητόν),[10] as the brightness of the sun; but contrariwise the more
invigorated thereby, and the better enabled to comprehend lesser and
smaller truths; because though sense is passion and organical, yet
knowledge is inorganical and an active power and strength of the mind,
which the more it is exerted, is the more thereby invigorated and
enlarged.

From hence likewise it is, as the same Aristotle hath observed, 'That
those knowledges which are more abstract and remote from matter, are
more accurate, intelligible, and demonstrable, than those which are
conversant about concrete and material things, as arithmetic than
harmonics',[11] which are numbers concrete with sounds; and so likewise
geometry than astronomy, or the mixed mathematics. Whereas if all
knowledge did arise from corporeal things by way of sense and passion,
it must needs be contrariwise true, that the more concrete and sensible
things were, the more knowable they would be. Moreover, from hence
it is also as experience tells us, that scientifical knowledge is best
acquired by the soul's abstraction from the outward objects of sense,
and retiring into itself,[12] that so it may the better attend to its own
inward notions and ideas. And therefore it is many times observed, that
over-much reading and hearing of other men's discourses, though
learned and elaborate, doth not only distract the mind, but also
debilitates the intellectual powers, and makes the mind passive and
sluggish, by calling it too much outwards. For which cause that wise
philosopher Socrates altogether shunned that dictating and dogmatical
way of teaching used by the sophisters of that age and chose rather an
aporetical and obstetricious method. Because knowledge was not to be
poured into the soul like liquor, but rather to be invited and gently
drawn forth from it; nor the mind so much to be filled therewith from
without, like a vessel, as to be kindled and awakened. Lastly, from hence
is that strange parturiency that is often observed in the mind, when it is
solicitously set upon the investigation of some truth, whereby it doth

---

[10] The Greek terms are from Aristotle, *De anima* 429b3 and 429b1.

[11] ἀκριβεστέραν [δ'] ἐπιστήμην τῆς ἐπιστήμης, τὴν μὴ καθ᾽ ὑποκειμένου τῆς καθ᾽ ὑποκειμένου,
οἷον ἀριθμητικὴν τῆς ἁρμονικῆς (Aristotle, *Posterior Analytics*, trans. H. Tredennick (London
and Cambridge, Mass., 1960 1.27). Greek varies from original.

[12] Compare John Smith,'We must shut the bright eye of Sense, and open that brighter Eye of our
Understanding' (*The True Way of Attaining to Divine Knowledge*, in *Select Discourses* (1660),
repr. in *The Cambridge Platonists*, ed. C.A. Patrides (Cambridge, 1969), p. 140).

endeavour, by ruminating and revolving within itself as it were to conceive it within itself, to bring it forth out of its own womb (*parturire*). By which it is evident, that the mind is naturally conscious of its own active fecundity, and also that it hath a criterion within itself, which will enable it to know when it hath found that which it sought.

7. Wherefore it is evident from what we have declared, that there are two kinds of perceptive cogitations in the soul: the one passive when the soul perceives by suffering from its body, and the objects without; the other active, when it perceives by exerting its own native vigour from within itself. The passive perceptions of the soul have two several names given unto them. For when the soul, by sympathizing with the body, seems to perceive corporeal things, as present and really existing without it, then they are called sensations (αἰσθήματα). But when the passive affections of the soul are looked upon not as things really existing without the mind, but only as pictures of sensible things in the mind, or more crass or corporeal cogitations, then they are called phantasms (φαντάσματα) or imaginations. But these phantasms and sensations being really the same things, as we said before, both of them being passions or affections in the soul, caused by some local motions in the body, and the difference between them being only accidental, insomuch that phantasms may be changed into sensations, and sometimes also sensations into phantasms, therefore all these passive perceptions of the soul may be called in general phantasms (φαντάσματα). But the active perceptions which rise from the mind itself without the body, are commonly called conceptions of the mind (νοήματα). And so we have the two species of perceptive cogitations, the one phantasms and the other conceptions of the mind.

8. Now that all our perceptive cogitations are not phantasms, as many contend, but that there is another species of perceptive cogitations distinct from them, arising from the active vigour of the mind itself, which we therefore call conceptions of the mind, is demonstrably evident from hence; because phantasms are nothing else but sensible ideas, images or pictures of outward objects, such as are caused in the soul by sense. Whence it follows, that nothing is the object of fancy (φάντασματον), but what is also the object of sense (αἴσθηματον), [and] nothing can be fancied by the soul but what is perceptible by sense. But there are many objects of our mind, which we can neither see, hear, feel, smell nor taste, and which did never enter into it by any sense; and

therefore we can have no sensible pictures or ideas of them, drawn by the pencil of that inward limner or painter which borrows all his colours from sense, which we call fancy. And if we reflect on our own cogitations of these things, we shall sensibly perceive that they are not fantastical, but noematical. As for example, justice, equity, duty and obligation, cogitation, opinion, intellection, volition, memory, verity, falsity, cause, effect, genus, species, nullity, contingency, possibility, impossibility, and innumerable more such there are that will occur to any one that shall turn over the vocabularies of any language, none of which can have any sensible picture drawn by the pencil of the fancy. And there are many whole propositions likewise, in which there is not any one word or notion that we can have any genuine phantasm of, much less can fancy reach to an apprehension of the necessity of the connection of the terms. As for example, *Nothing can be and not be at the same time* (*Nihil potest esse et non esse eodem tempore*). What proper and genuine phantasms can any perceive in his mind either of 'nothing', or 'can' or 'be' or 'and', or 'not be', or 'at the same', or 'time'?[13]

9. Neither was it asserted by Aristotle, as some have taken for granted, that all our perceptive cogitations are phantasms (φαντάσματα), but contrariwise, that there are conceptions of the mind (νοήματα) which are distinct things from phantasms, only that the latter were always individual companions of the former. This appears from those words of his, 'conceptions of the mind somewhat differ from phantasms, they are not phantasms, but neither are they without phantasms'.[14] Where he inclines to this, that the conceptions of the mind are not phantasms but that they have phantasms always joined with them. So again afterwards he asks, 'Whether intellection be fancy, or rather a different thing from fancy, but such as never goes without it.'[15] Which indeed he affirms in other places, that the mind doth never conceive (νοεῖν) without a phantasm. Now this is true of sensible and corporeal things, that we never understand them, but we have also some confused phantasms or other of them in our mind, and yet besides the phantasms the mind exerts conceptions also upon them, or else it could not understand them, phantasms being but imperfect, incomplete, and

[13] In the 1848 edition, the appropriate Latin word from the axiom is inserted alongside each English one in this list.
[14] Νοήματα τινὶ διοίσει τοῦ μὴ φαντάσματα εἶναι ἢ οὐδὲ ταῦτα φαντάσματα ἀλλ' οὐκ ἄνευ φαντασμάτων (Aristotle, *De anima* 432a13). Original has ταλλα for ταῦτα.
[15] τὸ νοεῖν φαντασία, ἢ μὴ ἄνευ φαντασίας (ibid., 403a9).

superficial cogitations, which sometimes go before, and invite or call in, meanwhile, the perceptions of the mind, and sometimes follow and attend upon the conceptions of the mind, as the shadow upon the substance, but never comprehend the thing. And indeed, as we ourselves consist of soul and body naturally united together, so are the cogitations that we have of corporeal things usually both noematical and phantasmatical together, the one being as it were the soul and the other the body of them. For when a geometrician considers a triangle, being about to demonstrate that it hath three angles equal to two right angles, no doubt but he will have the pha[n]tasmatical picture of some triangle in his mind. And yet notwithstanding he hath also a noematical perception or intellectual idea of it too, as appears from hence, because every express picture of a triangle must of necessity be either obtusangular or rectangular, or acutangular, but that which in his mind is the subject of this proposition thought on is the reason (*ratio*) of a triangle undetermined to any of these species. And the like might be observed also of the word angles in the same proposition. In like manner, whenever we think of a phantasmatical universal, or universalized phantasm, or a thing which we have no clear intellection of – as for example of the nature of a rose in general – there is a complication of something noematical, and something phantasmatical together. For phantasms in themselves alone, as well as sensations (αἰσθήματα) are always individual things. And by a rose we mean a thing which so affects our sense in respect of figure and colour.

10. But as for those other objects of cogitation which we affirmed before to be in themselves neither the objects of sense (αἰσθητά) nor the objects of fancy (φανταστά), but only things understood (νοητά), and therefore can have no natural and genuine phantasms properly belonging to them; yet it is true notwithstanding that the fantastic power of the soul, which would never willingly be altogether idle or quite excluded, will busily intend itself here also. And therefore many times when the intellect or mind above is exercised in abstracted intellections and contemplations, the fancy will at the same time busily employ itself below, in making some kind of apish imitations, counterfeit iconisms, symbolical adumbrations, and resemblances of those intellectual cogitations of sensible and corporeal things. And hence it comes to pass, that in speech, metaphors and allegories do so exceedingly please, because they highly gratify this fantastical power of passive and corporeal

81

cogitation in the soul, and seem thereby also something to raise and refresh the mind itself, otherwise lazy and ready to faint and be tired by overlong abstracted cogitations, by taking its old companion the body to go along with it, as it were to rest upon, and by affording to it certain crass, palpable, and corporeal images, to incorporate those abstracted cogitations in, that it may be able thereby to see those still more silent and subtle notions of its own, sensibly reflected to itself from the corporeal glass of the fancy.

Sometimes also there are other spurious phantasms that do little or nothing symbolize with the noetical cogitations, that yet are arbitrarily or customarily annected to them, merely because the fantastic power would not stand wholly idle and unemployed. So that when the mind thinks of such an intelligible idea, the fancy will presently hold forth such a customary phantasm before it, 'as those that use artificial memory, make certain phantasms at pleasure'[16] to signify certain cogitations.

But lastly, rather than the fancy shall quite stand out and do just nothing at all, it will sometimes exercise itself (especially in speech) in raising phantasms of the very sounds and names, by which the notions of the mind are signified respectively. So that it is very true both that there are active cogitations of the mind distinct from phantasms; and such of which there can be no natural and genuine phantasms or sensible pictures; and yet, according to Aristotle's opinion, that frequently those conceptions of the mind (at least in the vulgar, that are little accustomed to abstracted cogitation) have some kind of spurious and counterfeit, or verbal and nominal phantasms joined with and accompanying of them.

11. As for that opinion, that the conceptions of the mind and the intelligible ideas or reasons of the mind should be raised out of the phantasms by the strange chemistry of an agent intelligence:[17] this as it is founded on a mistake of Aristotle's meaning, who never dreamed of any such chimerical agent intelligence, as appears from the Greek interpreters that best understood him, so it is very like to that other

---

[16] ὥσπερ οἱ ἐν τοῖς μνημονικοῖς τιθήμενοι καὶ εἰδωλοποιοῦντες (ibid., 427b20).

[17] In *De anima* Aristotle distinguishes between the active intellect (*intellectus agens* or *nous poetikos*) and the potential intellect (*intellectus possibilis* or *nous pathetikos*). The distinction is not clear, but the former was conceived as a power of abstraction, by which universal content is abstracted from sense impressions. Inconsistencies in the text gave rise to divergent interpretations of the agent intellect (*intellectus agens*). See below, p. 115.

opinion called peripatetical, that asserts the eduction of immaterial forms out of the power of matter. And as both of them arise from the same sottishness of mind that would make stupid and senseless matter the original source of all things, so there is the same impossibility in both, that perfection should be raised out of imperfection, and that vigour, activity, and awakened energy should ascend and emerge out of dull, sluggish, and drowsy passion. But indeed this opinion attributes as much activity to the mind, if at least the agent intelligence be part of it, as ours doth. As he would attribute as much activity to the sun, that should say the sun had a power of educing light out of night or the dark air, as he that should say the sun had a power of exerting light out of his own body. The former being but an improper way of expressing the same thing, which is properly signified in the latter way. But that other opinion, that asserts that the abstract and universal reasons of things as distinct from phantasms, are nothing else but mere names without any signification, is so ridiculously false, that it deserves no confutation at all.

Chapter II

1. That there are some ideas of the mind which were not stamped or imprinted upon it from the sensible objects without, and therefore must needs arise from the innate vigour and activity of the mind itself, is evident, in that there are, first, ideas of such things as neither are affections of bodies, nor could be imprinted or conveyed by any local motions, nor can be pictured at all by the fancy in any sensible colours (such as are the ideas of wisdom, folly, prudence, imprudence, knowledge, ignorance, verity, falsity, virtue, vice, honesty, dishonesty, justice, injustice, volition, cogitation, nay of sense itself, which is a species of cogitation, and which is not perceptible by any sense, and many other such like notions as include something of cogitation in them) or refer to cogitative beings only. Which ideas must needs spring from the active power and innate fecundity of the mind itself, because the corporeal objects of sense can imprint no such things upon it. Secondly, in that there are many relative notions and ideas, attributed as well to corporeal as incorporeal things that proceed wholly from the activity of the mind

comparing one thing with another. Such as are cause, effect, means, end, order, proposition, similitude, dissimilitude, equality, inequality, aptitude, inaptitude, symmetry, asymmetry, whole and part, genus and species, and the like.

2. But that which imposes upon men's judgements here, so as to make them think, that these are all passive impressions made upon the soul by the objects of sense, is nothing else but this. Because the notions both of those relative ideas, and also of those other immaterial things (as virtue, wisdom, the soul, God) are most commonly excited and awakened occasionally from the appulse of outward objects knocking at the doors of our senses. And these men not distinguishing betwixt the outward occasion or invitation of those cogitations, and the immediate active or productive cause of them, impute them therefore all alike, as well these intelligible, as these other sensible ideas, or phantasms, to the efficiency or activity of the outward objects upon us. Wherefore that we may the better understand how far the passion of sense reaches, and where the activity of the mind begins, we will compare these three things together: first, a mirror, looking-glass or crystal globe; secondly, a living eye, that is a seeing or perceptive mirror or looking-glass; thirdly, a mind or intellect superadded to this living eye or seeing mirror.

3. First therefore, when the same objects are equally exposed or held before a crystal globe or looking-glass, and a living eye, there are all the same impressions made upon the crystal globe, that there are upon the living eye. Which appears from hence, because the eye looking upon the crystal globe or mirror, will see all the same images reflected to itself from thence, that it perceived before immediately from the objects themselves. The motion and pressure of the ethereal globulous particles, in which the nature of light is conceived to consist from every opaque object, bearing alike every way upon that which resists, and therefore as much upon the mirror as the eye: so that there is every jot as much corporeal passion in the mirror or crystal globe, as in the glassy part of the living eye; for, as we said before, the corporeal part of the eye is indeed nothing else but a mirror or looking-glass. And yet notwithstanding, the mirror or crystal globe doth not see or perceive anything as the eye doth; from whence we learn, first that things are never perceived merely by their own force and activity upon the percipient, but by the innate force, power, and ability of that which perceives. And therefore, secondly, that sense itself is not a mere corporeal passion, but

84

a perception of the bodily passions proceeding from some power and ability supposed to reside in a sensitive soul, vitally united to that respective body. Which perception, though it have something of energy in it, as being a cogitation, yet it is rightly called a passion of the soul, because it is not a clear intellective or cognoscitive perception of the motions of the body, but a passive or sympathetical perception only. Whereby, according to nature's instinct, it hath several seemings or appearances begotten in it of those resisting objects without it at a distance, in respect of colour, magnitude, figure, and local motion; by reason of the difference of those rectilinear motions communicated from them by the intermediate globulous particles, and impressed upon the optic nerves.

Wherefore the living eye immediately perceives nothing but these corporeal passions which are made equally upon it, and the mirror or crystal globe alike, by the motion of that intermediate or subtle body which causeth light; which corporeal passions being also passively perceived by that vital principle called the sensitive power residing in the eye, all passion from the outward object there ceaseth, and goes no further. But that power of the soul that next followeth, which is the third thing that we mentioned before, the intellect begins immediately to exert and display its activity upon the object passively perceived by sense.

4. But the better to illustrate the business in hand, let us again suppose some ingenious piece of mechanism, or artificial *automaton*, as for example, an horologe or watch,[18] at once held before the mirror or crystal globe, and also exposed to the particular view of the living or sentient eye, both in the outside and interior fabric of it, so that as every part in it is reflected from the mirror, so it may be consciously perceived also by the sentient eye, in a particular successive view. Now the sentient eye will be conscious or perceptive of nothing in all this, but only its being variously affected from different colours, figures, protuberancies, cavities, sculptures, local motions one after another, all the same things which were impressed on the crystal globe or mirror, and reflected from it, there being no difference at all betwixt the one and the

---

[18] S[imon] P[atrick] uses the clock metaphor when he argues for the relevance of philosophy, in particular Cartesianism, for Christian apologetics, in his *A Brief Account of the New Sect of Latitude Men* (London, 1662). This book was written in defence of latitudinarian divines like Cudworth. See also L. Laudan, 'The Clock Metaphor and Probabilism: the Impact of Descartes on English Methodological Thought 1660–1685', *Annals of Science*, 22 (1966), 73–104.

other, but that the eye was conscious or perceptive of what it suffered, but the mirror not. But now the mind or intellect being superadded to this sentient eye and exerting its active and more comprehensive power upon all that which was reflected from the mirror, and passively perceived by the sentient eye as it doth actually and intellectually comprehend the same things over again which sense had perceived before in another manner (of which we must speak afterward), so it proceeds further, and compares all the several parts of this ingenious machine or self-mover one with another, taking notice first of the spring as the original and cause of all motion in it, of the chain or string by the mediation of which that motion is communicated to the fusée, of the balance that reciprocating moderates the motion of the several wheels some greater, some lesser, propagating the motion from one to another, of the horary circle divided into equal parts, and lastly of the index[19] moving round about the circle through equal space in equal time, all these in their several relations (*scheses*) to one another and the whole. Whereupon the intellect besides figure, colour, magnitude, and motions raises and excites with itself the intelligible ideas of cause, effect, means, end, priority and posteriority, equality and inequality, order and proportion, symmetry and asymmetry, aptitude and inaptitude, sign and thing signified, whole and part, in a manner all the logical and relative notions that are. Whereas the sentient eye by which this whole mechanism was represented to the intellect perceived none of all these things, neither cause nor effect, nor equality nor irregularity, nor order nor proportions, nor symmetry nor asymmetry, nor sign nor thing signified, nor whole nor part, since there is no colour nor figure in any of these things. And if the sentient eye could dispute with the mind or intellect it would confidently avow and maintain that there were no such entities as those in this self-moving machine (*automaton*) and that the understanding was abused and deceived in those apprehensions, since all that was impressed from the object was by the sentient eye faithfully transmitted to it, and the intellect received all its intelligence or information from it. And to make its cause good, sense would appeal to the mirror or crystal globe standing by, in which there were no images of any of those invisible ideas or logical notions reflected. Wherefore, since sense doth freely conceive and ingenuously own that none of these

---

[19] That is, hand of the clock. The fusee is the wheel of a watch or clock, upon which the chain is wound, and by which the power of the mainspring is equalized.

ideas are passively and phantasmatically stamped upon it from the objects without, be they what they will, real or not real, certain it is that they are the objects of the intellect, and they must of necessity be raised in it by its own innate vigour and activity.

5. Indeed though it should be granted that the relations (*scheses*) of cause and effect, whole and parts, and the like, were mere notions of the mind and modes of conceiving in us that only signify what things are relatively to intellect, yet it would not follow from hence that they had no reality at all but were absolute non-entities because intellect, being a real thing and that which indeed hath more of entity in it than matter, or body, the modifications of intellect must needs be as real things as the modifications of matter. And therefore cause and effect, whole and part, symmetry and asymmetry and all the other logical notions would have as much reality in them as hard and soft, moist and dry, hot and cold, which though but modifications of matter are looked upon as very real things, and such intellectuals as were relative to intellect be as real as those sensible phantasms which are relative to sense. But this must not be granted, that the modes of conception in the understanding (where all truth is) are disagreeable to the reality of the things conceived by them and so, being unconformable, are therefore false. Wherefore, that these relations (*scheses*) are not (though sense doth not perceive them) mere notions or figments of the mind, without any fundamental reality in the things themselves without us corresponding to them, appears from hence because art and wisdom are most real things which beget real effects of the greatest moment and consequence in nature and human life of any thing, and yet are conversant about nothing else but only the relations, proportions, aptitudes of things to one another, and to certain ends. Now if these were all mere figments and nothing but logical notions or beings of reason (*entia rationis*), then there could be no such realities produced out of them. Nay, then art and wisdom themselves must need be figments and fancies. And likewise it would be indifferent whatever a man did in order to any end or effect. And all men (as Protagoras held) would be really alike wise and skilful. Then there would be no other extrinsical causality of any effect but that of efficiency, force, or power, which, in corporeal things, is nothing else but local motion. And no such thing as the causality of skill and art (that is commonly called the exemplary cause) distinct from force, power, and blind impetuosity. Nay, then virtue, justice, honesty must of

necessity be figments also, because moral good and evil are schetical and relative things, and, which is more yet, external convenience and inconvenience, utility and inutility themselves, be nothing else but fancies also.

6. But though the verdict and testimony of sense ought to be admitted as authentic in this particular, as to what is or is not passively impressed upon us from without, because it is not possible that anything should be impressed upon the intellect from sensible things, but it must needs pass through the medium of sense, and so be transmitted thereby unto the understanding, which cannot be, unless sense be conscious thereof. Yet, notwithstanding, sense is not at all to be heard as to the reality or non-reality of these relative ideas, it being no competent judge in that controversy. Because since the knowledge of things doth not arise from the activity, energy, and radiation of the objects without upon us passively received by sense, but from the active and comprehensive energy or activity of the mind itself, as we have already observed,

> That in knowing all things it rather useth its own power than that of things which are known. For since all judgement is the act of him that judgeth, it must needs be that every one perform his own work, not by the power of another, but by his own faculty,[20]

as the afore-commended Boethius expresseth it. We ought not to conclude that those relative ideas are therefore mere figments or modes of conceiving in us because sense is not conscious of any such things passively impressed upon it from without, and because that lower and narrow faculty comprehends them not, but rather acquiesce[s] in the sentiment of that larger and more comprehensive faculty the intellect that judges of things by exerting its own active power upon them.

7. Wherefore, if we well consider it, we shall find that not only the beauty and pulchritude, but also the strength and ability of natural and corporeal things themselves depend upon these relations and proportions of one thing to another. For what is pulchritude in visible objects, or harmony in sounds, but the proportions, symmetry, and commensuration of figures and sounds to one another, whereby infinity is

---

[20] 'In cognoscendo cuncta, sua potius facultate quam rerum quae cognoscuntur uti. Cum enim omne judicium judicantis actus existat, necesse est, ut suam quisque operam non ex aliena, sed ex propria facultate perficiat' (Boethius, *De consolatione philosophiae* v, pr. iv; Cudworth's translation). Cudworth cites the same passage more extensively in *TIS* I.iv, sect. iv, p. 856. He quotes from the same section of Boethius above, pp. 58 and 73.

measured and determined, and multiplicity and variety vanquished and triumphed over by unity, and by that means they become grateful and pleasing objects to the ear and eye of intellectual auditors and spectators, there being as it were certain ludicrous irritations and symbolical resemblances of art and wisdom, nay, and virtue too (as we shall show afterward) that is of intellectuality in general appearing in them, whereby the mind beholds as it were its own face and image reflected to itself from a corporeal glass.

But because many will be ready to say here that beauty is nothing but a fancy neither, and therefore cannot argue any reality in these schetical things, I add that even the strength and ability of corporeal things themselves depend upon the mutual relations (*scheses*) and proportions of one thing to another. And this all men will be sensible of as something. And the truth hereof evidently appears from the mechanical powers. Nay the health and strength of the body of animals arises from the configuration of the organical parts and the fit contemperation of humours and insensible parts with one another. So that if this harmonical temperature (*crasis*) of the whole body be disturbed and put out of tune, weakness and languishing will immediately seize upon it. Nay, doth not all the strength, as well as the comeliness and beauty, of an army consist in order? And therefore if we should suppose some subtle sophister and popular orator sent from the quarters of an enemy into a vast, numerous, and puissant army, that should insinuate to the common soldiers so far as generally to persuade them that order was nothing but a mere fancy or logical notion, a thing craftily devised by their commanders merely to keep them in subjection that they might the better tyrannize over them and rule them as they please, insomuch that they should all at length altogether neglect their ranks and files, and put themselves wholly into disorder and confusion, and in this fashion prepare themselves to encounter their approaching enemy, would they not hereby be betrayed to certain ruin though the enemy should be but a small handful of men, but well ordered and well commanded? For order is that which makes things with united forces (*junctis viribus*) to conspire all to one end, whereby the whole hath the force and ability of all the several particular strengths conjoined and united into one.

8. Therefore I say, in the next place, returning to our former instance of an automaton or horologe, that though those several relative ideas of cause, effect, symmetry, proportion, order, whole and part, and the like,

considered formally as conceptions of the mind (νοήματα) be only in the intellect itself (as the ideas and conceptions of all other things likewise are), yet, notwithstanding, the intellect doth not forge or falsify anything in apprehending of them in that material self-mover (*automaton*) represented to it by sense, because all the several relations (*scheses*) are fundamentally and really in the same, though they could not be stamped upon sense materially, and received passively from it. And therefore that the true nature, formal reason (*ratio*), essence, and idea of this self-mover (*automaton*), watch or horologe, is really compounded and made up of those several relations (*scheses*) as ingredients into it, so that it cannot possibly be understood without them, though sense could not reach to the comprehension of any one of them, much less of this whole logical system or collection (*compages*) of them. It being impossible that the nature of a self-mover (*automaton*), horologe, or watch should be otherwise understood than by the comprehension of these relative ideas, and by such a logical unitive, comprehensive power and activity as can frame out of them one idea of the whole. For an horologe or watch is not mere silver or gold, brass and steel any way jumbled, mingled, or confounded together. But it is such an apt and proportionable disposition of certain quantities of those several materials in to several parts of such certain figures, contempered together, as may harmoniously conspire to make up one equal and uniform motion. Which running as it were parallel with the motion of time, and passing round the horary circle, and being measured in that horary circle, may also measure out and distinguish the quantity of that silent and successive flux, which, like a still and deep river, carries down all things along with it indiscernible, and without any noise, and which in its progressive motion treads so lightly and softly that it leaves no traces, prints, or footsteps at all behind it.

9. Wherefore the eye of sense, though it be fixed never so much upon the material outside of this self-mover (*automaton*), yet it never comprehends the formal nature of it within itself, as it is a whole (*totum*) made up of several parts, united not so much by corporeal contact or continuity, as by their relative conspiration to one certain end. Sense, being like one of those narrow telescopes by which the eye looking upon the moon, can never view it all at once and see the site and configuration of all the several mountains and valleys and seas in it, and have one comprehensive idea of the whole, but taking it in the piecemeal part

after part leaves the intelligent spectator afterwards to compile and make up one entire draught or map of stenography out of all those several particular or partial views.

So that if we will speak properly, we cannot say that the eye sees any machine (*machina*) or self-mover (*automaton*), for it is but variously affected from the material part of it, perceiving several passions in itself from the several colours and figures of it, being so far from comprehending the formal reason (*ratio*) of it, as it is a whole (*totum*) made up of several parts, according to several relations (*scheses*) and proportions contributing thereto, that it cannot reach to any one relative idea, neither doth bare fancy go any further than sense. Or else the difference between intellect and sense may be resembled by the difference betwixt the sense of sight and touch. For touch groping perceives but as it were a point at once, the eye comprehends the whole superficies. Sense sees particular things absolutely; intellect compares them according to those relations they have one to another, has a comprehensive idea of a whole (*totum*) made up of several parts as one thing. And therefore the form, reason (*ratio*), or intelligible idea of a self-mover (*automaton*) or horologe, was never stamped or impressed upon the soul from without, but upon occasion of the sensible idea excited and exerted from the inward active and comprehensive power of the intellect itself.

10. There are many other such ideas of the mind, of certain wholes (*totums* (*sic*)) made up of several corporeal parts, which, though sometimes locally discontinued, yet are joined together by relations (*scheses*) and habitudes to one another (founded in some actions of them as they are cogitative beings) and by order all conspiring into one thing, which [ideas], though they are altogether imperceptible by sense and therefore were never stamped or impressed upon the mind from the objects without, yet notwithstanding are not mere figments or beings of reason (*entia rationis*), but things of the greatest reality, founded in certain actions of thinking and cogitative beings; which [ideas] are not altogether imperceptible by sense and therefore could not possibly be outwardly stamped upon the mind. As for example, a polity or commonwealth, called an artificial man, which is a company of many united together by consent or contract under one government, to be regulated by some certain laws as it were by one will for the good of the whole; where though the eye may see the particular persons (or at least

their outsides) that are the respective members thereof, yet it can neither see the bond which unites them together, which is nothing but relation, nor comprehend the whole (*totum*) that is made up of them, that is a polity or commonwealth, according to the formal nature of it, which is an idea that proceeds merely from the unitive power and activity of the mind itself.

In a word, all the ideas of things called artificial or mechanical contain something in them that never came from sense, nor was ever stamped upon the soul from the objects without, which, though it be not merely notional or imaginary, but really belongs to the nature of that thing, yet is no otherwise than intellectually comprehended. As for example, an house or palace is not only stone, brick, mortar, timber, iron, glass heaped together, but the very essence and formal reason (*ratio*) of it is made up of relative or schetical notions, it being a certain disposition of those several materials into a whole (*totum*) or collection (*compages*), consisting of several parts, rooms, stairs, passages, doors, chimneys, windows convenient for habitation, and fit for the several uses of men; in which there is the logic of whole and parts, order, proportion, symmetry, aptitude, concinnity, all complicated with wood, stone, iron, and glass, as it were informing and adorning the rude and confused mass of matter, and making it both beautiful and serviceable. And therefore, for this cause, no man that is in his wits will say that a stately and royal palace hath therefore less reality, entity, and substantiality in it than an heap of rubbish confusedly cast together, because forsooth the idea of it partly consists of logical notions, which are thought to be mere imaginary things, whereas the whole is all solid matter without this notional form. For this logical form (which is the passive stamp or print of intellectuality in it, the first archetypes contained in the idea or skill of the architect, and thence introduced into the rude matter, successively with much pains and labour) is the only thing that distinguishes it from mere dirt and rubbish, and gives it the essence of an house or palace. And it hath therefore the more of entity in it because it partakes of art or intellectuality. But the eye or sense of a brute, though it have as much passively impressed upon it from without as the soul of man hath, when it looks upon the most royal and magnificent palace, if it should see all the inside also as well as the outside, could not comprehend from thence the formal idea and nature of an house or palace, which nothing but an active intellectual principle can reach unto.

11. Neither is this true of such things only as are commonly called artificial, but also of natural compounded things, such as plants and animals are. And indeed if we consider things philosophically, we shall not find any such essential difference as is commonly supposed, betwixt things called artificial and natural. For there is a nature in all artificial things and again, an artifice in all compounded things. Plants and animals being nothing else but artificial mechanisms, the latter of which especially are contrived with infinitely more wit, variety, and curiosity than any mechanisms or self-movers (*automata*) that were ever yet produced by human art. Wherefore the true form of an animal, if we attend only to the mechanism of the body (for we must acknowledge something else not only in men but also in brutes, if they have any cogitation besides mechanism, which is a substance of another nature, or a cogitative being united to the body)[21] is an idea that includes many relative and logical notions in it, and therefore could never be stamped upon the soul by sense. For sense only takes notice of several colours and figures either in the outside or the inside of any animals, but doth not sum them up in one whole (*totum*). But the idea of it, as collected into one mechanical self-mover (*automaton*), consisting of many organical parts fitly proportioned together, and all harmoniously conspiring to one end, to make it every way a first habitation for a cogitative substance to reside in, in respect of nutrition, local motion, sense, and all other functions of life: such an idea, I say, that hath something of logic in it, is only conceivable by the unitive, active and comprehensive power of the intellect.

The same is to be affirmed of that huge and vast *automaton*, which some will have to be an animal likewise,[22] the visible world or material universe, the world, commonly called *cosmos* or *mundus*, from the beauty of it. Whether we mean thereby that one single vortex, to which our planetary earth belongs, or a system of as many vortices as we see fixed stars in the heavens,[23] their central suns and circumferential planets moving round about them respectively. Now sense looking round

---

[21] Cudworth, like Henry More, denied the Cartesian contention that animals were mere natural mechanisms, lacking a soul.

[22] A reference to the doctrine of world soul. See Plato, *Timaeus* 30b f. and 34b f.

[23] In Cartesian cosmology, the heavenly bodies were conceived as moving in a series of vortices. Through his wording, Cudworth alludes here directly to Descartes, *Principia philosophiae*, III.46.

about, and making many particular views, sees now one fixed star, and then another; now the moon, then the sun; here a mountain, there a valley; at one time a river, at another a sea, particular vegetables and animals one after another. But it cannot sum up or unite altogether, nor rise to any comprehensive idea of the whole at once, as it is one or many mechanical self-movers most curiously and artificially framed of innumerable parts; in which there are all manner of logical relations (*scheses*) possible offered to the mind, but also fitly proportioned with such admirable symmetries and correspondencies in respect of one another and the whole, that they perfectly conspire into one most orderly and harmonious form.

Hitherto therefore we have seen that the relative ideas that we have in our mind are not passions impressed upon the soul from the objects without, but arise from the innate activity of the mind itself. And therefore, because the essences or ideas of all things themselves, whether artificial or natural, that is whether made by the artifice of men or nature, always necessarily include these logical relations in them. We have demonstratively proved from thence, that no corporeal compounded thing whatsoever is understood by sense, nor the idea of it passively stamped upon the mind, from the objects without, but comprehended only by the large unitive power of the intellect, and exerted from the innate activity thereof.

12. But the case is still clearer concerning those other ideas beforementioned, of the several modes of cogitative beings, or such as involve or include some relation to them; that these are not by the passive impresses from outward objects by sense; although they are often occasionally invited and drawn forth by them. Which we shall illustrate by the former instance of an artificial self-mover exhibited first to the view of sense, and afterward actively comprehended by the understanding. After the mind hath framed a clear idea of this self-mover within itself, the end or design whereof is to measure the equal motion either of the sun and heavens, or earth (according to different astronomical hypothesis)[24] by the equal motion of this self-mover, and so to distinguish or mark out to us the quantities of that silent and undiscerned flux of time; and when it hath considered how aptly conducible every part of this mechanism is to that design, and how

---

[24] i.e. the Ptolemaic (geocentric) or Copernican (solar-centric).

there is neither the least redundancy nor deficiency in any thing in order thereunto, and of the beauty and elegancy of the fabric, making a further and a more inward reflection upon the same, it plainly perceives this accurate contrivance to be but a passive print or stamp of some active and living art or skill upon it. Wherefore the ideas of art and skill are upon this occasion naturally exerted from it. Neither doth it rest in considering of art and skill abstractedly, but because these are modes of an existent cogitative being, it thinks presently of some particular intelligent being, the artificer or author of this curious fabric, and looking further into it, finds his name also engraven in legible characters upon the same, whereupon he forthwith pronounces the sound of it. Whereas the living eye, that is, sense alone in its antecedent view, as it could not espy any logical relations or notions there, so neither can it perceive any ideas of art or skill in it, they having neither figure nor colour in them, nor of author and artificer, any more than it could see the sound of the artificer's name in the engraven sculptures or characters of it. For the eye could see no more than was represented in or reflected from the crystal globe or mirror. Wherefore the ideas of art and skill, author and artificer were not passively imprinted upon the intellect from the material self-mover (*automaton*), but only occasionally invited from the mind itself, as the figures of the engraven letters did not passively impress the sound of the artificer's name upon him, but only occasion him to exert from his own activity.

13. Just in the same manner it happens many times in the contemplation of that great self-mover (*automaton*) of the material universe, which is the artifice of God (θεοῦ τέχνασμα), the artifice of the best mechanist, though there be no more passively impressed upon us from it, than there is upon the diaphanous air, or liquid ether contiguous to all solid bodies by local motion, of which only sensitive beings have a conscious perception; yet there is a wonderful scene of various thoughts and motions raised in the mind thereupon, which are only occasionally invited by those stamps and impressions made from the material fabric, and its various furniture without, but owe their true original and efficiency to nothing else but the innate vigour and activity of the mind itself. Some of which we have already instanced in the ideas of those relative considerations (*scheses*) of corporeal things themselves and their parts to one another; by means of which the intellect rises up to that comprehensive view of the natures of particular corporeal things, and

the universal mundane system within itself all at once; which sense perceiving only by little and little, and taking in as it were point after point, cannot sum up its partial perceptions into the entire idea of any one whole (*totum*). But the intellect doth not rest here, but upon occasion of those corporeal things thus comprehended in themselves, naturally rises higher to the framing and exciting of certain ideas from within itself, of other things not existing in those sensible objects, but absolutely incorporeal. For being ravished with the contemplation of this admirable mechanism and artificial contrivance of the material universe, forthwith it naturally conceives it to be nothing else but the passive stamp, print, and signature of some living art and wisdom, as the pattern, archetype, and seal of it, and so excites from within itself an idea of that divine art and wisdom. Nay, considering further, how all things in this great mundane machine or animal (as the ancients would have it) are contrived, not only for the beauty of the whole, but also for the good of every part in it, that is endued with life and sense, it exerts another idea, *viz.* of goodness and benignity from within itself, besides that of art and wisdom, as the queen regent and empress of art, whereby art is employed, regulated, and determined. Now both these things whereof the first is art, wisdom, and knowledge, the second, goodness, benignity, and morality, being looked upon as modes of some intellectual being or mind in which they exist, it from hence presently makes up an idea of God, as the author or architect of this great and boundless machine, a mind infinitely good and wise, and so as it were resounds and re-echoes back the great creator's name, which from those visible characters impressed upon the material universe, had pierced loudly into its ears, but in such an indiscernible manner, that sense listening never so attentively, could not perceive the least murmur or whisper of it. And this is the most natural scale by which the intellectual mind in the contemplation of corporeal things ascends to God – from the passive prints and signatures of that one art and wisdom that appears in the universe, by taking notice from thence of the exemplary or archetypal cause, one infinite and eternal mind setting his seal upon all. For as he that hears a consort of musicians playing a lesson consisting of six or eight several parts, all conspiring to make up one harmony will immediately conclude that there was some other cause of that harmony besides those several particular efficients, that struck the several instruments, for every one of them could be but a cause of his own part which he played. But the unity of the whole harmony, into which all the several parts conspire, must needs proceed from the art and musical skill of some one mind, the exemplary and archetypal cause of that vocal harmony, which was but a passive print or stamp of it. So though the atheist might possibly persuade himself that every particular creature was the first author or efficient of that part which it played in the universe, by a certain innate power of its own, yet all the parts of the mundane system conspiring into one perfect harmony, there must of necessity be some one universal mind, the archetypal and exemplary cause of the whole mundane music, as one entire thing made up of so many several parts within himself.

14. But that oftentimes there is more taken notice of and perceived by the mind, both in the sensible objects themselves, and by occasion of them, than was impressed from them, or passively received by sense, which therefore must needs proceed from some inward active principle in that which perceives, I shall make it further appear by some other instances.

For, first, let a brute and man at the same time be made spectators of one and the same artificial statue, picture, or landscape. Here the brute will passively receive all that is impressed from the outward object upon sense by local motion, as well as the man, all the several colours and figures of it. And yet the man will presently perceive something in this statue or picture, which the brute takes not notice of at all, *viz.* beauty and pulchritude, and symmetry, besides the liveliness of the effigies and the portraiture. The eye of the brute being every jot as good as a glass or mirror, and perhaps endued with a more perspicacious sense or power of passive perception, than that of a man.

Or again, let both a man and a brute at the same time hear the same musical airs, the brute will only be sensible of noise and sounds. But the man will also perceive harmony in them, and be very much delighted with it; nay, even enthusiastically transported by it. Wherefore the brute perceiving all the sounds as well as the man but nothing of the harmony, the difference must needs arise from some inward active principle or anticipation in the man, which the brute hath not.

And indeed the reason is the same both in visibles and audibles. For the sense of a man, by reason of its vicinity and neighbourhood to reason and intellectuality, lodged in the same soul with it, must needs be coloured with some tincture of it; or have some passive impresses of the same upon it. And therefore when it finds or meets with insensible objects any footsteps or resemblances thereof, anything that hath cognation with intellectuality, as proportion, symmetry, and order have, being the passive stamps and impresses of art and skill (which are intellectual things) upon matter, it must needs be highly gratified with the same. But the soul of a brute having no intellectual anticipations in it, but barely suffering from the corporeal objects without, can have no sense of anything but what their activity impresseth upon it.

Nay further, the man will also espy some symbolical resemblances of morality, of virtue and vice in the variously proportioned sounds and airs. For there are *ethical* (*ἠθικαί*) (as Aristotle hath observed) as well as *enthusiastical harmonies* (*ἐνθουσιαστικαὶ ἁρμονίαι*), as the physiognomists in like manner observe signatures of morality in the countenances of men and their pictures, which it is yet less possible that a brute should be sensible of, these differences arising not from the absolute nature of the objects without, or their bare impression which they make, but [from] the different analogy which they have to some inward and active anticipations which they meet withal in the percipient. For the man hath certain moral anticipations and signatures stamped inwardly upon his soul, which makes him presently take notice of whatsoever symbolizes with it in corporeal things. But the brute hath none.

15. And this will still further appear if we again compare the judgement of some excellent artists in painting and music with that of an ordinary vulgar person, that hath not any acquired skill in either faculty. For the skilful and expert limner will observe many elegancies and curiosities of art, and be highly pleased with several strokes and shadows in a picture, where a common eye can discern nothing at all. And a musical artist hearing a consort of exact musicians playing some excellent composure of many parts, will be exceedingly ravished with many harmonical airs and touches, that a vulgar ear will be utterly insensible of. Nay such an one perhaps would be more pleased with the streperous noise of a single fiddle, or the rustical music of the country bagpipes, or the dull humming of a Jew's trump than the fullest and most exquisitely composed harmony.

And the reason is the same with what was before suggested, because the artists of either kind have many inward anticipations of skill and art in their minds, which being awakened by those passive impressions of the same skill or art in the outward objects that strike upon their senses, there arises immediately an inward grateful sense and sympathy from the correspondence and analogy that is betwixt them, art and skill in the mind of the musical hearer, finding something akin (συγγενές τι) to itself in those harmonious airs, some footsteps and resemblance of itself gratefully closing with them. Of which vital sympathy there is vulgarly thought to be some resemblance in nature, when upon the striking of a string on one viol, another string, that is in unison to it in a distant viol, will dance and leap, and that not from any mechanical cause (as some conceive) passively only, but from a vital active principle in nature, which is affected with concord and harmony.[25] Now there is yet a pulchritude of another kind, a more interior symmetry and harmony in the relations, proportions, aptitudes, and correspondencies of things to one another in the great mundane system, or vital machine of the universe, which is all musically and harmonically composed. For which cause the ancients made Pan, that is nature, to play upon an harp. But the sense, which only passively perceives particular outward objects, doth here, like the brute, hear nothing but mere noise and sound and clatter, but no music or harmony at all, having no active principle and anticipation within itself to comprehend it by and correspond or vitally sympathize with it, whereas the mind of a rational and intellectual being will be ravished and enthusiastically transported in the contemplation of it, and of its own accord dance this pipe of Pan, Nature's intellectual music and harmony.

16. But I shall yet further illustrate this business that the mind may actively comprehend more in the outward objects of sense, and by occasion of them, than is passively received and impressed from them by another instance. Suppose a learned written or printed volume held before the eye of a brute creature or illiterate person. Either of them will passively receive all that is impressed upon sense from those delineations, to whom there will be nothing but several scrawls or lines of ink drawn upon white paper. But if a man that hath inward anticipations of learning in him look upon them, he will immediately have another comprehension of them than that of sense, and a strange scene of thoughts presently represented to his mind from them. He will

---

[25] Cudworth alludes to the phenomenon of resonance here. The string of one instrument resonates with the same harmonic motion as another which is vibrating close by, without any physical contact between them apart from the air-waves which carry the sound from one string to another.

see heaven, earth, sun, moon and stars, comets, meteors, elements in those inky delineations. He will read profound theorems of philosophy, geometry, astronomy in them, learn a great deal of new knowledge from them that he never understood before, and thereby justly admire the wisdom of the composer of them. Not that all this was passively stamped upon his soul by sense from those characters. For sense, as I said before, can perceive nothing here but inky scrawls, and the intelligent reader will many times correct his copy, finding erratas in it. But because his mind was before furnished with certain inward anticipations that such characters signify the elements of certain sounds, those sounds certain notions or cogitations of the mind, and because he hath an active power of exciting any such cogitations within himself, he reads those sensible cogitations, the passive stamps or prints of another man's wisdom or knowledge upon them, and also learns knowledge and instruction from them, not as infused into his mind from those sensible characters, but by reason of those hints and significations thereby proposed to it, accidentally kindled, awakened, and excited in it. For all but the phantasms of black inky strokes and figures arises from the inward activity of his own mind. Wherefore this instance in itself shews how the activity of the mind may comprehend more in and from sensible objects than is passively imprinted by them upon sense.

But now, in the room of this artificial book in volumes, let us substitute the book of nature, the whole visible and material universe, printed all over with the passive characters and impressions of divine wisdom and goodness, but legible only to an intellectual eye. For to the sense both of man and brute there appears nothing else in it but as in the other, so many inky scrawls, *i.e.* nothing but figures and colours. But the mind or intellect, which hath an inward and active participation of the same divine wisdom that made it, and being printed all over with the same archetypal seal, upon occasion of those sensible delineations represented to it, and taking notice of whatsoever is cognate to it, exerting its own inward activity from thence, will not have only a wonderful scene and large prospect of other thoughts laid open before it, and variety of knowledge, logical, mathematical, metaphysical, moral displayed, but also clearly read the divine wisdom and goodness in every page of this great volume, as it were written in large and legible characters.

Chapter III

1. We have hitherto showed that there are many ideas of the mind which, though the cogitations of them be often occasionally invited from the motion or appulse of sensible objects without made upon our bodies, yet notwithstanding the ideas themselves could not possibly be stamped or impressed upon the soul from them, because sense takes no cognizance at all of any such things in those corporeal objects, and therefore they must needs arise from the innate vigour and activity of the mind itself. Such as are, first, the relative ideas of the several *scheses* or respects which are betwixt corporeal things themselves compared with one another. Which relative ideas being not comprehended by sense, and yet notwithstanding the natures of all compounded corporeal things, whether artificial or natural, that is whether made by the artifice of men or nature, consisting of them, we have demonstratively proved from thence, that the natures of no compounded corporeal things can possibly be known or comprehended by sense. And again the ideas of cogitative beings, and the several modes of them, together with all such notions as involve some respect or relation to them. For although these also be often occasionally invited and elicited by the objects of sense, when the mind, in the contemplation of them by its own active strength, perceives the signatures of art, counsels, contrivance, wisdom, nay, and goodness also (all which are modes of cogitative beings) printed upon them. Yet they cannot owe their being or efficiency to the activity of those outward objects, but merely to the activity of the mind itself.

I should now proceed to show, that even those simple corporeal things themselves, which by sense we have a passive perception of, in individual bodies without us, are also known and understood by the active power of the mind exerting its own intelligible ideas upon them.

2. That sensation is not knowledge of those corporeal things that we sensibly perceive, we have before largely showed. And indeed it sufficiently appears from hence, because upon the seeing of light and colours, though never so clearly, the feeling of heat and cold smartly, the hearing of loud sounds and noises, we naturally enquire further, what this light and colours, heat and cold, and sounds are, which is an undoubted acknowledgement that we have not a clear and satisfactory

comprehension of those things which make so strong a stroke and impression upon our senses. And therefore the mind desires to master and conquer them by its own active strength and power and to comprehend them by some ideas of its own, which are not foreign, but native, domestic, and intrinsical to it.

Now if sense itself be not knowledge, much less can any secondary or derivative result from sense be knowledge, for this would be a more obscure shadowy and evanid thing than sense itself is. As when the image of a man's face, received in a mirror or looking-glass, is reflected from thence into a ˚second mirror, and so forward into a third, still further it goes, the more obscure, confused, and imperfect it grows, till at last it becomes altogether imperceptible. Or as in the circlings and undulations of water, caused by the falling of a stone into it, that are successively propagated from one to another, the further and wider they go, the waves are still the less, slower and weaker, till at length they become quite undiscernible. Or as a secondary echo, that is, the echo of an echo, falls as much short of the primary echo in proportion, as that doth of the original in proportion, as that doth of the original voice. Or, lastly, if we could suppose a shadow to cast a shadow, this secondary shadow, or projection of a shadow, would fall as much short of the primary shadow as that did of the substance itself. So if the knowledge of corporeal things were but a secondary and derivative result from sense (though it cannot be conceived that the passion of sense should ray upon the intellect, so as to beget a secondary passion there, any more than one shadow should cast another) then knowledge would be much a weaker perception of them than sense itself is, and nothing but as it were the secondary reflection of an image, or the remote circlings and undulations of the fluid water, or the mere echo of the echo of an original voice. Or, lastly, nothing but the shadow of the shadow of a substance. Whereas it is a far more real, substantial, and satisfactory, more penetrative and comprehensive perception than sense is, reaching to the very inward essence of the things perceived. And therefore it must of necessity proceed from the active power of the mind itself, exerting its own intelligible ideas upon that which is passively perceived and so comprehending it by something of its own that is native and domestic to it. So that besides the sensations ($a\dot{i}\sigma\theta\dot{\eta}\mu a\tau a$) or phantasms ($\phi a\nu\tau\dot{a}\sigma\mu a\tau a$) the sensible ideas of corporeal things passively impressed upon us from without, there must be also conceptions or intelligible ideas of them (νοήματα) actively exerted from the mind itself, or otherwise they could never be understood.

3. Wherefore, that we may the better illustrate this business, let us suppose some individual body, as for example, a white or black triangular superficies, or a solid four-square (*tetrahedrum*) included all within a triangular superficies, exposed first to the view of sense or a living eye, and then afterward considered by the intellect, that we may see the difference betwixt the passive perception of it by sense, and the active comprehension of it by the understanding. Now sense, that is a living eye or mirror, as soon as ever it is converted toward this object, will here passively perceive an appearance of an individual thing, as existing without it, white and triangular, without any distinction concretely and confusedly together. And it will perceive no more than this, though it dwell never so long upon this object. For it perceives no more than is impressed upon it. And here the passion of sense ends and goes no further. But the mind or intellect residing in the same soul that hath a power of sensation also, then beginning to make a judgement upon that which is thus passively perceived, exerts its own innate vigour and activity, and displays itself gradually after this manner. For, first, with its subtle divisive power, it will analyse and resolve this concrete phantasmatical whole (*totum*) and take notice of several distinct intellectual objects in it. For considering that every white or black thing is not necessarily triangular, nor every triangular thing white or black, it finds here two distinct intellectual objects, the one white, the other triangular. And then again, because that which is nothing can have no affections, it concludes, that here is something as a common subject (*substratum*) to both these affections or modifications which it calls a corporeal substance, which being one and the same thing is here both white and triangular. Wherefore it finds at least three distinct objects of intellectual cogitation, corporeal substance, white, and triangular, all individual. But then reflecting again upon these several objects, and that it may further enquire into the natures and essences of them, it now bids adieu to sense and singularity, and taking a higher flight considers them all universally and abstractly from individuating circumstances and matter. That is, it no more seeks the knowledge and comprehension of these things without itself, from whence it hath already passively perceived them by sense. But revolving within itself upon its own inward notions and active anticipations (which must needs be universal) it looks for

some domestic ideas of its own to understand these general natures by, that so from thence with a descending view it may comprehend under them those individuals that now affect the sense.

4. First therefore, for corporeal substance in general, which is the subject (*substratum*) both of colour and figure, not to pursue any long and tedious processes, it quickly concludes that essence of it to be this: a thing extended impenetrably, or which hath impenetrable longitude, latitude, and profundity. And because it is not here considered merely as a notion or objective cogitation, but as a thing actually existing without the mind, therefore it exerts another notion (*ratio*) of existence or singularity also. Which added to the former makes it up a thing that hath impenetrable extension existing. Now none of these ideas, neither of essence nor existence, nor thing, nor substance, nor something, nor nothing, nor impenetrability, nor extension, nor longitude, latitude, and profundity, were impressed or stamped upon the mind, either from this individual, or any other sensible object. For they can be neither seen nor perceived by any corporeal sense, but are merely excited from the innate activity of the mind itself, that same power by which the mind is enabled to conceive of nothing (*nihil*) as well as something (*aliquid*) and certain it is that the idea of nothing was never impressed from any thing. And if the essence of body, or corporeal substance itself, be only comprehended and understood by the active ideas of the mind (for sense here perceived no such thing, but only was affected from the exterior induments thereof, colour and figure), then the several modes of it, such as whiteness and triangularity, which are but certain modes of an extended substance, must needs be understood in like manner, not by passive ideas and phantasms, but the noematical or intelligible ideas of the mind.

5. Wherefore in the next place, as for white colour or whiteness, here is a plain and palpable difference betwixt sense and intellection, betwixt the phantasm (φάντασμα) and conception (νόημα), betwixt a sensible and intelligible idea. For the sense or phantasm of white, that we have from the individual object is no clear comprehension of any essence or intelligible notion (*ratio*) but only a passion or affection in the soul, caused by some local motions communicated to the brain from the object without, that is, a drowsy, confused, and imperfect perceptive cogitation. But now the awakened mind or intellect revolving its own inward ideas, and being not able to comprehend any such mode or

quality in extended substance, as this sensible idea of white is, formally considered, for this very reason, boldly and confidently concludes that this is no real quality in that body itself absolutely considered, because no such thing is intelligible by it. In which opinion, it is confirmed by sense itself, in that the lower ends of the rainbow that reach to the earth do not stain or dye any thing with the several colours of it; and that the same drops of dew or rain to eyes at several distances have all those several colours of the rainbow in them and none at all. And by other experiments it appears that these things are only passions or affections in the sentient itself, caused by some peculiar modification of the superficies of that material object in respect of the figure, site, and disposition of its insensible parts, whereby the light or intermediate globulous particles are in a peculiar manner reflected upon the eye, and that probably the difference betwixt a white and a black object consists in this, that in one the small particles are polite and solid, and therefore vividly reflect the lighter globulous particles, but in the other, being differently disposed, the light, as a ball flung against a heap of sand, is not so smartly reflected from it, but as it were sinks into it, and its motion is stifled and smothered in the caverns of it. Wherefore the intelligible idea of a white colour is this, that it is a certain passion or sense in the soul, caused by a peculiar modification of the object without, in respect of the disposition of its insensible parts, whereby the light or globulous particles are more smartly and vividly reflected upon the eye. Which is another kind of comprehension of it, than the sensible idea or phantasm of white is, which is no intelligible idea, but a cogitative passion, that is, another species of cogitation, or an half-awakened perception. Neither are these intelligible ideas of passion and sense impressed upon the soul from the sensible objects without, for the eye sees neither passion nor sense, but they are actively exerted from the mind itself, and therefore mastered and conquered, and comprehended by it.

6. I now proceed to the last intellectual object comprehended in this individual body, which is triangularity, or some one particular species of a triangle, as for example, an equilateral, or a rectangular triangle. For there can be no individual triangle but must be of one determinate species or another.

Now because the phantasm of such a triangle doth not only bear a resemblance of the outward material object, which the phantasms of colours and the like do not, but also of the true intelligible idea of a triangle itself, and because when men think never so abstractedly and mathematically of a triangle, they have commonly some rude phantasm or picture of it before them in their imagination, therefore many confidently persuade themselves that there is no other idea of a triangle or other figure beside the bare phantasm or sensible idea impressed upon the soul from some individual object without – that is, no active noematical idea inwardly exerted from the mind itself. Which indeed is all one as to say, that there is no intellection or knowledge of a triangle at all, forasmuch as neither sense nor fancy, which are but superficial, imperfect, and incomplete perceptive cogitations, reach to the comprehension of the notion or essence of any thing. Wherefore now to make the contrary appear, we will again view this material triangle, or four-square (*tetrahedrum*) before our eyes, making a nearer approach to it, and upon this second contemplation of it we plainly observe much inequality in the superficies, unevenness and inequality in the lines, and bluntness in the angles. From whence it evidently appears that that idea that we had in our minds of a perfect triangle as a plain superficies terminated by three straight lines joined together in three angles, ending in so many points, was not impressed upon our soul from this individual object, it being different from it, and far more exact and perfect than that is. And therefore it must needs be granted that it was but occasionally or accidentally invited and drawn forth from the mind, upon the sight of it, just in the same manner as when a man looks upon certain lines drawn with ink upon a piece of paper something resembling the face of a man, his mind doth not fix and stay itself in the consideration of those inky lines, but presently upon this occasion excites within itself the idea of a man's face. Or when a man walking in a gallery where there are divers pictures hung upon the wall, chances amongst them to espy the picture of a friend or acquaintance of his, which, though perhaps far from an exact resemblance yet notwithstanding makes him presently to excite the idea of his friend in his imagination. Neither of which things could possibly be, if there had not been a previous and pre-existent idea of a man's face, or such a certain friend in his mind before. For otherwise a man in this case could think of nothing but just that was impressed upon him by sense, the figures of those inky delineations, and those several strokes and shadows of the pictures. In like manner, when we look upon the rude, imperfect and irregular figures of some corporeal things, the mind upon this occasion excites from within itself the ideas of a perfect triangle, square, circle, pyramid, cube, sphere, and the like, whose essences are so indivisible that they are not capable of the least additions, detraction, or variation without the destruction of them, because there was some rude and bungling resemblance of these regular figures in those material objects that we look upon, of which probably the maker had the ideas in his mind. And the mind naturally delights more to think of simple and regular, than of compounded and irregular figures.

7. But, if any one should here object, and say, that it doth not follow from hence that that more perfect idea which now I have of a triangle in my mind, the accuracy whereof this present visible idea before my eyes doth not reach unto, was actively excited from the mind itself, because it might be some time formerly impressed, from some other individual triangle which I had elsewhere seen, just in the same manner as when I looked upon a picture, that idea of a man's face in general, or of that particular friend, that was occasionally excited thereby, was not any innate idea, or an idea that sprung wholly from the activity of the mind, but was formerly impressed upon the soul, from individual sensible objects now remembered or called to mind. I say that this cannot possibly be true, because there never was any material or sensible straight line, triangle, circle, that we saw in all our lives, that was mathematically exact, but even sense itself, at least by the help of microscopes[26] might plainly discover much unevenness, ruggedness, flexuosity, angulosity, irregularity, and deformity in them, as will appear to any one that shall make a triangle upon the most accurate lines that wit or art of man can make. And therefore no material line could stamp or impress upon the soul in a mere passive way those exact ideas that we now have of a triangle or of a straight line, which is the shortest possible between two points, or a circle that is every where equidistant from an individual centre, &c. And if it should be again replied, that notwithstanding there being many such lines and circles as common sense cannot discern the least irregularity in them, howsoever they would be in the mean time really irregular to a perfect and lyncean sight, yet according to their appearance might impress those ideas that we have of

---

[26] The reference to microscopes shows that Cudworth was aware of recent scientific enquiries at the Royal Society and elsewhere which saw significant developments in microscopy. See Robert Hooke, *Micrographia* (London, 1665). Compare *TIS*, p. 732

a straight line or circle. I answer that this cannot be neither, there being a vast difference betwixt the confused indistinction of sense and fancy, by reason of their bluntness and imperfection and the express accuracy, preciseness, and indivisibility of those intelligible ideas that we have of a straight line, circle, triangle, four-square, and other geometrical figures. And therefore that imperfect, confused, indistinction of sense could never impress any such accurate ideas upon the mind, but only occasion the mind actively to exert them from within itself.

8. Nay, though it should be granted that there were material lines mathematically exact, perfect triangles, squares, pyramids, cubes, spheres, and the like, such as geometry supposes, as no doubt but the divine power can make such in fitting matter, yet sense could not at all reach to the discerning of the mathematical accuracy of these things, no more than it doth to the absolute equality of any quantities – as of lines, superficies, bodies, angles – which is found and determined only by the understanding in that intelligible matter (*materia intelligibilis*) which geometry is conversant about. So that sense could not be able to determine what triangle and what four-square (*tetrahedrum*) was mathematically exact, and what not. From whence it is demonstrably evident that neither the notion (*ratio*) of perfect equality, nor the perfect mathematical ideas of figures, triangle, square, circle, pyramid, cube, sphere, &c., were impressed upon the soul from without by sense, sense not at all reaching to the discernment of them.

9. But, lastly, if there were material lines, triangles, pyramids, perfectly and mechanically exact, yet that which made them such, and thereby to differ from other irregular lines, imperfect triangles and cubes, could be nothing but a conformity to an antecedent intellectual idea in the mind, as the rule and exemplar of them. For otherwise an irregular line and an imperfect triangle, pyramid, cube, are as perfectly that that they are, as the other is, only they are not agreeable to those anticipated and preconceived ideas of regular lines and figures actively exerted in the mind, or intellect, which the mind naturally formeth to itself, and delighteth to exercise itself upon them, as the proper object of art and science, which the other irregular figures are not. Wherefore whenever a man looking upon material objects judges of the figures of them, and says this is a straight line, this is a perfect triangle, that a perfect circle, but those are neither perfect triangles nor circles, it is plain that here are two several ideas of these lines and figures, the one outwardly impressed

from those individual material objects from without upon the sense of the beholder, the other actively exerted from his inward mind or intellect. Which latter busy anticipation of it is the rule, pattern, and exemplar whereby he judges of those sensible ideas or phantasms. For otherwise, if there were no inward anticipations or mental ideas, the spectator would not judge at all, but only suffer, and every irregular and imperfect triangle being as perfectly like to that, which is the most perfect triangle, the mind now having no inward pattern of its own before it, to distinguish and put a difference, would not say one of them was more imperfect than another; but only comparing them one with another, [the mind] would say that this individual figure was not perfectly like to that. Upon which account the perfect triangle would be as imperfectly the imperfect triangle as the imperfect was the perfect.

10. Wherefore, as I said before, this is just in the same manner as when a man looks upon the picture of an absent friend or familiar acquaintance, and presently judges of it, he hath plainly two several ideas in his mind at the same time: one outwardly impressed from the present picture, the other pre-existent in his mind before. By one of which he makes a judgement upon the other, and finds many faults in it, saving that here both the ideas were foreign and adventitious, the pre-existent idea having been some time formerly impressed from an outward material object, and thence retained in the memory or fancy. But in the other case, when a man looking upon a material triangle, square, circle, cube, sphere, in which there are some palpable irregularities, which he judges of by comparing them with some inward pre-existent ideas that he hath in his mind of a perfect individual triangle, square, circle, cube, and also conceives some dislike and displeasure at the disconformity of the one to the other. The pre-existent ideas here were no foreign or adventitious things, but native and domestic to him, nor at any time [were they] formerly passively received from any material objects without, but actively exerted from the mind itself. And I think there is no doubt to be made but if a perfect adult man, that was immediately framed out of the earth, having a newly created soul infused as the protoplast had, should look upon two several kinds of objects at the same time, whereof one was a perfect circle or sphere, equilateral triangle, four-square, square, or cube, the other having some resemblances of the same, had notwithstanding apparent irregularity in some parts of them, but notwithstanding apparent irregularity in some

parts of them, but that at first sight he would be more pleased with the one than with the other. Which could not be unless he had some native or active idea of his own within himself to compare them both with, to which one was more conformable than the other. For there could be no such thing as pulchritude and deformity in material objects, if there were no active power in the soul of framing ideas of regular, proportionate, and symmetrical figures within itself, but which it might put a difference between outward objects, and make a judgement of them; but that it only received stamps and impressions from without, for then it must needs be equally or indifferently affected with all alike, and not more pleased or displeased with one than with another. Now the judgement that men have of pulchritude and deformity in sensible things is not merely artificial from institution or instruction, or of taught things, but such as springs originally from nature itself.

11. But that there is an intelligible idea of a triangle inwardly exerted from the mind itself, distinct from the phantasm or sensible idea that is outwardly impressed from the material object, will yet further appear from that which follows. For the mind considers first the generical nature of it, that it is a plain figure, and that a plain figure is the termination of a plain superficies. Which superficies is nothing else but mere latitude without profundity, for plain figures are no otherwise conceived by geometricians. Now, it is certain that this idea of a superficies, which geometricians have, was never imprinted upon their minds by sense from any material objects, there being no such thing any where existing without the mind, as latitude without profundity. And therefore it must needs arise from the activity of the mind itself. And the idea of a plain superficies, that is, such a superficies as to all whose parts a straight line may be accommodated as well as the idea of a straight line, must needs be actively excited from the mind also. Again, it considers the difference betwixt a triangle and other plain figures, that it is included in and terminated by three straight lines joined together in three points. Which straight lines joined together being the extremities of those lines, have neither longitude, latitude, nor profundity in them. Which mathematical ideas, in like manner of a line without latitude or profundity, were never impressed upon Euclid, or any other geometrician from without, as is evident without further proof. Moreover, this intelligible idea of a triangle, as it includes some numerical considerations in it, which sense hath no idea of, perceiving only one and one and one: so

therein sides and angles are relatively considered also to one another. Nay the very notion of an angle, and the quantity thereof, is a relative thing, as Proclus hath observed, and therefore not impressed by sense.

Again, the mind considering the idea of its own, as it can find out the several properties of a triangle by mere cogitation without any thing of sense (as that the greater side always subtends the greater angle, nay and that the three angles are always equal to two right angles, as we shall show afterwards) so it also, by its own strength, is able to find out all the species that are possible in a plain triangle, in respect of the differences both of sides and angles. As in respect of the sides, that it is either equilateral or even-legged (*isosceles*) or having unequal sides (*scalenum*) or blunt-cornered (*amblygonium*) or sharp-cornered (᾽Οξυγώνιον) tri- angle, and that there can be no individual triangle but must of necessity belong to one of the three species of either sort. So that this is not gathered from sense, but exerted from the active power of the mind.

12. The mind can clearly understand a triangle in general without determining its thought to any particular species, and yet there can be no distinct phantasm of any such thing. For every distinct phantasm or sensible picture of a triangle must of necessity be either equilateral or equicrural or inequilateral, uneven-legged (*scalenum*). And so as we can in like manner clearly understand in our minds a thing with a thousand corners (*chiliogonum*) or one with ten thousand corners (*myriogonum*), though we cannot possibly have a distinct phantasm of either of them. But for those particular species of triangles which we may have distinct phantasms of, this doth not at all hinder but that we have, notwith- standing, intelligible ideas of the same besides, actively exerted from the mind itself. And so there is a phantasm (φάντασμα) and a conception (νόημα) at the same time concurring together, an active and a passive cogitation. The conception or intelligible idea being as it were embodied in the phantasm, which alone in itself is but an incomplete perceptive cogitation of the soul half awakened and doth not comprehend the indivisible and immutable notion (*ratio*) or essence of any thing.

Which thing to those that cannot better understand it by what we have already declared, might be illustrated in this manner: when an astronomer, thinking of the sun, demonstrates that it is a hundred and sixty times bigger than the globe of the earth, he hath all the while a phantasm or imagination of the sun in his mind, but as a circle of a foot diameter (ὥσπερ πεδαίον) nay he cannot for his life have a true phantasm of any such magnitude which contains the bigness of the earth so many times, nor indeed fancy the earth a hundredth part so big as it is. Now, as the astronomer hath an intelligible idea of the magnitude of the sun very different from the phantasm of the same, so in like manner have we intelligible ideas of corporeal things, when we understand them, besides the phantasms of them. The phantasm being as it were the crasser indument (*involucrum*) or corporeal vehicle of the intelligible idea (*νόημα*) of the mind.

13. Hitherto, by the instance of an individual and material triangle, we have shown how the soul, in understanding corporeal things, doth not merely suffer from without from the body, but actively exerts intelligible ideas of its own, and from within itself. Now, I observe that it is so far from being true, that all our objective cogitations or ideas are corporeal effluxes or radiations from corporeal things without, or impressed upon the soul from them in a gross corporeal manner, as a signature or stamp is imprinted by a seal upon a piece of wax or clay, that (as I have before hinted) this is not true sometimes of the sensible ideas themselves. For all perception whatsoever is a vital energy, and not a mere dead passion. And as the atomical philosophy instructs us, there is nothing communicated in sensation from the material objects without, but only certain local motions that are propagated from them by the nerves into the brain.[27] Which motions cannot propagate themselves corporeally upon the soul also, because it penetrates and runs through all the parts of its own body. But the soul, by reason of that vital and magical union which is between it and the body, sympathizing with the several motions of it in the brain, doth thereupon exert sensible ideas or phantasms within itself, whereby it perceives or takes notice of objects distant from the brain, either with or without the body. Many of which sentiments and phantasms have no similitude at all, either with those local motions made in the brain, or with the objects without, such as are the sentiments of pain, pleasure, and titillation, hunger, thirst, heat, and cold, sweet and bitter, light and colours, &c. Wherefore the truth is that sense if we well consider it, is but a kind of speech (*loquela*), if I may so call it, nature as it were talking to us in the sensible objects without, by certain motions as signs from thence communicated to the brain. For, as in speech, when men talk to one

---

[27] The 'atomical philosophy' to which he refers is Cartesianism. See the discussion in Book II, p. 38, above.

another, they do but make certain motions upon the air, which cannot impress their thoughts upon one another in a passive manner, but it being first consented to and agreed upon, that such certain sounds shall signify such ideas and cogitations, he that hears those sounds in discourse, doth not fix his thoughts upon the sounds themselves, but presently exerts from within himself such ideas and cogitations as those sounds by consent signify, though there be no similitude at all betwixt those sounds and thoughts. Just as in the same manner nature doth as it were talk to us in the outward objects of sense, and import various sentiments, ideas, phantasms, and cogitations not by stamping or impressing them passively upon the soul from without, but only by certain local motions from them, as it were dumb signs made in the brain; it having been first constituted and appointed by nature's law, that such local motions shall signify such sensible ideas and phantasms, though there can be no similitude at all betwixt them. For what similitude can there be betwixt any local motions and the senses of pain or hunger, and the like, as there is no similitude betwixt many words and sounds, and the thoughts which they signify. But the soul, as by a certain secret instinct and as it were by compact (*et tanquam ex compacto*) understanding nature's language, as soon as these local motions are made in the brain, doth not fix its attention immediately upon those motions themselves, as we do not use to do in discourse upon mere sounds, but presently exerts such sensible ideas, phantasms, and cogitations, as nature hath made them to be signs of, whereby it perceives and takes cognizance of many other things both in its own body, and without it, at a distance from it, in order to the good and conservation of it. Wherefore there are two kinds of perceptive powers in the soul, one below another: the first is that which belongs to the inferior part of the soul, whereby it sympathizes with the body, which is determined by the several motions and pressures that are made upon that from corporeal things without to several sensitive and fantastical energies, whereby it hath a slight and superficial perception of individual corporeal things, and as it were of the outsides of them, but doth not reach to the comprehension of the essence or indivisible and immutable notion (*ratio*) of any thing. The second perceptive power is that of the soul itself, or that superior, interior noetical part of it which is free from all passion or sympathy (ἀπαθὴς ἀσυμπαθής), free and disentangled from all that magical sympathy with the body. Which acting alone by

113

itself, exerts from within the intelligible ideas of things virtually contained in its own cognoscitive power, that are universal and abstract notions (*rationes*) from which as it were looking downward (*tanquam desuper spectans*) it comprehends individual things.[28] Now, because these latter which are pure active energies of the soul, are many times exerted upon occasion of those other passive or sympathetical perceptions of individual things anteceding, it is therefore conceived by many that they are nothing else but thin and evanid images of those sensible ideas, and therefore that all intellection and knowledge ascends from sense, and intellection is nothing but the improvement or result of sense. Yet, notwithstanding it is most certainly true that they proceed from a quite different power of the soul, whereby it actively protrudes its own immediate objects from within itself, and comprehends individuals without it, not passively or consequentially, but as it were proleptically, and not with an ascending, but with a descending perception. Whereby the mind first reflecting upon itself and its own ideas, virtually contained in its own omniform cognoscitive power, and thence descending downward, comprehends individual things under them. So that knowledge doth not begin in individuals, but ends in them. And therefore they are but the secondary objects of intellection, the soul taking its first rise from within itself, and so by its own inward cognoscitive power comprehending things without it. Else how should God have knowledge? And if we know as God knows, then do we know or gain knowledge by universals. In which sense (though not in that other of Protagoras) the soul may be truly said to be the measure of all things.[29]

Now I say, if the very sensible ideas and phantasms themselves be not mere stamps or impressions from individual things without in a corporeal manner impressed upon the soul, but active though sympathetical energies of the soul itself, it is much more impossible that the universal and abstract intelligible ideas of the mind, or essences of things, should be mere stamps or signatures impressed upon the soul, as upon a dead thing in a gross corporeal manner.

14. Wherefore here is a double error committed by vulgar philosophers: first that they make the sensible ideas and phantasms to be totally impressed from without in a gross corporeal manner upon the soul, as it were upon a dead thing; and secondly, that then they suppose the

---

[28] An allusion to Boethius. See above p. 58.
[29] Plato, *Theaetetus* 152A. Also 160D, 178B.

intelligible ideas, the abstract and universal notions of the mind to be made out of these sensible ideas and phantasms impressed from without in a corporeal manner likewise by abstraction or separation of the individuating circumstances, as it were by the hewing of certain chips from them, or by hammering, beating, or anvilling of them out into thin intelligible ideas, as if solid and massy gold should be beaten out into thin leaf-gold. To which purpose they have ingeniously contrived and set up an active understanding (*intellectus agens*),[30] like a smith or carpenter, with his shop or forge in the brain, furnished with all necessary tools and instruments for such work. Where I would only demand of these philosophers, whether this their so expert smith (*faber*) or architect, the active understanding, when he goes about his work, doth know what he is to do with these phantasms beforehand, what he is to make of them, and unto what shape to bring them? If he do not he must needs be a bungling workman. But if he do, he is prevented in his design and undertaking, his work being done already to his hand. For he must needs have the intelligible idea of that which he knows or understands already within himself. And therefore now to what purpose should he use his tools, and go about to hew and hammer and anvil out these phantasms into thin and subtle intelligible ideas, merely to make that which he hath already, and which was native and domestic to him?

But this opinion is founded in no less a mistake of Aristotle's text concerning the active understanding who never dreamed of any such as these men imagine (if we may believe the Greek scholiasts, that best understood him)[31] than it is of the text of nature, as if not only those phantasms, but also the intelligible ideas themselves were gross and corporeal things impressed from matter. Whereas even the first of these are passive energies of the soul itself, fatally united to some local motions in the body, and concurrently produced with them, by reason of that magical union betwixt the soul and body. But the other are pure active energies of the mind itself, as free from corporeal sympathy. Neither can these latter be made out of the former by any abstraction or separation, no nor by any depinxation or chymical distillation or sublimation neither. For it is a thing utterly impossible that vigour,

---

[30] See note 17 above. By 'vulgar philosophers', Cudworth must have scholastics in mind here.

[31] For instance, Alexander of Aphrodisias (fl. *c.* AD 200) and Simplicius (sixth century AD). Cudworth, like the humanists of the Renaissance, preferred the early commentators on Aristotle to more recent scholasticism.

activity, and awakened energy, as intellections are, should be raised out of dull, sluggish, and drowsy passion or sympathy. And this opinion is but like that other of the same philosopher's concerning the eduction or raising of substantial and immaterial forms out of the passive matter, both of them proceeding from one and the same sottishness of mind that induces them to think that dull, stupid, and senseless matter is the first original source of all activity and perfection, all form and pulchritude, all wisdom and knowledge in the world.

And things being rightly considered, this opinion doth in truth and reality attribute as much activity to the soul, that saith it hath a power of raising or educing of intelligible ideas or universal and abstract notions (*rationes*) out of phantasms as that other that affirms it hath a power of exerting them from itself, as it would attribute as much activity to the sun to say that he had a power of raising or educing light of the day out of night and darkness, as to say that he had a power of exerting it out of his own body.

15. Wherefore others of this kind of philosophers that will not acknowledge any immaterial substance that hath any active power of its own in it, or anything in the soul besides impression[s] from corporeal objects without, have found out another device, and that is this: plainly to deny that there are any universal notions, ideas, or reasons (*rationes*) in the mind at all, but that those things which are called universal are nothing else but names applied to several individuals. Which opinion as it was formerly held by those that were therefore called nominalists (*nominales*), so it hath been lately revived and taken up by some of these strenuous impugners of immaterial and incorporeal substances. There is nothing in the world (saith a late author)[32] universal, but names. For the things named are every one of them individual and singular. Now indeed this is true, and nobody denies it, of things existing without the mind. But this author's meaning herein is to deny all universal conceptions (*conceptus*) and reasonings (*rationes*) of the mind, as appears by his larger explication of the same opinion elsewhere:

> This universal is the name not of anything existing in the nature of things, nor of any idea or phantasm formed in the mind, but always the name of some word or name; so that when an animal or stone, or a spectre, or anything else is said to be universal, it is to be understood only that those words animal, stone, are universal names, that is names

[32] Hobbes. See below.

common to more things; and the conceptions answering to them in the mind are the images and phantasms of singular animals or other things. And therefore to understand the meaning of an universal, there is no need of any other faculty than that of the imagination, whereby we are minded that words of that sort have sometimes excited one thing sometimes another in our mind.[33]

That is, there are no other ideas in the mind but only phantasms of individual corporeal things; only there are universal names, which are applied in common to more individuals than one. But there is no other object of the mind or cogitation but only singular and individual things existing without the soul. Wherefore this author consentaneously hereunto defines understanding to be nothing else but conception caused by speech. And therefore if speech be peculiar to man, then is understanding peculiar to him also. This mysterious notion is insisted upon and explained likewise by the third objector against Cartesius' metaphysics after this manner:

Now what do we say, if perhaps reasoning be nothing else but the coupling and chaining together of names or appellations by these words, *it is*. Whence we gather nothing at all by reason concerning the nature of things, but concerning their appellations, to wit whether we join the names of things according to agreements or not. If this be so as it may be, reasoning will depend upon names, names upon the imagination, and the imagination upon the motion of the bodily organs. And so the mind will be nothing else but a motion in some parts of the body.[34]

According to which philosophy, reason and science do not superadd

---

[33] Cudworth's translation from Hobbes, *De corpore*, Philos. I. sect. 9. 'Est ergo nomen hoc universale non rei alicuius existentis in rerum natura, neque ideae sive phantasmatis alicuius in animo formati, sed alicujus semper vocis sive nominis nomen, ita ut cum dicatur animal, vel saxum, vel spectrum, vel aliud quicquam esse universale, intelligendum sit ullum hominem, saxum, &c. fuisse, esse, aut posse universale sed tantum voces eas animal, saxum, esse nomina universalia, id est nomina pluribus rebus communia, et respondentes ipsis in animo conceptus sunt singularium animalium vel aliarum rerum imagines et phantasmata. Ideoque non est opus ad vim universalis intelligendam alia facultate quam imaginativa qua recordamur voces ejusmodi modo unam rem, modo aliam in animo excitasse' (*Opera philosophica*, vol. I, pp. 17–18; cf. *English Works*, vol. I, p. 20).

[34] Cudworth's translation of Descartes,'Quid jam dicimus, si forte ratiocinatio nihil aliud sit, quam copulatio et concatenatio nominum sive appellationum, per verbum hoc, *Est*. Unde colligimus ratione nihil omnino de natura rerum, sed de earum appellationibus, nimirum utrum copulemus rerum nomina secundum pacta [...], vel non. Si hoc sit, sicut esse potest, ratiocinatio dependebit a nominibus, nomina ab imaginatione, et imaginatio [...] ab organorum corporeorum motu, et sic mens nihil aliud erit, praeterquam motus in partibus quibusdam corporis organici' (*AT* VII, 178). The 'third objector' was Thomas Hobbes. This is his fourth objection. (CSM, II, 125)

anything to sense, or reach any further in the knowledge of the nature of things, but only in making use of common names to express several individuals by at once.

16. Wherefore, although there be already enough said to prove that in the understanding of individual corporeal things, besides sense and the sensible phantasms from them, there are also intelligible ideas and universal notions (*rationes*) exerted from the mind itself, by which alone they are comprehended. Yet still to make this business clearer, and also to demonstrate that the knowledge of universal axiomatical truth and scientifical theorems is a thing which doth not passively result from sense, but from the actual strength and vigour of the intellect itself comprehending its own intelligible ideas, we will here propose that one geometrical theorem concerning a triangle; that it hath three angles equal to two right angles, and consider what the subject of it is scientifically (ἐπιστημονικῶς) comprehended.

First therefore, if there be no other object of the mind in knowledge but sensible individuals existing without us, then the subject of this theorem, when Euclid wrought it, was only some individual bodies by him compared together. Nay, Euclid himself did not carry this knowledge about with him in his mind, neither was he master of it any longer than he held those individual bodies in his hands, or looked upon them with his eyes. And if so, it could not signify anything at all, to any other person which either then or now had not the same individual bodies to compare, that Euclid had. Whereas it is plain that the subject of this theorem, whatsoever it be, is such a thing as every geometrician, though in never such distant places and times, hath the very same always ready at his hand, without the least imaginable difference. And they all pronounce concerning the same thing. Which could not possibly otherwise be, unless it were some universal notion (*ratio*) and intelligible idea of the mind.

17. Again, secondly, no individual or material thing is the subject of this theorem, as sense takes cognizance of it, that is the matter and colour and figure and magnitude, all concretely together. For the same individual matter may presently be made quadrangular or circular, but only precisely in respect of the figure, and of that also no otherwise than as it is conformable to the indivisible and immutable notion (*ratio*) or idea of a triangle, comprehended in the mind as the exemplar of it. Now as we have showed already, there is no material triangle any where to be

found that is mathematically exact and accurate, neither is the individual form of a material triangle immutable. And if there were any mathematically exact, our sense could be no criterion (κριτήριον) or rule to judge of it, nor discern when anything were invisibly such, nor judge of the absolute and mathematical equality of the three material angles of it, with two other angular superficies. Wherefore the subjects of this geometrical theorem are no sensible individual bodies, but the notions (*rationes*) of the mind itself, in which alone mathematical accuracy is to be found, and the exact equality of one thing to another certainly and infallibly known.

18. Nay if we should suppose that there were some individual material triangles and angles, absolutely and mathematically exact, and that our sense did infallibly perceive the indivisible points of them, or that we had an infallible pair of compasses, whose tops (*cuspides*) were mathematical points, whereby we could measure the several angles of the triangle and right angle in a perfect circle, accurately divided into infinite parts; or else cutting off those several angles of the triangles and laying them together upon an absolute plane we should thus mechanically find them equal to the two material right angles – this would not amount to the knowledge of this truth, that a triangle as such hath of necessity three angles equal to two right angles, we thus considering them only as material individuals, and things existing without the mind by corporeal sense. For though we had now found that these individual material triangles were equal to those two individual material right angles, yet looking no further than sense determined to individuals, we could not tell certainly that it was so with all individual triangles, much less understand any necessity of its being so, or attain to anything of the reason (διότι) of it, in which alone every true science consisteth. And this Aristotle hath observed very pertinently to our purpose:

> Neither is it necessary to understand by sense, but to perceive. But this regards a particular thing and manner, and the present time. But it is impossible to perceive by sense what relates to everything, and in all respects. For *this* and *now* relate not to an universal. For of an universal we say that it is always and everywhere. Since then demonstrations are of an universal, it is plain that there is no knowledge of the universal theorems of geometry by sense. For it is manifest, that if we could perceive by sense that the three angles of a triangle were equal to two right angles, yet should we not rest satisfied in this, as having therefore a

sufficient knowledge of it (as some say), but would seek further after a demonstration hereof, sense reaching only to singulars, but knowledge to universals.[35]

The mind would not be satisfied herewith, but would still further require a demonstration of it, which demonstrations are not of individuals perceived by sense, but only of the universal notions (*rationes*) comprehended in the mind. Knowledge, as I said before, being a descending comprehension of a thing from the universal ideas of the mind and not an ascending perception of them from individuals by sense.

19. Wherefore the apodictical knowledge of this truth is not otherwise to be attained than by the mind's ascending above sense, and elevating itself from individuals to the comprehension of the universal notions (*rationes*) and ideas of things within itself, making the object of its enquiry and contemplation not this nor that material individual triangle without itself, but the indivisible and immutable notion of a triangle. And thus it finds several ways that a triangle, as such, must of necessity have its three angles equal to two right angles.

For first, if one will consider any triangle as made out of a parallelogram (though this be the more compounded figure) divided by a diagonal line into two equal triangles, it is plain in every parallelogram there are four angles equal to four right angles, because when a straight line cuts two parallel lines, the two interior angles must of necessity be

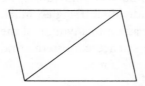 equivalent to two right angles, one of them being the complement of the other to a semicircle. But when the parallelogram is divided into two equal triangles by a diagonal line, the quantity of the three angles in each must of necessity be half the quantity of the four angles in the parallelogram.

---

[35] *Οὐδὲ δι' αἰσθήσεώς ἐστιν ἐπίστασθαι, [...] ἀλλ' αἰσθάνεσθαί γε ἀναγκαῖον· τὸ δέ τι καὶ που καὶ νῦν· τὸ δὲ καθόλου καὶ ἐπὶ πᾶσιν ἀδύνατον αἰσθάνεσθαι· οὐ γὰρ τόδε, οὐδε νῦν, οὐ γὰρ ἦν καθόλου. Τὸ γὰρ ἀεὶ καὶ πανταχοῦ καθόλου φαμὲν εἶναι. Ἐπεὶ οὖν αἱ μὲν ἀποδείξεις καθόλου, ταῦτα δὲ οὐκ ἔστιν αἰσθάνεσθαι, φανερὸν ὅτι οὐδὲ ἐπίστασθαι δι' αἰσθήσεώς ἐστιν. Ἀλλὰ δῆλον ὅτι καὶ εἰ ἦν αἰσθάνεσθαι ὅτι τὸ τρίγωνον δυσὶν ὀρθαῖς ἴσας ἔχει τὰς γωνίας, ἐζητοῦμεν ἂν ἀπόδειξιν, καὶ οὐχ (ὡς[περ] φασί τινες) ἠπιστάμεθα. Αἰσθάνεσθαι μὲν γὰρ ἀνάγκη καθ' ἕκαστον, ἡ δὲ ἐπιστήμη τὰ τοῦ καθόλου γνωρίζειν ἐστί* [v] (Aristotle, *Posterior Analytics* I.31). Compare *TIS*, p. 731.

Or if a man will consider the formation (*genesis*) of a plain triangle in this manner, first by a straight line cutting two parallel lines, and then one of these parallels moving upon its centre in the straight line out of its parallelism, and inclining towards the other line, if it move never so little out of its parallelism towards the other parallel, the continuation of it must needs cut the other line, and make a triangle. And so much as the interior angle, which with the other opposite, made up two right angles, so much is the third angle. And therefore all three make up two right angles.

20. Now here is a gross error of the vulgar to imagine, because geometricians demonstrating such theorems commonly make use of

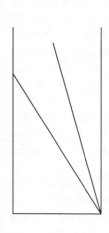

such sensible schemes or diagrams, that therefore the knowledge of this truth doth result from sense, or that the geometricians themselves have no other ideas in their minds of straight lines, parallels, right, acute, and obtuse angles, triangles, equality of angles, than what are impressed upon their fancy from these schemes. Whereas these are only made use of to entertain the fancy in the mean time, whilst the mind being intent upon the demonstration, actively exerts other intelligible ideas of these things from within itself, and from thence comprehends the apodictical necessity of the theorem. Neither is the true and proper knowledge of one theorem or universal and necessary truth, either in geometry or metaphysics, passively impressed upon the soul from individuals existing without, or the result of mere sense, but it proceeds from the active strength and vigour of the mind, comprehending the intelligible ideas and universal notions (*rationes*) of things within itself.

21. Wherefore we conclude, that the immediate objects of geometrical science, properly so called, are not individual bodies or superficies but the intelligible and universal ideas of a triangle, square, circle, pyramid, cube, sphere, actively exerted from the mind and comprehended in it. For the mind doth not seek its objects of knowledge abroad without itself, but must needs actively comprehend them within itself. Which also, as we shall show in the following chapter, are immutable things, and always the same.

Chapter IV[36]

1. No individual material thing is always necessarily the same with itself, but mutable and changeable. And our sensible perceptions of them are nothing but passions or affections in the soul from some local motions in our body caused by them. Which passions also are a kind of motions in the soul, whereby we do not comprehend the immutable *ratio* or essence of any thing. But intellection and knowledge are the active comprehension of something that is fixed and immutable, and hath always a necessary identity with itself. For that which is not one steady and immutable thing cannot, as such, be an object of intellection or knowledge, neither can the mind fix itself upon it. For it must needs mock and delude the understanding, perpetually gliding and rolling away from it when it endeavours to grasp or comprehend it. Neither can it be the basis or subject of any scientifical theorem or proposition. For how can any thing be certainly, constantly, and immutably affirmed of that which is no one certain thing, nor always immutably the same with itself. Whence it plainly follows that the immediate objects of intellection and knowledge cannot be these individual material things as such which our senses are passively affected from, but must of necessity be something else.

2. For which cause those flowing philosophers before mentioned, Heraclitus, Cratylus, and Protagoras,[37] that maintained that there were no other beings that could be the objects of cogitation besides these individual and material things, which they supposed always to flow, and never to stand still, did, consentaneously to this hypothesis of theirs, assert that there was no knowledge but sense, and no certain or immutable comprehension of any thing. For that this assertion of theirs was grounded merely upon this hypothesis that there was no other being or object of the mind besides individual material things as such. Which they signified after this manner, by saying that all things flowed, for these material things do so. Aristotle plainly instructs us in his Metaphysics:

---

[36] *TIS*, pp. 734–7 deals in summary form with the same content as this chapter, with many of the same examples.

[37] See above Book II, ch. II, pp. 32ff. In *TIS*, p. 735 Cudworth refers to 'the *Heracliticks* and other *Scepticks*'.

The ground of this opinion, which denied all certain and immutable knowledge was from hence, because truth and knowledge refer to beings or entities, and they supposed that there were no other beings besides these individual sensibles only. In which there is very much of undeterminateness ... And which they perceived to be liable to perpetual motion or mutation. Now concerning that which always changes, nothing can be affirmed as constantly and immutably true. And from this proposition sprung the highest sect of those which are called Heraclitical philosophers, and those that follow Cratylus, who at last came to this, that he only moved his finger, but thought that nothing at all ought to be affirmed, and reprehended Heraclitus for saying that one cannot twice enter into the same river because he thought that one could not so much as once do it.[38]

That is, that no material thing remained one moment the same.

3. Wherefore if there be any such thing as intellection, science, and knowledge, distinct from external sense, and any immutable truths, then there must of necessity be some other kind of beings or entities, besides these individual material things, as the immediate objects or subjects of them, such things as do not flow but 'always remain immutably the same' or 'permanent', and 'having always the same nature',[39] as Plato expresseth these immediate objects of knowledge. Or else in Aristotle's language, 'an immutable essence' (ἀκίνητος οὐσία). Who therefore confutes both these sects of philosophers, whereof one was extremely metaphysical, that made all things to stand still. Whom I confess I understand not, the other too grossly material and addicted to sense, that made nothing to stand still but all things to flow after this manner:

It is manifest that neither they speak truly who affirm all things to rest, nor they that affirm all things to move. For if all things rest, then the same things would always be true and false, which is not so, because he that affirms this, once was not, and again will not be. But if all things move, then nothing can be true, and therefore all things will be false.[40]

---

[38] Αἴτιον [δὲ] τῆς δόξης τούτοις ὅτι περὶ τῶν ὄντων μὲν τὴν ἀλήθειαν ἐσκόπουν· τὰ δ᾽ ὄντα ὑπέλαβον εἶναι τὰ αἰσθητὰ μόνον· ἐν δὲ τούτοις πολλὴ ἡ τοῦ ἀορίστου φύσις ἐνυπάρχει. ... Ἔτι δὲ πᾶσαν ὁρῶντες ταύτην κινουμένην τὴν φύσιν, κατὰ δὲ τοῦ μεταβάλλοντος οὐδὲν ἀληθευόμενον, περί γε τὸ πάντῃ πάντως μεταβάλλον, οὐκ ἐνδέχεσθαι ἀληθεύειν. Ἐκ γὰρ ταύτης τῆς ὑπολήψεως ἐξήνθησεν ἡ ἀκροτάτη δόξα τῶν εἰρημένων ἢ τῶν φασκόντων Ἡρακλειτίζειν, καὶ οἵαν Κρατύλος εἶχεν, ὃς τὸ τελευταῖον οὐθὲν ᾤετο δεῖν λέγειν, ἀλλὰ τὸν δάκτυλον ἐκίνει μόνον, καὶ Ἡρακλείτῳ ἐπετίμα εἰπόντι [ἐστιν] δὶς τῷ αὐτῷ ποταμῷ οὐκ ἐμβῆναι. αὐτὸς γὰρ ᾤετο οὐδ᾽ ἅπαξ (Aristotle, *Metaphysics* 1010a f).

[39] ἀεὶ ταυτὰ καὶ ὡσαύτως ἔχοντα, or νόμιμα καὶ μίαν ἀεὶ φύσιν ἔχοντα. Not quotations from Plato.

[40] Φανερὸν [δ᾽] ὅτι οὐδ᾽ οἱ πάντα ἠρεμεῖν λέγοντες ἀληθῆ λέγουσιν, οὐδ᾽ οἱ πάντα κινεῖσθαι. Εἰ

And both he and Plato compounded that controversy thus, by acknowledging two sorts of entities, the one mutable, or subject to flux and motion, such as are especially individual corporeal things, the other immutable, that always rest or stand still, which are the proper objects of certain, constant, and immutable knowledge, that therefore cannot be mere nothings, non-entities.

Which latter kind of being, that is, the immutable essence (ἀκίνητος οὐσία) as a distinct thing from individual sensibles, Aristotle plainly asserts against Heraclitus and those other flowing philosophers in these words: 'We would have these philosophers to know that besides sensible things', that are always mutable, 'there is another kind of being or entity of such things as are neither subject to motion, corruption nor generation'.[41] And elsewhere he tells us that this immoveable essence is the object of theoretical knowledge of the first philosophy and of the pure mathematics.

4. Now these immutable entities are the universal *rationes*, or intelligible natures and essences of all things, which some compare to unities, but Aristotle to numbers, which formally considered are indivisible. Saith he 'essences are like to numbers'[42] because if but the least thing be added to any number or subtracted from it, the number is destroyed.

And these are the objects of all certain knowledge. As for example, the objects of geometry are not any individual material triangles, squares, circles, pyramids, cubes, spheres, and the like. Which because they are always mutable, nothing can be immutably affirmed of them, but they are those indivisible and unchangeable *rationes* of a triangle, square, circle, which are ever the same to all geometricians in all ages and places of which such immutable theorems as these are demonstrated as that a triangle has necessarily three angles equal to two right angles.[43]

But if any one demand here, where these immutable entities do exist, I answer first that as they are considered formally, they do not properly exist in the individuals without us, as if they were from them imprinted

---

μὲν γὰρ ἠρεμεῖ πάντα, ἀεὶ ταῦτα ἀληθῆ καὶ ψευδῆ ἔσται· φαίνεται δὲ τοῦτο μεταβάλλον· ὁ γὰρ λέγων πότε αὐτὸς οὐκ ἦν, καὶ πάλιν οὐκ ἔσται, εἰ δὲ πάντα κινεῖται, οὐθὲν ἔσται ἀληθές, πάντα ἄρα ψευδῆ (ibid., 1012b3).

[41] Ἔτι δὲ ἀξιώσομεν αὐτοὺς ὑπολαμβάνειν καὶ ἄλλην [τινὰ] οὐσίαν εἶναι τῶν ὄντων, ᾗ οὔτε κίνησις ὑπάρχει, οὔτε φθορὰ, οὔτε γένεσις τὸ παράπαν (ibid., 1009a36).

[42] εἰσὶ πως ἀριθμοὶ αἱ οὐσίαι (ibid., 1043b33).

[43] Euclid, *Elements* I.31.

upon the understanding (which some have taken to be Aristotle's opinion) because no individual material thing is either universal or immutable. And if these things were only lodged in the individual sensibles, then they would be unavoidably obnoxious to the fluctuating waves of the same reciprocating Euripus,[44] in which all individual material things are perpetually whirled. But because they perish not together with them, it is a certain argument that they exist independently upon them. Neither in the next place do they exist somewhere else apart for the individual sensibles, and without the mind. Which is that opinion that Aristotle justly condemns, but either justly or unskilfully attributes to Plato. For if the mind looked abroad for its objects wholly without itself, then all its knowledge would be nothing but sense and passion. For to know a thing is nothing but to comprehend it by some inward ideas that are domestic to the mind, and actively exerted from it. Wherefore these intelligible ideas or essences of things, those forms by which we understand all things, exist nowhere but in the mind itself. For it was very well determined long ago by Socrates in Plato's *Parmenides* that these things are nothing else but *noemata*. 'These species or ideas are all of them nothing but *noemata* or notions that exist nowhere but in the soul itself.'[45] Wherefore to say that there are immutable natures and essences, and *rationes* of things, distinct from the individuals that exist without us, is all one as if one should say that there is in the universe above the orb of matter and body, another superior orb of intellectual being, that comprehends its own immediate objects, that is the immutable *rationes* and ideas of things with itself, by which it understands and knows all things without itself.

5.[46] And yet, notwithstanding, though these things exist only in the mind, they are not therefore mere figments of the understanding. For if the subjects of all scientifical theorems were nothing but figments, then all truth and knowledge that is built upon them would be a mere fictitious thing. And if truth itself and the intellectual nature be fictitious things, then what can be real or solid in the world? But it is evident that though the mind thinks of these things at pleasure, yet they are not

---

[44] The strait between Boeotia and Euboea.
[45] Τῶν εἰδῶν ἕκαστον [ἢ] τούτων νόημα, καὶ οὐδαμοῦ αὐτῷ προσήκαι ἐγγίνεσθαι ἄλλοθι ἢ ἐν ψυχῇ (Plato, *Parmenides* 132B).
[46] There is some confusion about the numbering of this and the following three sections in the first edition. I have changed the numbers to give a consistent series, and adjusted their positions.

arbitrarily framed by the mind, but have certain, determinate, and immutable natures of their own, which are independent upon the mind and which are blown away into nothing at the pleasure of the same Being that arbitrarily made them.

But we all naturally conceive that those things have not only an eternal, but also a necessary existence, so that they could not ever but be such and so many as they are, and can never possibly perish or cease to be, but are absolutely undestroyable.

Which is a thing frequently acknowledged in the writings of both those famous philosophers, Plato and Aristotle. The former of them calling those things, 'Things that were never made, but always are' and 'things that were never made, nor can be destroyed'.[47] 'Things ingenerable and unperishable', *'quae Plato negat gigni, sed semper esse'* (as Tully expresseth it).[48] And Philo, the Platonical Jew, calls the τὰ νοητά,[49] which are the same things we speak of, 'the most necessary essences' (ἀναγκαιόταται οὐσίαι), that is such things as could not but be, and cannot possibly not be. And Aristotle himself calls the *rationes* of things in his metaphysics not only 'things separate from matter and immutable' (χωριστά and ἀκίνητα), but also eternal (ἀΐδια). And in his ethics likewise he calls geometrical truths eternal things (ἀΐδια), *lib.* 3, *cap.* 5, where he makes the geometrical truth concerning the incommensurability betwixt the diameter and the side of a square to be an eternal thing.[50] Elsewhere he tells us that 'science properly so called is not of things corruptible and contingent'[51] but of things necessary, incorruptible, and eternal. Which immutable and eternal objects of science in the place before quoted he described thus: 'Such a kind of entity of things as has neither motion, nor generation, nor corruption',[52] that is, such

---

[47] τὰ μὴ γιγνόμενα ἀλλ᾽ ἀεὶ ὄντα, (not a quotation) μήτε γιγνόμενα μήτε ἀπολλύμενα (*Philebus* 61E22).

[48] Cicero, *Orator* III.10. Loeb translation: 'Plato [says these] do not "become"; they exist for ever and depend on intellect and reason.' Cicero, *Orator*, trans. H.M. Hubbell (London and Cambridge, Mass., 1939).

[49] Philo Judaeus (*c.* 20 BC–AD 40), Jewish Hellenistic philosopher from Alexandria. Through allegorical interpretation of Scripture he offered a Platonized reading of the Bible. *Inter alia*, he was the first to identify the intelligible realm of ideas as the thoughts of God.

[50] περὶ τῶν ἀϊδίων οὐδεὶς βουλεύεται, οἶον περὶ τοῦ [κοσμου ἢ τῆς] διαμέτρου καὶ τῆς πλευρᾶς, ὅτι ἀσύμμετροι (Aristotle, *Ethics* 1112a23–4). This is not an exact quotation, nor yet a close translation of the Greek.

[51] οὐ τῶν φθαρτῶν εἶναι ἐπιστήμην (Aristotle, *Posterior Analytics* 75b25).

[52] Οὐσίαν [εἶναι] τῶν ὄντων ἢ οὔτε κίνησις ὑπαρχει, οὔτε φθορὰ οὔτε γένεσις τὸ παράπαν (Aristotle, *Metaphysics* 1009a39).

things as were never made, and can never be destroyed. To which he saith the mind is necessarily determined. For science or knowledge has nothing either of fiction or of arbitrariness in it, but is 'the comprehension of that which immutably *is*'. (κατάληψις τοῦ ὄντος)

6. Moreover, these things have a consistent being, when our particular created minds do not actually think of them, and therefore they are immutable in another sense likewise, not only because they are indivisibly the same when we think of them, but also because they have a constant and never-failing entity, and always are, whether our particular minds think of them or not. For the intelligible natures and essences of a triangle, square, circle, pyramid, cube, sphere, &c. and all the necessary geometrical verities belonging to these several figures, were not the creatures of Archimedes, Euclid, or Pythagoras, or any other inventors of geometry, nor did then first begin to be, but all these *rationes* and verities had a real and actual entity before, and would continue still, though all the geometricians in the world were quite extinct, and no man knew them or thought of them. Nay, though all the material world were quite swept away, and also all particular created minds annihilated together with it, yet there is no doubt but the intelligible natures or essences of all geometrical figures, and the necessary verities belonging to them, would notwithstanding remain safe and sound. Wherefore these things had a being also before the material world and all particular intellects were created. For it is not at all conceivable that ever there was a time when there was no intelligible nature of a triangle, nor any such thing cogitable at all, and when it was not yet actually true that a triangle has three angles equal to two right angles, but that these things were afterward arbitrarily made and brought into being out of an antecedent nothing or non-entity, so that the being of them bore some certain date, and had a youngness in them, and so by the same reason might wax old, and decay again. Which notion he often harps upon when he speaks of forms (εἴδη) of things, as when he says 'There is no generation of the essence of a sphere',[53] that is, it is a thing that is not made, but always is. And elsewhere he pronounces universally of the εἴδη, 'The forms of material things are without generation and corruption',[54] and, 'That none makes the form

[53] τοῦ σφαῖραν εἶναι οὐκ ἔστι γένεσις. See Aristotle, *Metaphysics*,VII.8. Not actually a quotation.
[54] Ἄνευ γενέσεως καὶ φθορᾶς ὅλως εἶναι τὰ εἴδη. (ibid., 1033b5). Not an exact quotation.

of any thing, for it is never generated.'[55] Divers have censured Aristotle in some of such passages too much to confound physics and metaphysics together. For indeed these things are not true in a physical, but only in a metaphysical sense. That is, the immediate objects of intellection and science (τὰ νοητά), are eternal, necessarily existent, and incorruptible.

7. Now the plain meaning of all this is nothing else, but that there is an eternal wisdom and knowledge in the world, necessarily existing which was never made, and can never cease to be or be destroyed. Or, which is all one, that there is an infinite eternal mind necessarily existing, and that actually comprehends himself, the possibility of all things, and the verities clinging to them. In a word, that there is a God, or an omnipotent and omniscient Being, necessarily existing, who therefore cannot destroy his own being or nature, that is, his infinite power and wisdom.

For since the intelligible essences (*rationes*) and verities of things, as we observed before out of Plato, are nothing but *noemata*, that is objective notions or knowledges, which are things that cannot exist alone, but together with that actual knowledge in which they are comprehended, they are the modifications of some mind or intellect. It is all one to affirm that there are eternal *rationes*, essences of things, and verities necessarily existing, and to say that there is an infinite, omnipotent, and eternal Mind, necessarily existing that always actually comprehendeth himself, the essences of all things, and their verities, or, rather, which is the *rationes*, essences, and verities of all things. For the *rationes* and essences of things are not dead things, like so many statues, images, or pictures hung up somewhere by themselves alone in a world. Neither are truths mere sentences and propositions written down with ink upon a book, but they are living things and nothing but modifications of mind or intellect. And therefore the first intellect is essentially and archetypally all *rationes* and verities, and all particular created intellects are but derivative participations of it, that are printed by it with the same ectypal signatures upon them.

And we may undoubtedly conclude, that it is a thing altogether as certain, that there is an infinite and eternal Mind (that is, a God) necessarily existing in the world, as that there ever was the *ratio* or

---

[55] Τὸ εἶδος οὐδεὶς ποιεῖ οὐδὲ γεννᾶται. (ibid., 1043b17–18).

intelligible essence of a triangle, or circle, of unity and duality, and that it was ever actually true that a triangle hath three angles equal to two right angles, or that *aequalia addita aequalibus efficiunt aequalia* [equals added to equals make equals] or the like.

8. Neither does this hinder or contradict the truth of this assertion, that many that doubt concerning the existence of a God, yet notwithstanding confidently believe the necessary eternity of these things, and persuade themselves that, though there were no mind nor intellect, and so no God in the world, nay though there was no matter neither and no substantial entity at all, yet notwithstanding these *rationes* and verities of things would necessarily be as they are.

9. For there is an absolute impossibility in this assertion that these essences of things and verities should be, though there were no substantial entity or no mind existing. For these things themselves must of necessity be either substances or modifications of substance. For what is neither substance nor modification of a substance is a pure non-entity; and if they be modifications of substance they cannot possibly exist without that substance whose modifications they are. Which must either be matter or mind. But they are not the modifications of matter as such, because they are universal and immutable. Therefore they are the modifications of some mind or intellect, so that these cannot be eternal without an eternal Mind.

And these men do but deceive themselves in the hypothetical assertion, that there would have been these *rationes* and universal verities, though there had never been a God or intellect. Neither considering what the nature of God is, whose existence they would question or doubt of, nor what those *rationes* and verities are, which they would make so necessarily existent, by means whereof they do at once assert and question the same thing. For that which begets so strong a persuasion in their minds that the *rationes* of things and universal verities are so necessarily eternal, though they do not perceive it, is nothing else but an inward invincible prepossession of the necessary existence of God, or an infinite eternal omnipotent and omniscient mind (that always actually comprehends himself, and the extent of his own power, or the ideas of all possible things), so deeply radicated and infixed in their minds, as that they cannot possibly quit themselves of it, though they endeavour it never so much but it will unawares adhere to them, even when they force themselves to suppose the non-existence of God as a person, whose idea they do not clearly comprehend. That is, the force of nature is so strong in them as to make them acknowledge the thing when they deny the word. So that the true meaning of this phenomenon is nothing else but this, that God is a being so necessarily existent, that though men will suppose the non-existence of him, and deny the name, yet notwithstanding they cannot but confute themselves, and confess the thing.

10. Nay, it is clearly and mathematically demonstrable from what we have already proved, that there is some eternal mind. For as it is unquestionably certain that something in the world was eternal, merely from hence, because there is being which could not spring out of nothing, and therefore, if there were no God, matter of necessity must be eternal. So because there is mind and understanding and actual knowledge in the world, and these things could not spring out of matter, wisdom and knowledge must needs be eternal things, and there must be of necessity some eternal mind.

For, *ex hypothesi*, that once there had been no knowledge, no intelligible *rationes* or essences of things, no mind or intellect in the world, it would have been absolutely impossible that ever there should have been any such thing, because it could neither spring out of nothing, nor, which is all one, out of senseless and unknowing matter.[56]

11. Now because every thing that is imperfect must needs depend upon something that is perfect in the same kind, our particular imperfect understandings which do not always actually contain the *rationes* of things and their verities in them, which are many times ignorant, doubting, erring, and slowly proceed by discourse and ratiocination from one thing to another, must needs be derivative participations of a perfect, infinite, and eternal intellect, in which is the *rationes* of all things, and all universal verities are always actually comprehended. Which consideration is so obvious and unavoidable, that Aristotle himself could not miss of it. For he tells us that since our understandings are but potentially all things (δυνάμει πάντα), that is have not an actual but potential omniformity only, there must of necessity be *in rerum natura* [in nature] another intellect that is actually all knowledge, and is the same to our understandings, 'that active art is

---

[56] For Cudworth's argument for the existence of God, from the premiss that nothing can come of nothing, see *TIS* 738ff.

to passive matter' and, 'that the light is to our eyes', and that which does not, 'sometimes understand and sometimes not understand' but is always eternal, actual knowledge.[57] A sun that never sets, an eye that never winks. Wherefore though all our knowledges be not stamped or impressed upon our souls from the matter, they are all as it were ectypal prints (σφραγίσματα) and derivative signatures (ἐκμάγματα) from one archetypal intellect, that is essentially the *rationes* of all things and all verities.

12. And from hence it comes to pass, that all understandings are not only constantly furnished with forms and ideas to conceive all things by, and thereby enabled to understand all the clear conceptions of one another, being printed all over at once with the seeds of universal knowledge, but also have exactly the same ideas of the same things. Whereas if these things were impressed upon our souls from the matter without, all men would not be readily furnished with the ideas to conceive all things by at every time, it being merely casual and contingent what things occur to men's several senses. Neither could their ideas be exactly alike to one another, because no individual objects are so. And therefore when one spoke of one thing, another would mean another. Much less could men so promptly and expeditely exert them upon all occasions, if they were dead forms passively received only and not all virtually contained in some one active and vital principle that had a potential omniformity in it.

Wherefore, as Themistius observes, men could not possibly confer and discourse together in that manner as they do, presently perceiving one another's meaning, and having the very same conceptions of things in their minds, if all did not partake of one and the same intellect. Neither could one so readily teach, and another learn, 'if there were not the same ectypal stamps of things in the mind both of the teacher and the learner'.[58]

13. Moreover, from hence also it comes to pass that truths, though they be never so many several and distant minds apprehending them, yet they are not broken, multiplied, or diversified thereby, but that they are one and the same individual truths in them all. So that it is but one

---

[57] οἷον ἡ τέχνη πρὸς τὴν ὕλην (Aristotle, *De anima* 430a12). οἷον τὸ φῶς (ibid., 430a15). ὁτὲ μὲν νοεῖν, ὁτὲ δὲ οὐ νοεῖν. Not identified.

[58] Themistius (fl. *c.*317–*c* 388): εἰ μή τις ἦν εἰς νοῦς οὗ πάντες ἐκοινωνοῦμεν, and εἰ μὴ ταυτὸν ἦν τὸ νόημα τοῦ διδάσκοντος καὶ τοῦ μανθάνουτος. Not identified.

truth and knowledge that is in all the understandings in the world. Just as when a thousand eyes look upon the sun at once, they all see the same individual object. Or as when a great crowd or throng of people hear one and the same orator speaking to them all, it is one and the same voice, that is in the several ears of all those several auditors. So in like manner, when innumerable created understandings direct themselves to the contemplation of the same universal and immutable truths, they do all of them but as it were listen to one and the same original voice of the eternal wisdom that is never silent, and the several conceptions of those truths in their minds are but like several echoes of the same *verba mentis* [conceptions] of the divine intellect resounding in them.

14. From what we have already declared, it is evident that wisdom, knowledge, and understanding are eternal and self-subsistent things, superior to matter and all sensible beings, and independent upon them. Which mystery is thus acknowledged both in Christianity and Platonism, in that wisdom and intellect are made the eternal and first-begotten offspring of the first original goodness, the fountain of all things. 'The Lord possessed me in the beginning of his way, before his works of old. I was set up from everlasting, from the beginning, or ever the earth was. &c.' (Proverbs 8.22–3). And indeed that opinion that knowledge, wisdom, and understanding [are] in [their] own nature posterior to sensible and material things, and doth result out of them, or proceed only from the radiation and activity of the matter on that which understands, is nothing else but downright atheism. For if this were true, that wisdom, knowledge, and intellection were in its own nature posterior to sensible and corporeal things, as being nothing but the stamp or impress of them, then it must needs follow that this corporeal world was not made or framed by any antecedent wisdom or knowledge, but that it sprang up of itself from the blind, fortuitous, and giddy motions of eternal atoms, from whence all that knowledge that is in the world did afterward result. Which is all one as to say that there is no God at all.

But if any will here pretend that there is indeed a knowledge in God antecedent to all corporeal being, and therefore no passion but a thing independent upon matter and self-originated, but yet notwithstanding, the knowledge of all created understandings is not a thing immediately derived from thence, but only taken up at the rebound or second-hand from sensible and corporeal things; this is just as if one should say that there is indeed a brightness or lucidity in the sun, but yet notwithstanding the light which is in the air, is not derived from that light which is in the body of the sun, but springs immediately out of the power of the dark air. Which being a thing apparently absurd, it may be presumed that this assertion is nothing but a verbal and pretended acknowledgement of a God, that has an antecedent and an independent knowledge made by such as deny the same. For otherwise to what purpose should they so violently and distortedly pervert the natural order and dependency of things in the universe, and cut off that cognation and connection which is betwixt things imperfect and things perfect of the same kind, betwixt created minds and the increated mind, which is the intellectual scale or ladder by which we climb up to God, if they did really believe and acknowledge any such thing. But he that can believe that all human knowledge, wisdom, and prudence has no other source and original than the radiations and impresses of the dark matter, and the fortuitous and tumultuous jumblings thereof, it is justly to be suspected that he is too near akin to those ancient theologues that Aristotle speaks of that fetched the original of God and all things out of night or the dark chaos of matter,[59] that held there is no God at all, or that blind and senseless matter and chance are the only original of all things.

Chapter v

1. We formerly showed that the perception of external sense as such is a mere relative and fantastical thing, there being nothing absolutely true and real in it, but only this, that the soul hath such a passion, affection, phantasm, appearance, or seeming in it. But sense being but an idiopathy, we cannot be absolutely certain by it that every other person or animal has the same passion or affection or phantasm in it from the same corporeal object that we ourselves have. 'Are you certain that every other animal has the same sense or phantasm of every colour that you have', saith Socrates, according to Protagoras' sense, 'nay that every other man has the same. Or, lastly, can you be so much as sure that yourself shall always have the same phantasm from the same object,

---

[59] *οἱ ἐν νυκτὸς πάντα γεννῶντες* (Aristotle, *Metaphysics* 1071b27).

when you are not always the same with yourself?'[60] and passions are diversified by the ἰδιοσυγκρασία [idiosyncrasy] of the patient. Wherefore we cannot be sure merely by the passions of sense, what the absolute nature of a corporeal object is without us, our perception being only relative to ourselves, and our several organs and bodily *crasis*.

Nay, we cannot be sure that there is any object at all before us, when we have a phantasm of sensation of something. Forasmuch as not only in our dreams, but also when we are awake we have phantasms and sensations in us of things that have no reality.

The reason of all which is, because by external sense we do but suffer from corporeal things existing without, and so do not comprehend the nature of the thing as it is absolutely in itself, but only our own passion from it. Neither is our sense a passion immediately from the thing itself that is perceived, for then it would not be altogether so uncertain as it is, but only from certain local motions in that body which the soul is vitally united to, by the mediation whereof it perceives other things at a distance, which local motions and passions may be produced when there are no such objects.

So that if there were no other perceptive power or faculty distinct from external sense, all our perceptions would be merely relative, seeming and fantastical, and not reach to the absolute and certain truth of any thing. And every one would but, as Protagoras expounds it, 'think his own private and relative thoughts truths',[61] and all our cogitations being nothing but appearances, would be indifferently alike true phantasms and one as another.

2. But we have since also demonstrated that there is another perceptive power in the soul superior to outward sense, and of a distinct nature from it, which is the power of knowing or understanding, that is, an active exertion from the mind itself. And therefore has this grand pre-eminence above sense, that it is no idiopathy, not a mere private, a relative, seeming, and fantastical thing, but the comprehension of that which absolutely IS and IS NOT.

---

[60] Ἦ σὺ διϊσχυρίσαιο ἂν ὡς οἷόν σοι φαίνεται ἕκαστον χρῶμα τοιοῦτον [...] καὶ ὁτῳοῦν ζῴῳ; θεαιτ. μὰ Δί οὐκ ἔγωγε· Σωκ· τί δ' ἄλλῳ ἀνθρώπῳ ἆρ' ὅμοιον καὶ σοὶ φαίνεται ὅτι οὖν ἔχεις τοῦτο ἰσχυρῶς ἢ πολὺ μᾶλλον ὅτι οὐδέ σοι αὐτῷ ταὐτόν, διὰ τὸ μηδέποτε ὁμοίως αὐτὸν σεαυτῷ ἔχειν (Socrates to Protagoras in *Theaetetus*, 154A). Cudworth's English translation omits the names of the speakers, rendering the dialogue between Theaetetus and Socrates as a monologue by Socrates. He also omits 'καὶ κυνί', reference to a dog.

[61] τὰ ἴδια μόνον δοξάζειν (compare Plato, *Theaetetus* 161D).

For whereas the objects of external sense (τὰ αἰσθητά) are nothing but individual corporeal things existing without us, from which by sense we receive only idols, images, and passions, of which, as Plotinus observes, 'that which is known by sense, is but an image of that individual body existing without, which sense suffers from. But the object of sense is a being not inwardly comprehended, but remaining without'[62] and, 'for this cause the truth of the thing is not in sense, but only opinion'.[63]

Yet the proper and immediate objects of science rightly so-called and intellection (τὰ νοητά), being the intelligible essences of things and their necessary verities, that exist nowhere but in the mind itself, the understanding by its active power is fully master of them, and comprehends 'not idols or images of them',[64] but the very things themselves within itself. 'Knowledge is not the perception of things abroad without the mind',[65] but is the mind's comprehending itself. 'The mind, in considering things, will not apprehend the things themselves, but only their images, &c.'[66]

Wherefore it is most true as Aristotle often observeth, 'that the knowledge of any scientifical theorem is one and the self-same thing with the thing known',[67] 'that which knows and that which is known are really the same thing',[68] 'The knowledge of any metaphysical or mathematical truth is the very thing',[69] 'or truth itself known' and not any passion or picture of it.[70] And though the same philosopher writes elsewhere that sense is the same with sensible things and understanding the same with the things understood,[71] yet the difference betwixt those

---

[62] τὸ [τε] γιγνωσκόμενον δι᾿αἰσθήσεως, τοῦ πράγματος εἴδωλόν ἐστι, καὶ οὐκ αὐτὸ τὸ πρᾶγμα ἡ αἴσθησις λαμβάνει· μένει γὰρ ἐκεῖνο ἔξω (Plotinus, *Enneads* v.v.1, 17–20).

[63] διὰ τοῦτο [γὰρ καὶ] ἐν ταῖς αἰσθήσεσιν [οἶμαι] οὐκ [ἐν] ἔστιν ἀλήθεια ἀλλὰ δόξα, ὅτι παραδεχομένη καὶ διὰ τοῦτο δόξα οὖσα ἄλλο παραδέχεται, ἄλλου ὄντος ἐκείνου ἐξ οὗ τοῦτο ὃ παραδέχεται ἔχει (ibid., v.v.1, 62–6).

[64] αὐτὰ τὰ πράγματα. καὶ οὐκ εἴδωλα μονον (ibid., iv.vi.1.32). A 'portmanteau' quotation made up of two separate phrases conjoined.

[65] ὁ νοῦς τὰ νοητὰ γιγνώσκων οὐκ ἕτερα ὄντα γινώσκει (ibid. v.v.1, 20–3). Not an exact quotation.

[66] θεωρήσει αὐτὰ οὐκ ἔχων αὐτά, εἴδωλα δι᾿αὐτῶν ... τὸ τοίνυν ἀληθινὸν οὐκ ἔχων, εἴδωλα δὲ τοῦ ἀληθοῦς παρ᾿ αὐτῷ λαβών, τὰ ψευδῆ ἕξει, καὶ οὐδὲν ἀληθές (Plotinus, *Enneads* v.v.1, 55–9).

[67] ὁ νους ὁ κατ᾿ἐνέργειαν τὰ πράγματα νοῶν (*De anima* 430a5).

[68] τὸ αὐτό ἐστι τὸ νοῦν καὶ τὸ νοούμενον (ibid.).

[69] Ἡ ἐπιστήμη ἡ θεωρητικὴ καὶ τὸ ἐπιστητὸν τὸ αὐτό ἐστι (ibid.).

[70] τὸ [δ᾿]αὐτό ἐστιν ἡ κατ᾿ἐνέργειαν ἐπιστήμη τῷ πράγματι (ibid., 430a20).

[71] αἴσθησις ἐστι τὰ αἰσθητὰ, and νόησις τὰ νοητά. Not quotation.

two is very great, for the sensible things really exist without, and sense has only a passive and phantasmatical representation of them. But intellectual conceptions properly so-called, the primary objects of science and intellection, that is the 'separate eternal and immutable *rationes* of things',[72] exist nowhere but in the mind itself, being its own ideas. For the soul is as Aristotle speaks, 'the place of forms and ideas',[73] and they have no other entity at all but only in being known or understood. And by and through these inward ideas of the mind itself, which are its primary objects, does it know and understand all external individual things, which are the secondary objects of knowledge only.

3. Moreover, that the intellection and knowing perception of the soul is not relative and fantastical as the sensitive, is evident from hence, because it is liable to falsehood, which it could not be, if it had not a power of comprehending absolute truth.

For external sense, for this very reason, is not capable of falsehood, because as such it does not comprehend the absolute truth of any thing, being only a phantasm ($\phi\alpha\nu\tau\alpha\sigma\iota\alpha$) or appearance, and all appearances as such are alike true.

So in like manner, if the noetical perceptions of the soul were only fantastical, and did not extend to the comprehension of the absolute truth of things, then every opinion would of necessity be alike true, neither could there be any absolute falsehood in any, because 'every fancy is true',[74] that is, every fancy is a fancy or an appearance, and nothing more is required to it. For absolute truth belongs not to the nature of it. But it is evident to all that are not sunk and degenerated below men into brutish sottishness, that there are false opinions. Whence it follows undeniably that the noetical knowing and intellective power extends to the absolute truth of things. So that whatever theoretical universal proposition in geometry or metaphysics is true to one mind, the same is absolutely true in itself, and therefore true to all minds whatsoever throughout the whole world, that clearly understand it.

Wherefore, though the immediate objects of knowledge, which are the intelligible essences of things and their relations to one another or verities, exist nowhere but in minds, yet notwithstanding they are not

---

[72] τὰ χωριστὰ ἀΐδια καὶ ἀκίνητα (cf. Aristotle, *Metaphysics* 1026a10–11).
[73] τόπος εἰδῶν (Aristotle, *De anima* 429a27).
[74] πᾶσα φαντασία ἐστὶν ἀληθὴς (Sextus, *Against the Logicians* cf. n. 72 1.390). See above p. 44.

figments of the mind, because then every opinion or cogitation would be alike true, that is a true figment having no other truth but relative to that particular mind whose figment it is. But these things have an absolute and immutable nature in themselves, and their mutual respects to one another are alike immutable. And therefore those opinions and cogitations of the mind which are not conformable to the immutable reality of those objective ideas have an absolute falsehood in them. As for example, the nature of a triangle is an immutable thing, and this is demonstrable of it as immutably and necessarily true that it hath three angles equal to two right ones. Neither can any man's opinion or thinking make it otherwise. For it is a false opinion, unless it be agreeable to the immutable nature of a triangle. So likewise the plain regular geometrical solids as such have an immutable nature or essence. And it is demonstrable of them that there are five such bodies, and that there can be no more. And any opinion to the contrary will be an absolute falsehood. Wherefore every opinion or thinking is not knowledge, but only a right opinion. And therefore knowledge is not relative (πρὸς τὸ κρίνον), as sense is. Truth is the most unbending and incompatible, the most necessary, firm, immutable, and adamantine thing in the world.

4. Moreover, because these intelligible essences of things, as before was observed, are like unities indivisible, so that if the least be added to them, or detracted from them, they are not the same, but something else. Whenever the same things are rightly understood by any minds, they must of necessity have all the same truths belonging to them every where. Nay, these truths are not all multiplied, as we observed before, by the multiplicity of minds that apprehend them, but are as one and the same individual truths in those several minds, forasmuch as wisdom, truth, and knowledge are but one and the same eternal original light shining in all created understandings.

To conclude therefore, whenever any theoretical proposition is rightly understood by any one particular mind whatsoever, and wheresoever it be, the truth of it is no private thing, nor relative to that particular mind only. But it is a catholic and universal truth (ἀληθὲς καθολικόν), as the Stoics speak, throughout the whole world. Nay, it would not fail to be a truth throughout infinite worlds, if there were so many, to all such minds, as should rightly understand it.

5. But probably it may be here demanded, how a man shall know

when his conceptions are conformed to the absolute and immutable natures or essences of things and their unchangeable relations to one another? Since the immediate objects of intellection exist in the mind itself, we must not go about to look for the criterion of truth without ourselves, by consulting individual sensibles, as the exemplars of our ideas, and measuring our conceptions by them. And how is it possible to know by measuring of sensible squares, that the diameter of every square is incommensurable with the sides? Nay, as was observed before, the necessary truth of no geometrical theorem can ever be examined, proved, or determined by sensible things mechanically. And though the eternal divine intellect be the archetypal rule of truth, we cannot consult that neither to see whether our conceptions be commensurate with it. I answer therefore, that the criterion of true knowledge is not to be looked for any where abroad without our own minds, neither in the height above, nor in the depth beneath, but only in our knowledge and conceptions themselves. For the entity of all theoretical truth is nothing else but clear intelligibility, and whatever is clearly conceived is an entity and a truth. But that which is false, divine power itself cannot make it to be clearly and distinctly understood because falsehood is a non-entity, and a clear conception is an entity. And omnipotence itself cannot make a non-entity to be an entity.

Wherefore no man ever was or can be deceived in taking that for an epistemonical truth which he clearly and distinctly apprehends, but only in assenting to things not clearly apprehended by him, which is the only true original of all error.

6. But there is another opinion that seems to have gained the countenance of some very learned philosophers, which differs but a little from the Protagorean doctrine. Though for my part I conceive it not to be an opinion, but only a certain scheme of modesty and humility, which they thought decorous to take upon themselves that they might not seem to arrogate too much either to themselves, or to their excellent performances, by not so much as pretending to demonstrate any thing to be absolutely true, but only hypothetically, or upon supposition that our faculties are rightly made.

For if we cannot otherwise possibly be certain of the truth of any thing, but only *ex hypothesi* that our faculties are rightly made, of which none can have any certain assurance but only he that made them, then all created minds whatsoever must of necessity be condemned to an eternal *scepsis*. Neither ought they ever to assent to any thing as certainly true, since all their truth and knowledge as such is but relative to their faculties arbitrarily made, that may possibly be false, and their clearest apprehensions nothing but perpetual delusions.

Wherefore according to this doctrine, we having no absolute certainty of the first principles of all our knowledge, as that *quod cogitat, est* [whatever thinks, is], *Aequalia addita aequalibus efficiunt aequalia* [Equals added to equals make equals], *Omnis numerus est vel par vel impar* [Every number is either even or odd]. We can neither be sure of any mathematical or metaphysical truth, nor of the existence of God, nor of ourselves.

For whereas some would endeavour to prove the truth of their intellectual faculties from hence, because there is a God, whose nature also is such as that he cannot deceive,[75] it is plain that this is nothing but a circle, and makes no progress at all, forasmuch as all the certainty which they have of the existence of God, and of his nature, depends wholly upon the arbitrary make of their faculties, which for aught they know may be false. Nay, according to this doctrine, no man can certainly know that there is any absolute truth in the world at all, because it is nothing but his faculties which makes him think there is, which possibly may be false. Wherefore upon this supposition, all created knowledge as such is a mere fantastical thing.

Now this is very strange to assert, that God cannot make a creature which shall be able certainly to know either the existence of God, or of himself, or whether there be any absolute truth or no.

7. It is evident that this opinion plainly supposes that intellectual faculties may be so made, as clearly and distinctly to understand that to be true which is absolutely false and impossible (for unless they did acknowledge that we do clearly understand some things, they could not undertake so much as hypothetically to demonstrate any thing). As for example, that the whole is not greater than one of its parts, or that the three angles of a triangle are never equal to two right angles.

Now, we have already demonstrated that a falsehood can never be clearly conceived or apprehended to be true, because a falsehood is a mere non-entity. And whatsoever is clearly conceived or understood is an entity. But a non-entity can never become an entity. Nay the true

---

[75] Descartes, *Meditations* I and II, CSM II, 15 and 17ff. See *TIS*, p. 716ff.

knowledge or science which exists nowhere but in the mind itself has no other entity at all besides intelligibility, and therefore, whatsoever is clearly intelligible is absolutely true. Hence it comes to pass that both philosophers and divines have without scruple measured the divine omnipotence itself, and the possibility of things by their own clear intellections concerning them, and so pronounce that God himself cannot make contradictions to be true at the same time. Whereas it were a high and unpardonable presumption thus to venture to measure the divine omnipotence, if there were not an absolute certainty of the truth of clear intellections, as being nothing else but the immutable wisdom of God participated and imparted to us. And if it be absolutely impossible even to omnipotence, that contradictories should be true together, then omnipotence itself cannot make any such faculties as shall clearly understand that which is false to be true, since the essence of falsehood consists in nothing else but non-intelligibility.

But if they will say that it is not impossible that contradictories should be true, because our faculties, which make us think so, may be false and deceive us in every thing, the necessary consequence from hence will be that it is possible that there may be no certain knowledge at all, because if contradictories may be true, then nothing can be certainly affirmed or denied of any thing.

8. Wherefore, be our faculties what they will, and let them be supposed to be made how you will, yet notwithstanding whatsoever is clearly understood and conceived, has an objective entity in it, and must of necessity be true. For a clear conception cannot be nothing. And though intellectual faculties may be made obscure more or less, yet it is not possible that they should ever be made false, so as clearly to apprehend whatsoever is true to be false, and what is false to be true.

So that if there were a world of men created either in the moon or elsewhere, that should affirm the contradictories to all the theorems in geometry, forasmuch as we certainly know that we clearly understand them to be true, and that falsehood can never be clearly understood, we ought not in the least to question from hence whether our faculties or theirs were made true, or to suspect that truth and knowledge were such whiffling things, as that they merely depended upon an arbitrary make of faculties. But [we ought] to conclude without any controversy that this was but a bedlam world of mad, frantic, and distracted souls, that had no clear apprehensions of any thing, and either by mere chance or humour happened to assent to every thing that was false as true.

9. But yet if any one will still pertinaciously urge that it is nothing but our faculties which instruct us thus, that every clear conception is an entity, and that the entity of truth is nothing but clear intelligibility, that contradictions cannot be true, or if they could, then there were no possibility of any certain knowledge, that all this is from our faculties, but that still our faculties themselves may be false – nay it is not reasonable to think that the intellectual faculties of any creatures should be absolutely infallible in any thing, because this seems to be the peculiar privilege and sole prerogative of the Deity.

I answer that this is the thing we contend for, that the ultimate resolution of theoretical truth and the only criterion (κριτήριον) of it is in the clearness of the apprehensions themselves, and not in any supposed blind and unaccountable make of faculties. So that the certainty of clear apprehensions is not to be derived from the contingent truth of faculties, but the goodness of faculties is only to be tried by the clearness and distinctness of apprehensions. For be these faculties what they will, clear intellectual conceptions must of necessity be truths, because they are real entities. And to suppose that faculties may be so made, as to beget clear apprehensions of things that are not, as if knowledge were an arbitrary fictitious thing, is much like that opinion of some, that all the new celestial phenomena, as of the jovial planets,[76] and the mountains in the moon, and the like, are no real things, but that the clear diaphanous crystal of the telescopes may be so artificially cut, ground, polished, as to make all those, and any other phenomena, clearly to appear to sense, when there is no such thing. Nay, it is more absurd and ridiculous to imagine, that that more than crystalline pellucid intellectual faculty, by which we perceive the truth of things, can be arbitrarily so made or polished as to represent any non-entities whatsoever, as clear and real objects of intellection.

10. Nay, to make the certainty of all truth and knowledge, not to be determined by the clearness of apprehensions themselves, but a supposed unaccountable truth and rectitude of faculties, and so by the uncertainty thereof quite to baffle all our clearest intellections, is quite to pervert the nature of knowledge, which is the 'comprehension of that

---

[76] 'Jovial', of Jove, i.e. Jupiter. This and mention of mountains in the moon is an allusion to Galileo's discoveries.

which absolutely is' (κατάληψις τοῦ ὄντος), which is not terminated in appearance (τὸ ὄν φαινόμενον) only, as sense is, but in that which is (τὸ ὄν) and 'whose evidence and certainty is no extrinsical and borrowed thing, but native and intrinsical to itself'.

For if knowledge have no inward κριτήριον [criterion] of its own, but the certainty of all truth and knowledge depends upon an arbitrary peculiar make of faculties, which is not a thing knowable in itself, neither can there be any assurance of it given but what is extrinsical by testimony and revelation (inartificial arguments), there will be no such thing as knowledge, but all will be mere credulity and belief.

11. It is a fond imagination for any to suppose that it is derogatory to the glory of God to bestow or import any such gift upon his creatures as knowledge is, which hath an intrinsical evidence within itself, or that creatures should have a certainty of the first principles which all men are conscious that they do so clearly understand, that they cannot doubt of them, as that *Nihil nulla est affectio* [No effect results from nothing], *Aequalia addita aequalibus efficient* (*sic*) *aequalia* [Equals added to equals make equals], without which they can know nothing at all, though they be notwithstanding ignorant, doubting, and erring in many things, and slowly proceed in their ratiocinations from one thing to another. Whereas, on the contrary, it is plainly derogatory to it to suppose that God cannot make any creature that can possibly have any certain knowledge of God's own existence, or any thing more than a bare credulity of the same.

12. Wherefore since it cannot be denied but every clear apprehension is an entity, and the essence of truth is nothing but clear intelligibility,[77] those philosophers must lay the stress of their cause here, that intellectual faculties may be so made as that men can never certainly tell when they have clear apprehensions but may think they have them when they have not.

And it cannot be denied but that men are oftentimes deceived and think they clearly comprehend what they do not. But it does not follow from hence, because men sometimes think that they clearly comprehend what they do not, that therefore they can never be certain that they do clearly comprehend any thing. Which is just as if we should argue that because in our dreams we think we have clear sensations, we cannot

---

[77] Compare *TIS*, p. 718.

therefore be ever sure, when we are awake, that we see things that really are.

I shall conclude this discourse with that of Origen against Celsus, 'Science and knowledge is the only firm thing in the world',[78] without a participation of which communicated to them from God, all creatures would be mere *ludibria* [playthings] and vanity.

Chapter VI

1. We have now abundantly confuted the Protagorean philosophy, which, that it might be sure to destroy the immutable natures of just and unjust, would destroy all science or knowledge, and make it relative and fantastical. Having shown that this tenet is not only most absurd and contradictious in itself, but also manifestly repugnant to that very atomical physiology on which Protagoras endeavoured to found it, and, than which nothing can more effectually confute and destroy it: as also [having] largely demonstrated, that though sense be indeed a mere relative and fantastical perception as Protagoras thus far rightly supposes. Yet notwithstanding there is a superior power of intellection and knowledge of a different nature from sense, which is not terminated in mere seeming and appearance only (ἐν τῷ φαινομένῳ), but in the truth and reality of things (ἐν τῷ ὄντι), and reaches to the comprehension of that which really and absolutely is, whose objects are the eternal and immutable essences and natures of things, and their unchangeable relations to one another.

2. To prevent all mistake, I shall again remember what I have before intimated, that where it is affirmed that the essences of all things are eternal and immutable (which doctrine the theological schools have constantly avouched) this is only to be understood of the intelligible essences and *rationes* of things, as they are the objects of the mind. And that there neither is nor can be any other meaning of it than this, that there is an eternal knowledge and wisdom, or an eternal mind or intellect, which comprehends within itself the steady and immutable

---

[78] Μόνον τῶν ὄντων βέβαιον ἐπίστημα (Origen, *Contra Celsus* III.72). This is the only quotation from Origen in *EIM*. Cudworth quotes him at length in *FW*, pp. 161–3. He quotes the same passage in the same connection in *TIS*, p. 721.

rationes of all things and their verities, from which all particular intellects are derived, and on which they do depend. But not that the constitutive essences of all individual created things were eternal and uncreated, as if God in creating the world did nothing else but as some sarcastically express it, '*Sartoris instar rerum essentias vestire existentia*', only clothe the eternal, increated and antecedent essences of things with a new outside garment of existence, and not create the whole of them. And as if the constitutive essences of things could exist apart separately from the things themselves, which absurd conceit Aristotle frequently and no less deservedly chastises.

3. Wherefore the result of all that we have hitherto said is this, that the intelligible natures and essences of things are neither arbitrary nor fantastical, that is, neither alterable by any will whatsoever, nor changeable by opinion. And therefore every thing is necessarily and immutably to science and knowledge what it is, whether absolutely or relatively, to all minds and intellects in the world. So that if moral good and evil, just and unjust, signify any reality, either absolute or relative, in the things so denominated, as they must have some certain natures which are the actions or souls of men, they are neither alterable by mere will nor opinion.

Upon which ground that wise philosopher Plato, in his Minos, determines that a law (νόμος) is not any arbitrary decree of a city or supreme governors (δόγμα πόλεως) because there may be unjust decrees which therefore are no laws but the invention of that which *is* (τοῦ ὄντος ἐξεύρεσις) or what is absolutely or immutably just in its own nature.[79] Though it be very true also that the arbitrary constitutions of those that have lawful authority of commanding, when they are not materially unjust, are laws also in a secondary sense, by virtue of that natural and immutable justice or law that requires political order to be observed.

4. But I have not taken all these pains only to confute scepticism or fantasticism, or merely to defend and corroborate our argument for the immutable natures of just and unjust. But also for some other weighty purposes that are very much conducing to the business that we have in hand. And first of all that the soul is not a mere naked and passive thing, a *rasa tabula*, which has no innate furniture or activity of its own, nor

---

[79] ps.-Plato, *Minos* 314E.

any thing at all in it, but what was impressed upon it [from] without. For if it were so then there could not possibly be any such thing as moral good and evil, just and unjust, forasmuch as these differences do not arise merely from the outward objects or from the impresses which they make upon us by sense, there being no such thing in them. In which sense it is truly affirmed by the author of the *Leviathan*, 'That there is no common rule of good and evil to be taken from the nature of the objects themselves',[80] that is either considered absolutely in themselves, or relatively to external sense only, but according to some other interior analogy which things have to a certain inward determination in the soul itself, from whence the foundation of all this difference must needs arise, as I shall show afterwards. Not that the anticipations of morality spring merely from intellectual forms and notional ideas of the mind, or from certain rules or propositions arbitrarily printed upon the soul as upon a book, but from some other more inward and vital principle, in intellectual beings as such, whereby they have a natural determination in them to do some things and to avoid others, which could not be, if they were mere naked passive things. Wherefore since the nature of morality cannot be understood, without some knowledge of the nature of the soul, I thought it seasonable and requisite here to take this occasion offered and to prepare the way to our following discourse[81] by showing in general that the soul is not a mere passive and receptive thing, which hath no innate active principle of its own, because upon this hypothesis there could be no such thing as morality.

5. Again, I have the rather insisted upon this argument also, because that which makes men so inclinable to think that justice, honesty, and morality are but thin, airy, and fantastical things, that have little or no entity or reality in them besides sensuality, is a certain opinion in philosophy which doth usually accompany it, that matter and body are the first original and source of all things; that there is no incorporeal substance superior to matter and independent upon it; and therefore that sensible things are the only real and substantial things in nature; but souls and minds springing secondarily out of body, that intellectuality and morality belong unto them, are but thin and evanid shadows

---

[80] Hobbes, *Leviathan*, part 1, ch. 6. in *The English Works of Thomas Hobbes*, ed. William Molesworth, III.41. It is apparent from the reference that Cudworth gives that he was using the 1651 edition of *Leviathan*.

[81] Presumably a reference to one of the treatises on freewill, but we cannot be certain which, if any, of the three extant versions was to follow.

of sensible and corporeal things, and not natural, but artificial and factitious things that do as it were border upon the confines of non-entity.

6. This is a thing excellently well observed by Plato, and therefore I shall set down his words at large concerning it:

These men making this distribution of things, that all things that are, are either by nature, or art, or chance, they imagine that the greatest and most excellent things that are in the world, are to be attributed to nature and chance; which working upon those greater things which are made by nature, does form and fabricate certain smaller things afterward, which we commonly call artificial things. To speak more plainly, fire, water, air and earth, they attribute wholly to nature and chance, but not to any art or wisdom. In like manner those bodies of the earth, the sun, moon and stars, they will have to be made out of them fortuitously agitated; and so by chance causing both divers systems and compages of things. Thus they would have the whole heavens made, and all the earth and animals, and all the seasons of the year, not by any mind, intellect or God, not by any art or wisdom, but all by blind nature and chance. But art and mind afterwards springing up out of these, to have begotten certain ludicrous things, which have little truth and reality in them, but are like images in a glass, such as picture and music produces. Wherefore these men attribute all ethics and politics, morality and laws, not to nature, but to art, whose productions are not real and substantial.[82]

7. Now this philosopher, that he may evince that ethics, politics, and

[82] Λέγουσί που τινές ὡς πάντα ἐστὶ τὰ πράγματα [...] τὰ μὲν φύσει, τὰ δὲ τέχνῃ, τὰ δὲ διὰ τύχην. [...] Ἔοικε δὲ φασί, τὰ μὲν μέγιστα αὐτῶν καὶ κάλλιστα ἀπεργάζεσθαι φύσιν καὶ τύχην, τὰ δὲ σμικρότερα τέχνην· ἣν δὲ παρὰ φύσεως λαμβάνουσαν τὴν τῶν μεγάλων καὶ πρώτων γένεσιν ἔργων πλάττειν καὶ τεκταίνεσθαι πάντα τὰ σμικρότερα, ἃ δὴ τεχνικὰ πάντες προσαγορεύομεν. [...] Ὧδ᾽ ἔτι σαφέστερον ἐρῶ. Πῦρ καὶ ὕδωρ καὶ γῆν καὶ ἀέρα φύσει πάντα εἶναι καὶ τύχῃ φασί, τέχνῃ δὲ οὐδὲν τούτων· καὶ τὰ μετὰ ταῦτα αὖ σώματα γῆς τε καὶ ἡλίου καὶ σελήνης ἄστρων τε πέρι, διὰ τούτων γεγονέναι παντελῶς ὄντων ἀψύχων. Τύχῃ δὲ φερόμενα τῇ τῆς δυνάμεως ἕκαστα ἑκάστων, ᾗ ξυμπέπτωκεν ἁρμόττοντα οἰκείως πως θερμὰ ψυχροῖς, ἢ ξηρὰ πρὸς ὑγρά, καὶ μαλακὰ πρὸς σκληρά· καὶ πάντα ὁπόσα τῇ τῶν ἐναντίων κράσει κατὰ τύχην ἐξ ἀνάγκης συνεκεράσθη. Ταύτῃ καὶ κατὰ ταῦτα οὕτω γεγεννηκέναι τόν τε οὐρανὸν ὅλον καὶ πάντα ὁπόσα κατ᾽ οὐρανόν· καὶ ζῷα αὖ καὶ φυτὰ ξύμπαντα ὡρῶν πασῶν ἐν τούτων γενομένων· οὐ διὰ νοῦν φασιν, οὐδὲ διά τινα θεὸν, οὐδὲ διὰ τέχνην, ἀλλὰ ὃ λέγομεν φύσει καὶ τύχῃ. Τέχνην δὲ ὕστερον ἐκ τούτων ὑστέραν γενομένην αὐτὴν θνητὴν ἐκ θνητῶν, ὕστερα γεγεννηκέναι παιδείας τινὰς, ἀληθείας οὐ σφόδρα μετεχούσας, ἀλλ᾽ εἴδωλα ἄττα συγγενῆ ἑαυτῶν· οἷα ἡ γραφὴ γεννᾷ, καὶ Μουσικὴ, καὶ ὅσαι ταύταις εἰσὶ συνέριθοι τέχναι· [...] οὕτω δὲ καὶ τὴν νομοθεσίαν πᾶσαν οὐ φύσει, τέχνῃ δὲ, ἧς οὐκ ἀληθεῖς· εἶναι τὰς θέσεις. εἶναι τὰς θέσεις (Plato, *Laws* 889A–B). This is not a very exact quotation: the first seven words come from a point several lines earlier in Plato's text (888E), and a portion is omitted from the centre of the text. Another example of Cudworth rendering a dialogue as if it were a monologue 'or Wisdom' interpolated.

morality are as real and substantial things, and as truly natural as those things which belong to matter, he endeavours to show that souls and minds do not spring secondarily out of matter and body, but that they are real things in nature, superior and antecedent to body and matter. His words are these:

> These men [...] are all ignorant concerning the nature of mind and soul, as in other regards, so especially in respect of its original, as it is in order of nature before matter and body, and does not result out of it, but does command it, govern it, and rule it.[83]

And I have in like manner in this antecedent discourse, endeavoured to show that wisdom, knowledge, mind, and intellect, are not thin shadows or images of corporeal and sensible things, nor do result secondarily out of matter and body, and from the activity and impressions thereof, but have an independent and self-subsistent being, which in order of nature is before body, all particular created minds being but derivative participations of one infinite eternal mind, which is antecedent to all corporeal things.

8. Now from hence it naturally follows, that those things which belong to mind and intellect, such as morality, ethics, politics and laws are, which Plato calls, 'the offspring and productions of mind, are no less to be accounted natural things, or real and substantial', than those things which belong to stupid and senseless matter.[84] For since the mind and intellect are first in order of nature before matter and body, those things which belong to the mind must needs be in order of nature before those things which belong to the body.

> Wherefore mind and intellect, art and law, ethics and morality are first in order of nature, before hard and soft, light and heavy, long and broad, which belong to body.[85]

---

[83] *Ψυχὴν, ὦ ἑταῖρε, ἠγνοηκέναι κινδυνεύουσι μὲν ὀλίγου ξύμπαντες, οἷόν τε ὄν τυγχάνει καὶ δύναμιν ἥν ἔχει, τῶν τε ἄλλων αὐτῆς πέρι, καὶ δὴ καὶ γενέσεως ὡς ἐν πρώτοις ἐστὶ σωμάτων ἔμπροσθεν πάντων γενομένη, καὶ μεταβολῆς τε αὐτῶν καὶ μετακοσμήσεως ἁπάσης ἄρχη παντὸς μᾶλλον* (ibid. p. 892A). Cudworth 'these men': Loeb, 'nearly all men'. Cudworth, 'mind and soul': Loeb, 'mind'.

[84] *νοῦ γεννήματα οὐχ ἧττον φύσει εἶναι ἤ φύσεως* (*Laws* 890D).

[85] *Ἆρα οὐκ ἐξ ἀνάγκης τὰ ψυχῆς συγγενῆ πρότερα ἄν εἴη γεγονότα τῶν σώματι προσηκόντων, οὔσης ταύτης πρεσβυτέρας ἤ σώματος, νοῦς καὶ τέχνη καὶ νόμος καὶ τρόπος καὶ ἤθη σκληρῶν καὶ μαλακῶν, βαρέων καὶ κούφων, μήκους σωμάτων καὶ πλάτους πρότερα.* This appears to be *Laws* 892D; Cudworth interpolates 'ethics', 'long and broad, which belong to body'.

And therefore more real and substantial things. For since mind and intellect are a higher, more real and substantial thing than senseless body and matter, and what hath far the more vigour, activity, and entity in it, modifications of mind and intellect, such as justice and morality, must of necessity be more real and substantial things than the modifications of mere senseless matter, such as hard and soft, thick and thin, hot and cold, and the like are. And therefore that grave philosopher excellently well concludes:

> the greatest and first works and actions are of art or of mind, which were before body; but those things which are said to be by nature (in which they abuse the word nature appropriating it only to senseless and inanimate matter) are afterwards being governed by mind and art.[86]

9. Wherefore I thought our former discourse seasonable to confute the dullness and grossness of those philosophasters that make corporeal things existing without the soul, to be the only solid and substantial things and make their grossest external senses the only judges of [the] reality of things, 'and so conclude nothing is or has any reality but what they can grasp in their hands, or have some gross or palpable sense of'.[87]

Whereas notwithstanding it is most true that those corporeal qualities, which they think to be such real things existing in bodies without them, are for the most part fantastic and imaginary things, and have no more reality than the colours of the rainbow, and, as Plotinus expresseth it, 'have no reality at all in the objects without us, but only a seeming kind of entity in our own fancies',[88] and therefore are not absolutely any thing in themselves, but only relative to animals. So that they do in a manner mock us, when we conceive of them as things really existing without us, being nothing but our own shadows, and the vital passive energies of our own souls.

Though it was not the intention of God or nature to abuse us herein, but a most wise contrivance thus to beautify and adorn the visible and material world, to add lustre or embellishment to it, that it might have

---

[86] Τὰ μεγάλα καὶ πρῶτα ἔργα καὶ πράξεις τέχνης ἂν γίγνοιτο ὄντα ἐν πρώτοις, τὰ δὲ φύσει καὶ φύσις (ἣν οὐκ ὀρθῶς ἐπονομάζουσιν) αὐτὸ τοῦτο, ὕστερα καὶ ἀρχόμενα ἂν ἐκ τέχνης εἴη καὶ νοῦ (ibid., 892B). 'or of mind' interpolated.

[87] οἱ οὐδὲν ἄλλο οἰόμενοι εἶναι ἢ οὗ ἂν δύνωνται ἀπρὶξ τοῖν χεροῖν λαβέσθαι. Not Plotinus, but Plato, *Theaet.* 155E.

[88] καὶ οὐκ ἐν ὑποκειμένοις ἀλλ᾽ ἐν τοῖς πάθεσιν ἔχει τὴν ὑπόστασιν. Plotinus, *Enneads* V.V.1.14. Not an exact quotation.

charms, relishes, and allurements in it, to gratify our appetites. Whereas otherwise really in itself, the whole corporeal world in its naked hue, is nothing else but a heap of dust or atoms, of several figures and magnitudes, variously agitated up and down. So that these things which we look upon as such real things without us, are not properly the modifications of bodies themselves, but several modifications, passions, and affections of our own souls.

10. Neither are these passive and sympathetical energies of the soul, when it acts confusedly with the body and the pleasures resulting from them, such real and substantial things as those that arise from the pure noetical energies of the soul itself intellectually and morally. For since the mind and intellect is in itself a more real and substantial thing, and fuller of entity than matter and body, those things which are the pure offspring of the mind (νοῦ γεννήματα) and sprout from the soul itself, must needs be more real and substantial than those things which blossom from the body, or from the soul enfeebled by it, and slumbering in it.

11. Wherefore that philosopher professing and understanding to confute Atheists, and to show, 'that all Atheists, though they pretend to wit never so much, are but bunglers at reason and sorry philosophers'.[89] He not without cause fetches his discourse from hence, that 'They that thus infect men's minds with impiety and atheism, make that which is the first cause of all generation and corruption to be the last thing in the universe, and that which is the last to be the first. From hence proceeds their error concerning the being of God.'[90] That is, they make mind and soul to be the last thing, and body and matter to be the first.

This therefore is the only course and method which this philosopher proceeds in to confute the atheists, to show, 'that mind and soul, in the order of the universe, are before body, and not posterior to it, mind and soul being that which rule in the universe and body that which is ruled and ordered by it'.[91] And there is no phenomenon in the world but may be solved from this hypothesis. Now this he demonstrates, even from local motion, because body and matter has no self-moving power, and therefore it is moved and determined in its motion by a higher principle, a soul or mind. Which argument is further improved by the author of that excellent philosophical treatise, Book II, chapter 2.[92]

---

[89] Apparently a free rendering of *Laws* 891D.   [90] ibid., 891E.   [91] ibid., 896c.
[92] It is not clear which the 'excellent philosophical treatise' is here. Cudworth's reference would

12. Now, for the self-same cause I have endeavoured to demonstrate in the foregoing discourse, that knowledge and intellection cannot possibly spring from sense, nor the radiation or impresses of matter and body upon that which knows, but from an active power of the mind, as a thing antecedent to matter, and independent upon it, whereby it is enabled from within to exert intelligible ideas of all things.

13. Lastly, I have insisted the rather so largely upon this argument for this further reason also, because it is not possible that there should be any such thing as morality, unless there be a God, that is, an infinite eternal mind that is the first original and source of all things, whose nature is the first rule and exemplar of morality. For otherwise it is not conceivable whence any such thing should be derived to particular intellectual beings. Now there can be no such thing as God, if stupid and senseless matter be the first original of all things, and if all being and perfection that is found in the world, may spring up and arise out of the dark womb of unthinking matter. But if knowledge and understanding, if soul, mind, and wisdom may result and emerge out of it, then doubtless everything that appears in the world may. And so night, matter, and chaos must needs be the first and only original of all things.

14. Wherefore Plato, as I have already intimated, taking notice of the opinion of divers pretenders to philosophy, 'that first water, air, and earth are the first beings of all, to which senseless and inanimate things they appropriate the title of nature. But that soul did spring up afterward out of these as a secondary thing'[93] and as a mere shadow of them, he immediately adds concerning it, 'We have here found and discovered the true fountain of all atheistical madness that possesses most of those that deal in physiology or questions of natural philosophy',[94] *viz.*, that they are all possessed with this sottishness, that matter and body is the first original of all things. And therefore it is observed by the same author, that the same persons that held all things were derived from body, blind nature, and chance, did both deny the existence of God, and, which is consentaneous thereunto, asserted that justice and morality have no nature or entity at all, saying, they were

suggest it is Henry More in his *Immortality of the Soul* (London, 1659). But see also Plato, *Laws* 896ff.

93 πῦρ καὶ ὕδωρ καὶ γῆν καὶ ἀέρα πρῶτα ἡγεῖσθαι τῶν πάντων εἶναι καὶ τὴν φύσιν ὀνομάζειν ταῦτα αὐτά, ψυχὴν δὲ ἐκ τούτων ὕστερον (ibid., 891c).

94 Οἷον πήγην τινὰ ἀνοήτου δόξης ἀνευρήκαμεν ἀνθρώπων ὁπόσοι πώποτε τῶν περὶ φύσεως ἐφήψαντο ζητημάτων (ibid.).

nothing but passion from corporeal things, without the sentient or the renitence, or the reaction made upon local motion in a body duly mixed and tempered. That is, if soul and mind, knowledge and wisdom may thus arise from the contemplation of mere senseless matter, and radiation or impression that is the mere local motion of corporeal objects without, then as we said before, there cannot possibly be the least shadow of argument left to prove a Deity by. Since not only the souls of men, but also all that wisdom, counsel, and contrivance that appears in the frame of the whole visible world, might first arise in like manner from the mere casual concourse and contemperation of the whole matter, either in those particular bodies of the sun and stars, or else in the whole system and compages of the material world itself.

15. Wherefore we have not only showed that all intellection and knowledge does not emerge or emane out of sense, but also that sense itself is not a mere passion or reception of corporeal impresses [from] without, but that it is an active energy and vigour though sympathetical in the sentient. And it is no more possible that this should arise out of senseless matter and atoms, by reason of any peculiar contemperation or contexture of them in respect of figure, site, and motion, than that which all atheists stoutly deny, that something should arise out of nothing.

And here we can never sufficiently applaud that ancient atomical philosophy, so successfully revived of late by Cartesius,[95] in that it shows distinctly what matter is, and what it can amount unto, namely nothing else but what may be produced from mere magnitude, figure, site, local motion, and rest. From whence it is demonstrably evident, and mathematically certain, that no cogitation can possibly arise out of the power of matter; whereas that other philosophy which brings in a dark unintelligible matter that is nothing and everything, out of whose potentiality not only innumerable qualities, but also substantial forms and sensitive souls (and therefore why not rational also, since all reason emerges out of sense?) may be educed, must of necessity perpetually brood and hatch atheism. Whereas we cannot but extremely admire that monstrous dotage and sottishness of Epicurus, and some other spurious

---

[95] Cudworth, like Henry More, regarded Descartes as the reviver of atomistic natural philosophy that had been known to the ancient Greeks. Cf. Add. MS 4980, fol. 221: 'Cartesius lately reviving yᵉ antient Atomicall Philosophy according to its pristine purity as it was before Democritus explodes all substantiall forms & reall Qualities from motion.'

pretenders to this atomical philosophy, that notwithstanding they acknowledge nothing else in matter besides magnitude, figure, site, and motion, yet would make not only the power of sensation, but also of intellection and ratiocination, and therefore all human souls to arise from the mere contexture of corporeal atoms, and utterly explode all incorporeal substances. Than which two assertions nothing can be more contradictious. And this is far more absurd, to make reason and intellection to arise from magnitude, figure, and motion, than to attribute those unintelligible qualities to matter which they explode.

A Treatise of Freewill

Chapter 1

We seem clearly to be led by the *instincts of nature* to think that there is something ἐφ᾽ ἡμῖν,[1] in nostra potestate, *in our own power* (though dependently upon God Almighty), and that we are not altogether passive in our actings, nor determined by inevitable necessity in whatsoever we do. Because we praise and dispraise, commend and blame men for their actings, much otherwise than we do inanimate beings or brute animals. When we blame or commend a clock or automaton, we do it so as not imputing to that automaton its being the cause of its own moving well or ill, agreeably or disagreeably to the end it was designed for, this being ascribed by us only to the artificer. But when we blame a man for any wicked actions, as for taking away another man's life, either by perjury or by wilful murder, we blame him not only as doing otherwise than ought to have been done, but also than he might have done, and that it was possible for him to have avoided it, so that he was himself the cause of the evil thereof. We do not impute the evil of all men's wicked actions to God the creator and *maker* of them, after the same manner as we do the faults of a clock or watch wholly to the watchmaker. All men's words at least free God from the blame of wicked actions, pronouncing ὁ θεὸς ἀναίτιος, God is causeless and guiltless of them, and we cast the blame of them wholly on the men themselves, as principles of action; and the true causes of the moral defects of them.[2] So also do we blame men's acting viciously and immorally in another sense than we blame a halting or a stumbling horse; or than we blame the natural and necessary infirmities, of men themselves when uncontracted by vice. For in this case we so blame the

---

[1] This is a term used in Stoicism to denote moral responsibility. Stough translates *ta eph'hemin* as 'things that are attributed to us', C. Stough, 'Stoic Determinism and Moral Responsibility', in J.M. Rist (ed.), *The Stoics* (London, 1957), pp. 203–31. R.W. Sharples, renders *to eph'hemin* as 'what depends on us', in Alexander of Aphrodisias, *On Fate*, trans. R.W. Sharples (London, 1983). The likely source for this passage is the discussion of freewill in Origen's *Peri Archon* (Latin title *De principiis*) III.i.1: 'it lies within our own power to devote ourselves to a life worthy of praise or of blame'. Origen employs the Stoic terminology, *eph hemin* (*in nostra potestate*). See J.P. Migne, *Patrologiae cursus completus. Series Graeca*, XI.

[2] Descartes uses the same analogy in, *Principia philosophiae*, I.37: 'it is a supreme perfection in man that he acts voluntarily, that is, freely; this makes him in a special way the author of his actions and deserving of praise for what he does. We do not praise automatons for accurately producing all the movements they were designed to perform, because the production of these movements occurs necessarily. It is the designer who is praised for constructing such carefully-made devices' (CSM, I, 205).

infirmities as to pity the men themselves, looking upon them as unfortunate but not as faulty. But we blame men's vices, with a displeasure against the persons themselves.

The same sense of nature's instincts appears yet more plainly, from men's blaming, accusing, and condemning themselves for their own actions, when done either rashly, inconsiderately, and imprudently, to their own private disadvantage, or else immorally and viciously, and against the dictate of honesty. In which latter case men have an inward sense of guilt (besides shame), remorse of conscience, with horror, confusion, and astonishment; and they repent of those their actions afterward with a kind of self-detestation, and sometimes not without exercising revenge upon themselves as being a piece of justice due. No man accuses or condemns himself, nor looks upon himself as guilty for having had a fever, the stone, or the gout, when uncontracted by vice. And if all human actions were necessary, men would be said no more to repent of them than of diseases, or that they were not born princes, or heirs to a thousand pounds a year.

Lastly, we have also a sense of retributive, punitive, vindictive justice, as not mere fancy, but a thing really existing in nature, when punishments are inflicted upon malefactors for their unjust and illegal actions past, by civil magistrates in particular commonwealths. For though it be true that these civil punishments do in part look forward to prevent the like for the future, by terrifying others from doing the same, or to hinder these malefactors themselves from doing the like mischief again by cutting them off by death, as we kill noxious animals, wolves, and vipers, and serpents, and mad dogs, yet it is not true that this is all the meaning of them, and that they have no retrospect to the actions past; as being satisfaction to the equitable nature of rational beings, when they see wicked men who have both abused and debased themselves, and also acted injuriously to others, to have disgrace and pain for their reward.

But men's natural instincts do more strongly suggest to them a notion of vindicative justice, in the Supreme Governor of this great mundane republic, God Almighty, in inflicting punishments upon notorious wicked persons, even here in this life, though sometimes but slowly, as Plutarch has observed.[3] But besides this which, the generality of

---

[3] ὡς τῆς ἀδικίας τον μὲν καρπὸν εὐθὺς ὡραῖν καὶ προυπτον ἀποδιδούσης, τὴν δὲ τιμωρίαν ὀψὲ καὶ πολὺ τῆς ἀπολαυσέως καθυστεροῦσαν (Plutarch, *Moralia* 548A, 'De sera numinis vindicta').

mankind have always had a strong presage of punishments to be inflicted by the Deity after death. And the Scripture assures us that there is a solemn day of judgement appointed, in which God will conspicuously, palpably, and notoriously render to every one according to his works or actions past. And that these punishments in Hell, after death, will respect only the future, and are no otherwise designed than as iatrical and medicinal, in order to the curing or recovering of the deceased souls punished, as some have imagined (from whence they infer that there can be no eternal punishments) is neither agreeable to Scripture nor sound reason. But if all actions be necessary, there seems to be no more reason why there should be a day of judgement appointed to punish men for murders and adultery, injustice and intemperance, than for agues and fevers, palsies and lethargies.

Hence it is that moralists, looking upon men's free and voluntary actions as blameworthy in a peculiar sense, have called the evil of them *malum culpae*, an evil of fault, in way of distinction from those other necessary evils which are without fault, that is of which the doer himself was not properly the cause. Concerning which Cicero thus – *Hoc tibi persuade nihil homini pertimescendum praeter culpam*;[4] i.e. that no evil is to be feared by a man, comparatively to the evil of fault, according to that Stoical doctrine that the truest and greatest goods and evils of rational beings, consist ἐν τοῖς προαιρετικοῖς or ἐν τοῖς ἐφ᾽ ἡμῖν, in their own free willed actions or things in their own power.

Wherefore, I conclude therefore, according both to the genuine instincts of nature, rightly interpreted, and the tenor of the Christian religion, we are to conclude that there is something ἐφ᾽ ἡμῖν, in our own power, and that absolute necessity does not reign over all human actions, but that there is something of contingent liberty in them. This being an article of Christ's faith, that God hath appointed a day in which he will judge the world, and render rewards and punishments to men for their actions past in this life, good and evil. Glory, honour, and power, to every man that hath done well, but tribulation and anguish to every soul or man that hath done evil. We cannot possibly maintain the justice of God in this, if all men's actions be necessary either in their own nature, or by Divine decrees and influx. That is, we cannot possibly maintain the truth of Christianity without a liberty from necessity.[5]

---

4 A rendition of Cicero, *Epistulae familiares* v, letter 21, section 5.
5 'punishments ... liberty from necessity' on verso of previous page in MS.

Chapter II

Notwithstanding which, there have not wanted some in all ages who have contended that there is no such thing as *liberum arbitrium* [freewill], nothing in our own power, no contingent liberty in human actions, but whatsoever is done by men was absolutely and unavoidably necessary.

And this upon two different grounds, first, because according to some, this contingent liberty is πρᾶγμα ἀνύπαρκτον or ἀνυπόστατον, a thing both unintelligible and impossible to exist in nature. Secondly, because though there be such a thing possible, and actually existing, yet is the exercise thereof peculiar only to God Almighty – so that he is the only self-determining Being, and the actions of all creatures were by his decrees from all eternity made necessary.[6]

The reasons alleged why there should be no such thing in nature existing anywhere, as a contingent liberty or freewill, are chiefly such as these. First, because nothing can move itself, but *quicquid movetur movetur ab alio* [whatever is moved is moved by something else], therefore whatsoever is moved is moved by something else which moveth necessarily. Secondly, because though it should be granted that there is something self-active, or moving from itself, yet nothing can change itself, or act upon itself, or determine its own action. Since the same thing cannot be both agent and patient at once. Thirdly, because οὐδὲν ἀναίτιον, nothing can come to pass without a cause; or whatsoever is done or produced had a sufficient cause antecedent; and, as Hobbes adds, 'Every sufficient cause is a necessary cause'.[7] Fourthly, because all volition is determined by the reason of good, or the appearance of the greater good; now the appearances and reasons of good are in the understanding, and therefore not arbitrary but necessary, wherefore all volitions must be necessary. Fifthly, because that which is indifferent in itself can never to eternity determine itself, but will stand indifferent for ever, without motion, volition, or action, either way. Lastly, Hobbes sophistically argues the necessity of every disjunctive proposition. From these and such like grounds have many of the ancients concluded that there is a chain of causes from eternity to eternity, every link whereof is

---

[6] 'Yet ... necessary': insertion written on opposite page, and followed by a long passage scored out.

[7] Hobbes, *Of Liberty and Necessity*, in *Works*, ed. Molesworth, vol. IV, p. 274.

necessarily connected both with that which went before, and that which
follows after, according to that in Ennius:

> Utinam ne in nemore Pelio securibus,
> Caesae cecidissent abiegna ad terram Trabes.
>
> ['Would that in Pelius' glade the pine-tree beams
> Had never fallen to earth by axes hewn!']⁸

to which Cicero adds,

> Licuit vel altius; utinam ne in Pelio nata ulla unquam esset arbor; etiam
> supra, utinam ne esset mons ullus Pelius, similiterque superiora repe-
> tentem regredi in infinitum licet,
>
> > Neve inde navis inchoandae exordium coepisset.
>
> Quorsum haec praeterita? quia sequitur illud.
>
> > Nam numquam Hera errans mea domo ecferret pedem
> > Medea animo aegro, amore saevo [Saucia].
>
> ['He might have gone even further back, "Would that no tree had ever
> grown on Pelius!" and even further, "Would that no Mount Pelius had
> existed" and similarly one may go on
>
> > Nor thence had made inception of the task
> > Of laying down a ship.
>
> What is the point of recounting these past events? because
>
> > For were it so, my roving royal mistress,
> > Medea, from her home had ne'er set forth
> > Heart sick and by love's cruel weapon wounded.']⁹

Though this, as the same Cicero observeth, is only the chain or series of
causes *sine qua non* [necessary causes]. For though there were never so
many ships ready at hand in Medea's time, yet was there therefore no
necessity that she should commit herself to sea, or be transported in any
one of them. But Mr Hobbes carries the business much further, when
he dogmatizes in this manner: 'That there is no one action, how casual
soever it seem, to the causing whereof concur not whatsoever is *in rerum*

---

8 From Ennius, *Scenica*, lines 246–7, in *Ennianae poesis reliquis*, ed. J. Vahlen (Leiden, 1903). As
quoted in Cicero, *De fato*, 15.35. Translation by H. Robinson, in Cicero, *De oratore*, vol. II
(London and Cambridge, Mass., 1939).
9 ibid. Adaptation of the opening lines of Euripides, *Medea*.

natura' [in the nature of things],[10] which he saith truly is a great paradox, and which depends upon many antecedent speculations. So that according to him every action doth not only depend upon one single chain, but is implexed and entangled with infinite chains.[11]

But the reasons assigned why though there be such a thing as contingent liberty in nature, yet the exercise thereof must needs be peculiar to the Deity, are commonly such as these: first, because to suppose any creature determine itself, is to make it independent upon its Creator, which is contradictious to the idea of God, from whence it will follow that God must be the sole determiner of all actions in the universe, and indeed properly the only actor. Secondly, because if there be contingent liberty in any creaturely agents, there could be no Divine prescience of such future events. Thirdly, nevertheless, if it should be supposed that there is a prescience notwithstanding contingency of men's wills, yet this prescience itself will consequently infer necessity of them,[12] because if there be any liberty of will as to moral things, this will be a ground of Pelagianism,[13] a denying the necessity of Divine grace being taken away by this so much cried up αὐτεξούσιον, self-power, or freewill. Lastly, it seems absurd and unjust too, that men should be damned to all eternity for a contingent turn of their own will. (This takes away the reason of it, men may as well be damned for what they were necessitated to by Divine Decrees.)

Chapter III

If there were nothing ἐφ' ἡμῖν, in our own power, no αὐτεξούσιον or *sui potestas*, no self-power, no contingent liberty of acting, but everything whatsoever acted necessarily. Then upon supposition that God Almighty should, after the conflagration of this earth, put the whole frame of this world again exactly in the very same posture that it was in at the

---

[10] Hobbes, *Of Liberty and Necessity*, in *Works*, ed. Molesworth, vol. IV, p. 267.
[11] ibid., 'time, yet was there ... infinite chains': insertion written on verso of previous page in MS.
[12] 'Thirdly ... infer necessity': insertion written on verso of previous page in MS.
[13] Pelagianism is the heresy that human beings can initiate the process of salvation by their own efforts, without the aid of Divine Grace. Called after the late-fourth-century Briton, Pelagius, whose teachings emphasized human freedom to choose good. Later the heresy included denial of Original Sin.

beginning of this mundane revolution; and make another Adam and another Eve perfectly like the former, without the least difference either of body or mind, and they propagating or multiplying in successive generations, it should continue or run out such another period of time as this world hath lasted before, seven thousand years or more; then would everything, every motion and action in it be the very same that had been in the former periodic revolution without the least difference or variation. Another such like Cain and Abel, another Enoch, and another Noah, another Abraham, Isaac, and Jacob, another Moses, another Pythagoras, another Socrates, another Jesus Christ, another Pontius Pilate, another Caiaphas,[14] another everything, and another every person, exactly the same, wearing all the same clothes, dwelling all in the same or like houses, sitting upon the same stools, making all the same motions, writing all the same books, speaking all the same words, and doing all the same actions over again.

This was the doctrine of the Stoics, that there had been and should be infinite such worlds or mundane periods, and circuits from eternity to eternity, exactly alike to one another.[15] They supposing God Almighty himself to be a necessary agent too, and, therefore, that after the several conflagrations, he must needs put things in the very same posture he had before. And then all acting necessarily, there must be all along the same or like men, doing all the same things exactly.

Celsus, who for the most part personates a Platonist, having vented this Stoical dogma, the learned Origen animadverts upon him after this manner:

> I know not why Celsus, writing against us Christians, should think it necessary to assert this Stoical dogma, that has not so much as a seeming or probable demonstration. That from the beginning to the end (or rather without beginning or end) there should be always the same periods or circuits of mortal things, and that of necessity in certain appointed revolutions, all things that have been, are, and shall be, should be the very same again repeatedly. From whence it will follow, that of necessity Socrates shall always be about to philosophize, and to be accused for holding new gods and corrupting of the youth, and Anytus

---

14 See the quotation from Origen, *Contra Celsum*, below. Origen makes the same point in *Contra Celsum* IV.67 and V.20, where he makes the link with Stoicism. The same biblical examples occur in Origen, *De principiis* II.3, 4.

15 Cudworth refers to the Stoic doctrine of cosmic cycles, at the end of each of which the universe is destroyed and then recreated.

and Melitus be always about to bear witness against him, and the senate of Areopagus about to condemn him to drink poison.[16] And after the same manner (saith this same Origen) will it be necessary that, according to appointed revolutions, Phalaris should always be about to tyrannize, and the Pheraean Alexander to act the same cruelties, and men condemned to Phalaris' bull, always be about to roar.[17] Which, if it be admitted, I know not how any liberty of will can be defended, or how there should be any place left for praise or dispraise.[18] Likewise, according to this hypothesis of Celsus (that this period of mortal things, from the beginning to the end, shall be repeated the same over again infinitely, and that always the same things of necessity will be past and present and to come without end), Moses should always, in every revolution, lead the children of Israel out of Egypt, through the Red Sea; and Jesus being born again and again, should do the same thing which he had, not once, but infinite times, done before; and all the same Christians, also, should be in appointed times infinitely; and Celsus should write this very same book against Christians, which he had written ten thousand times before. Now Celsus asserteth such periodical revolutions of mortal things only, wherein of necessity the same that have been, are, and shall be, in this world, should have been heretofore, and shall be again, infinitely. But the Stoics generally maintain such periodical revolutions of immortal things too, or, at least, of those which they account gods, for after the universal conflagration which hath been infinitely, and shall be again infinitely, all things without exception, according to them, run round in the same order, from the beginning to the end; all the same gods, as well as the same men, doing the same things. Nevertheless, to lessen the absurdity hereof, these Stoics, indeed, pretend that they shall not be all numerically the same, but ἀταράκτους, exactly alike in everything. So that not the same numerical Socrates shall be again but one in all things exactly alike to Socrates, who shall marry one in all things exactly alike to Xanthippe,[19] and shall be accused by two persons, in all things alike to Anytus and Melitus. But I understand not this (saith Origen), how since the world is always numerically the same, and not another exactly alike to another; the things in it should not be numerically the same too, and not exactly alike only.[20]

---

[16] Plato, *Phaedo* 117.   [17] Lucian, *Phalaris*.

[18] 'Which, if it be ... dispraise' on verso of previous page in MS.

[19] Wife of Socrates. See *Phaedo* 60A. Chadwick points out that all these examples were commonplace. Origen, *Contra Celsum*, trans. H. Chadwick (Cambridge, 1953), pp. 237–8.

[20] Origen, *Contra Celsum* IV.67–8. Cudworth refers to Spencer's edition (Cambridge, 1677), Book 4, pp. 208–9. Cudworth owned the 1658 edition of this. See Musca, in Further Reading. For a modern translation of Origen, see Chadwick, pp. 237–8.

But the case will be the same, should we suppose two numerically distinct worlds, made by God Almighty, at the same or contemporary time, exactly alike to one another, two Adams and two Eves indistinguishably the same, both in soul and body, multiplying themselves by propagation for several thousands of years. If there was no such thing as contingent liberty in nature, they must needs all along, at the same time, make the same motions, speak the same words, write the same books, all as exactly alike to one another as the motions of the image in the glass are to the body without it.

Now if we cannot think this to be possible, but that, two such worlds being made in all things perfectly alike, and the first parents, men and women, in them perfectly alike too; yet, in process of time, there would grow a great dissimilitude and diversity between them. But though this diversity were never so little, yet must it needs[21] be granted that there is a contingent liberty, and that men have something in their own power, add something of their own, so that they can change themselves and determine themselves, and all things are not linked and tied in a fatal adamantine chain of causes.

Chapter IV

Now that this is not true, *quod cuncta necesse intestinum habeant* ['that all things have internal necessity'],[22] or that nothing *in rerum natura*[23] can possibly act otherwise than it suffers or is acted upon; but that, on the contrary, there is some contingent liberty in nature, and that men, and other rational creatures, can add or cast in something of their own to turn the scales which even may, I think, sufficiently appear from hence. Because it cannot be denied but that there are, and may be, many cases in which several objects propounded to our choice at the same time, are so equal, or exactly alike, as that there cannot possibly be any reason or motive in the understanding necessarily to determine the choice to one of them rather than to another of them. As for example, suppose one

---

[21] 'But though ... must it needs' on verso of previous page in MS.

[22] This appears to be a variant on Lucretius, *De rerum natura*, II.289–90, 'sed ne mens ipsa necessum intestinum habeat cunctis in rebus agendis' ('what keeps the mind itself from having necessity within it in all actions').

[23] An allusion to Hobbes, *Of Liberty and Necessity*, in *Works*, ed. Molesworth, vol. IV, p. 267.

man should offer to another, out of twenty guinea pieces of gold, or golden balls, or silver globulites, so exactly alike in bigness, figure, colour, and weight, as that he could discern no manner of difference between them, to make his choice of one and no more. Add also that these guineas or golden balls may be so placed circularly as to be equidistant from the chooser's hand. Now it cannot be doubted but that, in this case, any man would certainly choose one, and not stand in suspense or demur because he could not tell which to prefer or choose before another. But if being necessitated by no motive or reason antecedent to choose this rather than that, he must determine himself contingently, or fortuitously, or causelessly, it being all one to him which he took, nor could there be any knowledge *ex causis* [from causes][24] beforehand which of these twenty would certainly be taken. But if you will say there was some hidden, necessarily determinating in this case, then if the trial should be made a hundred times over and over again, or by a hundred several persons, there is no reason why we must not allow that all of them must needs take the same guinea every time, that is either the first, or second, or third, &c., of them, as they lie in order from the right or left hand.

From hence, alone, it appears that rational beings, or human souls, can extend themselves further than necessary natures, or can act further than they suffer, that they can actively change themselves and determine themselves contingently or fortuitously, when they are not necessarily determined by causes antecedent. Here is, therefore, a great difference between corporeal and incorporeal things. Bodies that cannot move themselves, can never act further than they suffer, and therefore if causes of motions or impulsions made upon them be of equal force or strength, they cannot move at all, neither one way nor t'other. If two equal scales in a balance have equal weights put into them, they will rest to eternity, and neither of them be able to move up or down. But rational beings and human souls standing in equipoise as to motive reasons, and having the scales equiponderant, from the weight of the objects themselves without them, will not perpetually of necessity always thus hang in suspense, but may themselves add or cast in some grains into one scale rather than the other, to make that preponderant, so that the determination here will be contingent or loose, and not

[24] 'But if . . . *ex causis*' on verso of previous page in MS.

necessarily linked with what went before. Here, therefore, is a sufficient cause which is not necessary. Here is something changing itself, or acting upon itself, a thing which, though indifferent as to reason, yet can determine itself and take away that passive indiff[erence].

But it cannot be denied by any theist, but that this liberty, at least, must be acknowledged to belong to God Almighty. There being many things in the frame and constitution of the world for which no reason could possibly be given, why they should be of necessity so as they are and not otherwise, and, therefore, must be determined by his arbitrary will and pleasure. As for example, the world being supposed not to be infinite, there could not be any necessity in the thing itself, why it should be just so big as it is, and not an inch nor an hairbreadth bigger or lesser. There could be no necessity why the number of stars should be even or odd, whereas one of them it must needs be, and is so as it seemeth good to him to appoint. So likewise Christianity assures us that God hath appointed a day in which he will judge the world. Of which it is said, Mark 13.32, 'But of that day and hour, knoweth no man, no not the angels which are in heaven, neither the Son, but the Father.' In which words, it is implied that this is a thing determined by the arbitrary goodwill and pleasure of God the Father. There being no necessity in the nature of the thing itself, why it should be cast at such a precise time, and not an hour nor a moment sooner or later. Nay, it is commonly conceived that this whole created world, with all things in it, having no necessary existence, but precarious both, might not have been, and again is destroyable, was made by the arbitrary will and pleasure of God, according to that, Rev. 4.11, 'Thou Lord hast created all things, and for thy pleasure they are and were created.' The creation being not a natural and necessary emanation, as the word and the Son is from the Father, but a free and self-determined emanation, it being as it were but the Λογὸς προφορικός of God Al[mighty]. 'He spake the word, and they were made.'[25]

But this arbitrary and contingent liberty of the Deity is carried on much too far by those who extend it to the necessitating of all creaturely actions and volitions, by a Divine predetermination of everything, with a consequent irresistible influence; and to the reprobating of far the greater part of mankind, by absolute decrees from eternity, and without

---

[25] Psalm 33.9, 'He spake, and it was done.' Psalm 148.5, 'He commanded and they were created.' Compare *TIS*, pp. 574 and 599. See Athanasius in Migne, *Pg* vol. xxv, p. 501c.

any respect to their own actions, also, the future execution thereof, by damning of them for what they were necessitated unavoidably to do by G[od] Al[mighty] himself.

'Tis, indeed, an absurd saying of some that *Deus tenetur ad optimum*, God is bound to do the best. For God hath no law but the perfection of his own nature. Nevertheless, it may be well concluded, that God can act nothing contrary to the same law of his own perfections, that is, can do nothing either foolishly or unjustly. And it may be piously believed, that when he did create the world, he made the whole after the best manner that (all things considered) it could have been made in, and, consequently, that as he cannot be liable to any blame for making the whole worse than it might have been, so neither is he to be [given] such praise and commendation, as men are, for doing better when he might have done worse.

Chapter v

But this contingent liberty of self-determination, which we have hitherto spoken of (called by some of the Greek philosophers epeleustick liberty), when there is a perfect equality in objects and a mere fortuitous self-determination, is not that αὐτεξούσιον, that *liberum arbitrium*, which is the foundation of praise or dispraise, commendation or blame. For when two objects, perfectly equal and exactly alike, are propounded to a man's choice, as two eggs, or two guineas, or two golden balls, of equal bigness, and weight, and value, he cannot be justly blamed by any other or himself, for choosing one of them rather than another. And the case must needs be the same in all other objects of choice, that have a perfect equality of good in them, or are means equally tending and conducing to the same end. There can be no just blame or dispraise, but only where the objects, being in themselves really unequal, the one better, the other worse, a man refuseth the better and chooseth the worse. As in the difference between the dictate of honesty or conscience, and the suggestion of the lower appetites, inclining either to sensual pleasure or private utility. He that resisting these lower and worser inclinations, firmly adhereth to the better principle or dictate of honesty and virtue, hath in all ages and places in the world been accounted ἐπαινετός, praiseworthy, as being κρείττων ἑαυτῷ, superior to himself, or a self-conqueror. But he that yieldeth up himself as vanquished or succumbeth under the lower affections, called the law of the members, in opposition to that superior dictate of honesty, or law of the mind, is accounted blameworthy as being ἥσσων ἑαυτῷ, inferior to himself, or conquered by his worser part. Now that there is such an αὐτεξούσιον as this too, such a liberty or will (where there is an inequality in the objects) of determining oneself better or worse, and so of deserving commendation or blame (though it be not rightly taken by some for an absolute perfection as will be showed elsewhere) is undeniably evident, both from the common notions of mankind,[26] and from the sense of conscience in all men, accusing or excusing them.

Nevertheless, it must be granted that there is no small difficulty in the explaining of this phenomenon rightly; so as clearly to make out and vindicate the same from all exceptions made against it, especially since the vulgar psychology, or the now generally received way of philosophizing concerning the soul, doth either quite baffle and betray this liberty of will, or else render it absurd, ridiculous, or monstrous.

For the vulgarly received psychology runs thus. That in the rational soul there are two faculties, understanding and will,[27] which understanding hath nothing of will in it, and will nothing of understanding in it. And to these two faculties are attributed the actions of intellection and volition; the understanding (say they) understandeth, and the will willeth.

But then follows a *bivium* [parting of the ways], wherein these philosophers are divided: for, first, many of them suppose this understanding to be the beginner and first mover of all actions. For this reason, because *ignoti nulla cupido* ['there is no desire of the

---

[26] The concept derives from the Stoic *koinai ennoiai*, common notions, or principles of knowledge innate to the mind.

[27] Cudworth here summarizes scholastic debates about freewill. He refers to the traditions deriving from St Thomas and from Duns Scotus respectively. The former put forward an intellectualist position, according to which will follows the dictates of intellect. Scotist voluntarists stressed the self-determining power of will. For a good general introduction to these issues, see N. Fiering, *Moral Philosophy at Seventeenth-Century Harvard* (Chapel Hill, N.C., 1981). See also, V.J. Bourke, *Will in Western Thought: an Historico-Critical Survey* (New York, 1964), N. Kretzman *et al.* (eds.), *The Cambridge History of Later Medieval Philosophy* (Cambridge, 1982), ch. 32. There is more extensive discussion of the same topic in the other Cudworth manuscripts on freewill.

unknown'],[28] there can be no desire nor no will of that which is unknown. And, secondly, they conclude that the understanding acteth necessarily upon its several objects, without anything of will to determine either its exercise or specification of them (which necessity some call a train of thoughts)[29] because the will being blind, therefore cannot determine the understanding, either to exercise or specification of object. Thirdly, that the understanding judgeth necessarily of all things, not only as to the truth or falsehood of speculative things, but also as to eligibility of practicals, what is to be done or not done. Lastly, that the blind faculty of will always necessarily follows the last practical judgement of the necessary understanding.

But others there are, who, in order to the salving of this phenomenon of liberty of will, think it necessary to suppose, that first of all, the will, though blind, yet determines the understanding, both to exercise, and specification of object. And though the understanding, being necessary in its judgements, doth only propound to the blind will what he thinks ought to be done, or his last practical judgement in the case, and no more, only to allure and invite the will thereunto. But that this sovereign queen, or empress of the soul, the blind will, still remaineth as free, and indifferent to do or not this or that, as if the understanding had given no judgement at all in the case, and doth at last fortuitously determine itself without respect to the same either way. Which is the meaning of that definition of liberty of will commonly given, that *Voluntas, positis omnibus ad agendum requisitis, potest agere, vel non agere*, that the will after all things put, the last dictate or judgement of the understanding, itself therein included, is yet free and absolutely indifferent, both as to exercise and to specification, and doth determine itself to do or not, to this or that, fortuitously. There being no other way, as these men conceive, to salve the liberty of the will but this only.

Chapter VI

But, I say, if this psychology be true, then either can there be no liberty at all, no freedom from necessity, or else no other than such as is absurd

---

[28] Ovid, *Ars amatoria* VII.397. A key *locus* in discussions of will.
[29] An allusion to Hobbes, *Leviathan*, ch. 3.

and ridiculous or monstrous. For, first, if the blind will do alway[s] necessarily follow a necessary dictate of the understanding antecedent, then must all volitions and actions needs be necessary – that pretence which some here make to salve liberty of will, notwithstanding, from the amplitude of the understanding, as having a larger scope and prospect before it; these fancies and *hormae* [impulses, desires], each whereof is determined to one, signifying nothing at all, so long as the understanding in its approbations and judgements, concerning the difference of those objects, acts altogether necessarily. But whereas some others of those philosophers, who contend that the will must, therefore, of necessity follow the last dictate or practical judgement of the necessary understanding, because it is in itself a blind faculty, do nevertheless, in order to maintain liberty, assert that this blind faculty of will doth first of all move and determine the understanding, both as to its exercise and objects, this is a manifest contradiction in itself. Besides, they are here forced to run round in an endless circle: they maintaining that the will can will nothing, but as represented to it first by the understanding (since otherwise it must will it knows not what), and again that the understanding cannot act about this or that but as it is moved and determined thereunto by the will, so that there must be both an action of the understanding going before every act of the will, and also an act of the will going before every act of the understanding, which is further contradictious and impossible.

But if the blind will do not necessarily follow[30] the last dictate of practical judgement of the necessary understanding, but still remains indifferent and doth fortuitously determine itself either in compliance with the same or otherwise, then will liberty of will be mere irrationality, and madness itself acting or determining all human actions. Nor is this all, but that which willeth in every man will perpetually will not only it knows not why, but also it knows not what. Then is all consideration and deliberation of the mind, all counsel and advice from others, all exhortation and persuasion, nay the faculty of reason and understanding itself, in a man, altogether useless, and to no purpose at all. Then can there be no habits either of virtue or vice, that fluttering uncertainty and fortuitous indifference, which is supposed to be essential to this blind

---

[30] 'not only at first fortuitously determ[ine] the understanding both to exercise and object, but also after all is done remains indifferent to follow the last dictate of it or not', on verso of previous page in MS.

will, being utterly uncapable of either. Nor, after all, could this hypothesis salve the phenomena of commendation and blame, reward and punishment, praise and dispraise. For no praise, commendation, or blame, could belong to men for their freewilled actions neither, since when they did well they acted but fortuitously and temerariously and by chance, and when they did ill their wills did but *uti jure suo*, use their own natural right and essential privilege, or property of acting ὁπότερον ἐτυγχάνει as it happeneth, or any way, without reason. Lastly, as for this scholastic definition of freewill, *viz.* that it is, after all things put, besides the volition itself, even the last practical judgement in the soul too, an indifferency of not doing or of doing this or that. This is an upstart thing, which the ancient peripatetics, as Alexander[31] and others, were unacquainted with, their account thereof being this, that αὐτοῖς περιεστῶσι the same things being circumstant, the same impressions being made upon men from without, all that they are passive to being the same, yet they may, notwithstanding, act differently. The last practical judgement also, as according to these, being that which as men are not merely passive to, so is it really the same thing with the βούλησις, the will, or volition.

Chapter VII

But this scholastic philosophy is manifestly absurd, and mere scholastic jargon. For to attribute the act of intellection and perception to the faculty of understanding, and acts of volition to the faculty of will, or to say that it is the understanding that understandeth, and the will that willeth – this is all one as if one should say that the faculty of walking walketh, and the faculty of speaking speaketh, or that the musical faculty playeth a lesson upon the lute, or sings this or that tune.

Moreover, since it is generally agreed upon by all philosophers, that *actiones sunt suppositorum*, whatsoever acts is a subsistent thing, therefore by this kind of language are these two faculties of understanding and will made to be two *supposita*, two subsistent things, two agents, and two

---

[31] Alexander of Aphrodisias, Aristotelian philosopher, author of *De fato* which was very influential with Pietro Pomponazzi. See below, n. 87. Cudworth speaks respectfully of Alexander in *TIS*, where he calls him 'that safe and sure-footed interpreter' (p. 171).

persons, in the soul. Agreeable to which are these forms of speech commonly used by scholastics, that the understanding propounds to the will, represents to the will, allures and invites the will, and the will either follows the understanding, or else refuses to comply with its dictates, exercising its own liberty. Whence is that inextricable confusion and unintelligible nonsense, of the will's both first moving the understanding, and also the understanding first moving the will, and this in an infinite and endless circuit. So that this faculty of will must needs be supposed to move understandingly, or knowingly of what it doth, and the faculty of understanding to move willingly, or not without will. Whereas to intellect as such, or as a faculty, belongs nothing but mere intellection or perception, without anything of will; and to will as such, or [as] a faculty, nothing but mere volition, without anything of intellection.

But all this while it is really the man or soul that understands, and the man or soul that wills, as it is the man that walks and the man that speaks or talks, and the musician that plays a lesson on the lute. So that it is one and the same subsistent thing, one and the same soul that both understandeth and willeth, and the same agent only that acteth diversely. And thus may it well be conceived that one and the same reasonable soul in us may both will understandingly, or knowingly of what it wills; and understand or think of this or that object willingly.

It is not denied but that the rational soul is πολυδύναμος, hath many powers or faculties in it, that is, that it can and doth display itself in several kinds of energies, as the same air or breath in a Pneumatic Instrum[ent],[32] passing through several pipes, makes several notes. But there is a certain order or method that may be conceived wherein the soul puts itself forth in these its several operations and affections, of which I shall proceed to treat in the next place.

Chapter VIII

It is a very material question which Aristotle starteth, τί τὸ πρώτως κινοῦν – what is that that first moveth in the soul and setteth all the

---

[32] 'organ' deleted.

other wheels on work? That is, what is that vital power, and energy, which the soul first displayeth itself in, and which in order of nature precedes all its other powers, it implying them, or setting them on work?[33] First, therefore, I say the outward observations of corporeal sense are not the only beginning and first movers or causes of all cogitations in us, as the Epicureans, Hobbians, and Atheists suppose who, indeed, make all cogitation to be nothing but local motions in the brain; these being intercurrent they only occasionally raising a variety of cogitations. But there is a thread of life always spinning out, and a living spring or fountain of cogitation in the soul itself. Now[34] divers of the scholastics, as we said before, tell us that it is no other than an indifferent or blind will which first moveth the understanding, and causeth deliberation, and yet after this, itself blindly chooseth and determineth all human actions. Whereas, if the first mover be perfectly blind, then must it move to it knows not what, and it knows not why. And be perfectly indifferent to move any one thing rather than another. Moreover it is not conceivable that mere indetermination and indifferency should be the first mover of all actions. Besides which, necessary nature must be the beginner and spring of all action.[35] Whereas, if there were any such faculty of the soul as a blind will (which is impossible) knowledge must of necessity go before it, to represent things to it, and to hold a torch to light it and show it its way, and this must come after it, it must follow it as its guide. Wherefore knowledge and understanding, counsel and reason, and deliberation, seem to bid the fairest for the first mover in the soul, and that which leads the vanguard. Nevertheless it is certain that neither this speculative nor deliberative understanding doth alway[s] act in us necessarily of itself and uninterruptedly, but we are sensible that our minds are employed and set awork by something else, that we apply them both in contemplation and deliberation to this or that object, and continue or call them off at pleasure, as much as we open and shut our eyes, and by moving our eyes determine our sight to this or that object of sight. Were our souls in a constant gaze or study, always spinning out a necessary thread or series of uninterrupted concatenate thoughts; then could we never have any presence of mind, no attention to passing occas[ional] occur[rences],

---

[33] Aristotle, *De anima* 415b9–29. See also III.ix.

[34] 'First ... Now': insertion written on opposite page.

[35] 'Whereas, if the first mover ... spring of all action' on verso of previous page in MS.

always thinking of something else, or having our wits running out a
wool-gathering, and so be totally inapt for action. Or, could we do
nothing at all, but after studied deliberation, then should we be often in
a puzzle, at a stand, demur, and fumble a long time before we could act
or will any thing. Aristotle himself determines that βουλή, counsel,
cannot be the first moving principle in the soul, because then we must
consider, to consider, to consider infinitely. Again, the principle of all
actions, and therefore intellection itself is ends and good. Every thing
acting for the sake of some end and good. And concerning ends, the
same Aristotle hath rightly observed, that they are οὐκ αὐθαίρετα φῦναι
δεῖ, that they are not chosen, studied out, or devised by us, but exist in
nature, and preventively obtrude themselves upon us.

Wherefore, we conclude that the τὸ πρώτως κινοῦν, that which
first moveth in us, and is the spring and principle of all deliberative
action, can be no other than a constant, restless, uninterrupted desire,
or love of good as such, and happiness. This is an ever bubbling
fountain in the centre of the soul, an elater or spring of motion, both a
primum and *perpetuum mobile* [first and perpetual mover] in us, the first
wheel that sets all the other wheels in motion, and an everlasting and
incessant mover.[36] God, an absolutely perfect being, is not this love of
indigent desire, but a love of overflowing fulness and redundancy,
communicating itself. But imperfect beings, as human souls, especially
lapsed, by reason of the *penia* [need] which is in them, are in continual
inquest, restless desire, and search, always pursuing a scent of good
before them and hunting after it.[37] There are several things which
have a face and mien, or alluring show, and promising aspect of good
to us. As pleasure, joy, and ease, in opposition to pain, and sorrow,
and disquiet, and labour, and turmoil. Abundance, plenty, and
sufficiency of all things, in opposition to poverty, straitness, scantiness,
and penury. Power, not only as it can remove want, and command
plenty, and supply pleasures, but also in the sense of the thing itself.
Honour, worship, and veneration, in opposition to evils of disgrace,
contempt, and scorn. Praise, commendation, and applause, in opposition to censure of others, ignominy, and infamy. Clarity, and celebrity,

[36] At the foot of the page in the MS the following is deleted: 'God almighty a Perfect Being is an
overflowing Fountain ever Displaying Himselfe wisely and Powerfully, but in Humane Souls in
this lapsed state by Reason of their [naturall] Poverty and defectiveness in the'.
[37] An allusion to the tale of *Poros* and *Penia*, Resource and Need, the parents of Love, told by
Socrates in Plato's *Symposium* 203b, and discussed in Plotinus, *Enneads* III.5.

in opposition to private obscurity, and living in corners. Prae-excellency over others, superiority, victory, and success – in opposition to being worsted or foiled, left behind, outdone, and disappointed. Security, in opposition to anxiety, and fear of losing whatsoever,[38] pulchritude, in opposition to ugliness, and deformity. Knowledge, and truth, in opposition to the evils of ignorance, folly, and error, since no man would willingly be foolish, no man would err or be mistaken. Liberty, in opposition to restraint, bondage, servility, to be subject to commands and prohibitions.[39]

But above all these, and such like things, the soul of man hath in it μάντευμά τι, a certain vaticination, presage, scent, and odour of one *summum bonum*, one supreme highest good transcending all others, without which, they will be all ineffectual as to complete happiness, and signify nothing, a certain philosopher's stone that can turn all into gold.

Now this love and desire of good, as good in general, and of happiness, traversing the soul continually, and actuating and provoking it continually, is not a mere passion or *horme*; but a settled resolved principle, and the very source, and fountain, and centre of life. It is necessary and nature in us which is immutable, and always continues the same, in equal quantity. As Cartesius supposed the same quantity of motion to be perpetually conserved in the universe,[40] but not alike in all the same bodies, but being transferred, and passing from one to other, and so, more or less, here and there. So is there the same stock of love and desire of good always alive, working in the soul by necessity of nature, and agitating it, though by men's will and choice, it may be diversely dispensed out, and placed upon different objects, more and less.

But there are many other powers and energies of the soul, that are necessary and natural in us too, besides that lowest of the plastic life,[41] subject to no command of [the] will. Its vital sympathy with the body displaying itself in the perceptions of the outward sense and of bodily pleasure and [pain], the sentiments whereof the soul, as willing, hath no *imperium* [command] over, though it have a despotic and undisputed power locomotive in other [...] and members of the body. Then fancy or imagination, sudden passions and *hormae*, and commo-

---

38 'or loosing the prize' insertion written on verso of previous page in MS.
39 'Liberty ... prohibitions', insertion written on verso of previous page in MS.
40 Descartes, *Principles*, II.37–42 and III.46. Also, *The World*, ch. 7.
41 A reference to Cudworth's doctrine of Plastic Nature. For a full account of this see his 'A Digression Concerning the Plastick Life of Nature', *TIS*; pp. 146–72.

tions called concupiscible and irascible, whose first assaults prevent our will, intended by nature as spurs to action, and the quickeners of life, which else without them would grow dull and languid, and sometimes, as it were, fall asleep; these are natural too, come upon us unawares, invade us, and surprise us with their sudden force, and we have no absolute, despotic, easy, undisputed power over them, notwithstanding which the hegemonic of the soul may by conatives and endeavours acquire more and more power over them. Above all these is the dictate of honesty, commonly called the dictate of conscience – which often majestically controls them [and] clashes with the former. This is necessary nature too, when here the hegemonic, sometimes joins its assistance to the better one, and sometimes takes part with the worser against it. Lastly, the understanding, both speculative understanding, or the soul, as considering the truth and falsehood of things, and the practical, considering their good and evil, or what is to be done and not done, both of them inferring consequences from premises in way of discursive reason. The perceptions of which, are all natural and necessary, subject to no command of will, though both the exercise, and their specification of objects, be determinable by ourselves.

Chapter IX

The next grand enquiry is, what is τὸ ἡγεμονικόν, the ruling, governing, commanding, determining principle in us. For here, or nowhere else, is to be found the τὸ ἐφ' ἡμῖν and the τὸ αὐτεξούσιον, *sui potestas*, self-power, or such a liberty of will as whereby men deserve praise or dispraise, commendation or blame. This hegemonic of the soul is a thing that was much taken notice of by the Greek philosophers, after Aristotle, and to this is ascribed by them the original of those moral evils that deserve blame and punishment. Thus the learned Origen, *Nam sua cuique ratio causa est existentis in ipso malitiae, quae ex ea proveniunt: nec aliud quicquam est malum juxta nostrum examen exquisitissimum* [Each person's mind is responsible for the evil which exists in him, and this is what evil is. Evils are actions which result from it. In our view nothing else is strictly speaking evil.],[42] where the τὸ ἑκάστου ἡγεμονικόν is rendered by Gelenius[43] *sua cuique ratio*, every man's own reason, as if this were the thing whereby he is the cause of moral evil. He taking it for granted that Origen's hegemonic, in every man, is reason; which is a thing commonly supposed to be natural and necessary in its perception, whereas necessary nature can be no foundation for blame and punishment. And if moral evil were to be imputed wholly to necessary nature, then must that, and the blame of it, needs be imputed to God himself, as the cause thereof. Whereas Origen's design here, and elsewhere, is to free both God and nature from the blame of moral evils, and cast it upon men themselves, as being something, besides necessary nature, loose and at their own disposal, and therefore ἀρχαὶ πράξεων, principles of action, and thus, according to Origen, every man's own hegemonic, or that which rules or commands in his soul, is the only cause of moral evil, vice, or wickedness, which is truly evil, as also are the actions that proceed from it. And in strictness or exactness of philosophy (saith he) there is nothing else evil to a man; that is nothing besides the evil of sin and fault. But I know saith he that this is a matter of great subtlety and nicety, and therefore it would be an operose thing to explain it, &c. and require longer ambages of discourse than would be proper for this place. Now the herd of modern philosophers and theologers, who zealously maintain the phenomenon of *liberum arbitrium*, or freewill, think there is no other way to do it but only to make an indifferent and blind will fortuitously determining itself, to be both the first mover, and the hegemonic or ruling principle in the soul too. Nevertheless they themselves acknowledge that there is so much of necessary nature even in this blind and fortuitous will, that it is notwithstanding always determined to good, or some appearance of it, and can never possibly choose evil when represented to it by the understanding as wholly such. But within that latitude and compass of apparent good in the understanding, the will to them is free to determine itself to either greater or lesser, and so to any of the lowest degrees and appearances thereof. Nay, though a thing have never so much more of good than evil appearing in it, yet

---

[42] τὸ γὰρ ἑκάστου ἡγεμονικὸν αἴτιον τῆς ὑποστάσεως ἐν αὐτῷ κακίας ἐστὶν ἥτις ἐστι τὸ κακόν· καὶ ἄλλο οὐδὲν, ὡς πρὸς ἀκριβῆ λόγον καθ᾽ ἡμᾶς ἐστι κακόν. ἀλλ᾽ οἶδα τὸν λόγον δεόμενον πολλῆς ἐξεργασίας καὶ κατασκευῆς (Origen, *Contra Celsum* IV.65, trans. Chadwick, p. 237).

[43] Sigismundus Gelenius, whose commentary on Origen William Spencer translated in his edition of *Contra Celsum* (Cambridge 1658).

the least glimpse of good glimmering in it, is enough for the blind will to exercise its lordly and unaccountable liberty in preferring it, before such another good as hath not any the least shadow of evil apprehended in it. And when any great end is proposed, and upon deliberation concerning means, it clearly appears to the understanding that there is one means, which, if chosen, cannot fail but reach and attain to that end; but another, which is only not impossible to do it, but hath ten thousand to one odds against it. In this case (they say) it is the perfection of the blind indifferent will to be able to determine itself fortuitously that way as well as the other.

But as it is very absurd to make active indifference blindly and fortuitously determining itself, that is active irrationality and nonsense, to be the hegemonic and ruling principle in every man; and as it is indeed impossible, there should be any such thing in nature as a blind faculty of will, which does nothing else but will, acting temerariously or fortuitously, where there are different degrees of good and evil in the objects such as shall be perfectly indifferent, to never so much greater or lesser good; a will that is nothing else but will, mere impetus force and activity without any thing of light or understanding – a will which acts both it knows not why or wherefore, and even it knows not what – so could not such a blind, indifferent, and fortuitous will ruling salve the phenomenon of moral good and evil of commendation or blame, because this being supposed to be the perfection of this will's own nature, and a man's essential liberty and privilege to act thus, there can be no fault nor blame in him for his exercising the same, and acting according to his nature – no nature being sin.

Wherefore it cannot be supposed that the hegemonic, or ruling principle in a man is utterly devoid of all light, and perception, or understanding. Notwithstanding which, in peccable beings reason, understanding, and knowledge, as such, or as necessary nature cannot be the only hegemonic or ruling principle. Because reason, as such, can never act unreasonably, understanding, as such, and clear perceptions, can never err. There is no such thing as false knowledge, nor erroneous understanding, nor can sin ever be the result of reason, understanding, clear perceptions, and knowledge, any more than error.[44] Nor is error any more from God and the necessary nature of understanding, than sin

44 Here Cudworth is arguing against the Calvinist stress on the depravity of human reason. He takes a specifically Cartesian line on clarity and distinctness of ideas. His argument here echoes

is. But the hegemonic of created souls may err, and judge falsely, and sin. Moreover we know, by certain experience, that speculation or deliberation about particular things is determined by ourselves both as to objects and exercise; we can call it off from one thing, and employ it or set it a work upon another, and we can surcease, suspend, and stop the exercise of it (when we please) too, diverting ourselves into action. From whence it is plain that there is something in us superior thereunto, something more universal and comprehensive, and yet withal more simple, which is hegemonic to it, and doth manage and determine the same.

Chapter x

I say, therefore, that the τὸ ἡγεμονικόν [hegemonicon] in every man, and indeed that which is properly we ourselves (we rather having those other things of necessary nature than being them), is the soul as comprehending itself, all its concerns and interests, its abilities and capacities, and holding itself, as it were in its own hand, as it were redoubled upon itself, having a power of intending or exerting itself more or less in consideration and deliberation, in resisting the lower appetites that oppose it, both of utility, reason, and honesty; in self-recollection and attention, and vigilant circumspection, or standing upon our guard; in purposes and resolutions, in diligence in carrying on steady designs and active endeavours – this in order, to self-improvement and the self-promoting of its own good, the fixing and conserving itself in the same. Though by accident and by abuse, it often proves a self-impairing power, the original of sin, vice, and wickedness, whereby men become to themselves the causes of their own evil, blame, punishment, and misery. Wherefore this hegemonicon [*sic*] always determines the passive capability of men's nature one way or other, either for better or for worse. And [it] has a self-forming and self-framing power, by which every man is self-made, into what he is. And accordingly deserves either praise or dispraise, reward or punishment.

Now I say, in the first place, that a man's soul as hegemonical over

his appraisal of Descartes' argument for the existence of God in *Meditations* III. See *TIS*, pp. 717–19.

itself, having a power of intending and exerting itself more or less in consideration and deliberation, when different objects, or ends, or mediums, [are] propounded to his choice, that are in themselves really better and worse, may, upon slight considerations and immature deliberations (he attending to some appearance of good in one of them without taking notice of the evils attending it), choose and prefer that which is really worse before the better, so as to deserve blame thereby. But this not because it had by nature an equal indifferency and freedom to a greater or lesser good, which is absurd, or because it had a natural liberty of will either to follow or not follow, its own last practical judgement, which is all one as to say a liberty to follow or not follow its own volition. For upon both these suppositions there would have been no such thing as fault or blame. But here also the person being supposed to follow the greater apparent good at this time and not altogether to clash with his last practical judgement neither. But because he might have made a better judgement than now he did, had he more intensely considered, and more maturely deliberated, which, that it [*sic*] did not, was its [*sic*] own fault. Now to say that a man hath not this power over himself to consider and deliberate more or less, is to contradict common experience and inward sense. And to deny that a man is blameworthy for inward temerity in acting in any thing of moment without due and full deliberation, and so choosing the worser is absurd. But if a man have this power over himself to consider and deliberate more or less; then is he not always determined thereunto by any antecedent necessary causes. These two things being inconsistent and contradictious. And consequently there was something of contingency in the choice.

From what has been declared it appears that though perception be nature or necessary understanding in us, yet for all that, we are not merely passive to our own practical judgements and to the appearances of good, but contribute something of our own to them, to make them such as they are. Because these may be very different accordingly as we do more or less intensely consider or deliberate, which is a thing ἐφ' ἡμῖν in our own power. A man who does but slightly consider, may hastily choose that as better, which upon more serious and leisurely consideration, he would judge should be refused as what is much the worser. The same motives and reasons propounded have not always the same force and efficacy upon different persons, nor yet upon the same persons, neither at several times, but more or less as they are differently apprehended, or more or less attended to, pondered or considered, which we are not merely passive to, but determined by ourselves.

Besides which, it is certain, that in our practical judgements we often extend ourselves or [our] assents further than our understanding, as necessary nature goes, that is, further than our clear and distinct perceptions. For when upon a slighter consideration we are sometimes become doubtful which of two or more things should be preferred, not clearly discerning at that time any greater eligibility in one than another of them, though in reality there were much difference, we are not hereupon necessitated to arrest and stop and suspend action, but may and often do proceed to making a judgement in the case one way or other, stochastically or conjecturally (which itself is not without some contingency neither) and so go forward to action.

It hath seemed very strange to some, what Cartesius hath written, that it is not the understanding but the will that judgeth,[45] and that this is the cause of error as well as of sin. And indeed this may well seem strange according to that notion, which men commonly have of will, as a mere blind faculty. But it is most certain that even in speculative things, about truth and falsehood, as well as [in] practical [things], the hegemonic of the soul (which is the soul self-comprehensive, and having the conduct and management of itself in its own hand) doth sometimes extend itself further in way of assent than the necessary understanding goes, or beyond clear and distinct perception. That is when we have no clear and distinct conception of the truth of a proposition (which is the knowledge of it and can never be false) we may notwithstanding, extend our assents further and judge stochastically, that is opine, this way or that way concerning it, and that sometimes with a great deal of confidence and assurance too. And this is undoubtedly the original of all error in speculative things also, which cannot be imputed to necessary nature in us without casting the blame of them upon God the maker of it. The understanding as necessary nature in us, or clear distinct conception, can never err because there cannot possibly be any clear conception of falsehood in eternal things as geometry and metaphysics. Clear conceptibility is the essence of truth, and clear distinct conception is knowledge, which can never be false.[46] Wherefore if we did always suspend our assents, when we had no clear

---

[45] Descartes, *Meditations*, IV. CSM, II, 25–7.
[46] For Descartes' enunciation of this principle, see his *Principles* I.30. See *EIM*, pp. 138–42 above.

distinct conceptions of the connection between the predicate and subject of a proposition, we should never err. But we do often opine and judge stochastically, concerning truth and falsehood even in speculative things, beyond our clear conceptions and certain knowledge. That of Aristotle, ἡ κακία φορτικὴ τῶν ἀρχῶν[47] and the common opinion that interest and vicious inclinations bribe the judgement, shows that the judging power in us is not the understanding or necessary nature in us, for then it could not be bribed, corrupted, and swayed. And indeed the necessary understanding that is our clear conception and knowledge going so little way, there is need and use of this stochastical judging and opining beyond it concerning truth and falsehood, going further and beyond it, in human life, our actions and volitions depending much upon our speculative opinions concerning the truth and falsehood of things. The weakness of human understanding is such that there are very few things which men do so certainly know as that no manner of doubt may be raised in their minds against them, either by sophistical arguments or bigotry in religion. Hence is it, that divine faith is so much commended to us in the Gospel, which is undoubtedly an assent to things beyond clear conception and certain necessary knowledge. The belief of the existence of a God, of the natural immortality of the soul, and consequently of rewards and punishments after this life, are things which the generality of mankind, have no clear conceptions nor demonstrative science of, and yet they are highly necessary to be believed in order to a morally virtuous and good life. And it was truly and wisely said by Plato that πίστις and ὀρθαὶ δόξαι[48] faith and true opinions are things no less useful and effectual in life, than certain science and demonstrations. Nevertheless it cannot be denied, but that by the rash uncautious use of this power of the hegemonic in our souls, of extending its assent further than our clear conception, and beyond our understanding as necessary nature in us, we frequently fall into many errors, which errors are therefore no more to be imputed to God than our sins are, they being not from necessary nature as made by him but from the ill conduct or management of ourselves, and the abuse of that αὐτεξούσιον or *sui potestas*, that larger power, which we have over ourselves, given for necessary uses and purposes in extending our

---

[47] Aristotle, *Nichomachean Ethics*, VI, v.6.

[48] Δόξα ἄρα ἀληθὴς ὀρθότητα, οὐδέν χεῖρον ἡγεμὼν φρονήσεως (Plato, *Meno*, 97b). Not an exact translation.

assents and judgements beyond our clear conception, understanding, or knowledge, without sufficient grounds. And there may be very sufficient grounds sometimes to believe beyond knowledge, as well as beyond sense and yet notwithstanding is this divine faith a virtue or grace.

Chapter XI

Again in that contest betwixt the dictate of honesty or of conscience, and the suggestion of the lower appetites urging and impelling to pleasure or present good or profit, I say in this contest there is no necessary understanding interposing and coming in to umpire between, that does unavoidably and irresistibly determine one way or other. But the matter wholly depends upon the soul's hegemonic or power over itself, its exerting itself with more or less force and vigour in resisting these lower affections, or hindering the gratification of them, according to which the issue or event of action will be determined. But this is not one single battle or combat only, but commonly a long lasting or continued war [and] colluctation betwixt the higher and the lower principle, in which there are many vicissitudes, reciprocations, and alternations upward and downward, as in the scales of a pair of balances, before there come to be a perfect conquest on either side, or fixation and settling of the soul either in the better or the worse. During which struggling and colluctation was that pronounced, 'the good that I would do I do not, the evil that I would not do that do I'.[49] And then according to the issue of this intestine war will men either receive praise from God or deserve blame and punishment from him, glory and honour to him that doth well, but 'tribulation and anguish to every soul that doth evil'.[50] And 'I have fought a good fight and now there is laid up for me a crown of life.'[51] And that we have a power more and less to exert ourselves to resist the lower inclinations, or hinder the gratifications of them, and to comply with the dictate of conscience or honesty, we being not wholly determined therein by necessary causes antecedent, but having something at least of it ἐφ᾽ ἡμῖν, in our own power, every man's own conscience bears witness, in accusing and condemning him when-

---

[49] Romans 7.19.   [50] Romans 2.9, 10.   [51] 2 Timothy 4.7.

ever he does amiss. Whereas it is plain that if we be determined by necessity of nature here, then is there nothing in our own power, nor can we be blameworthy or deserve punishment.

Moreover we are certain by internal sense, that our souls as comprehending themselves, and hegemonical or having a ruling power over themselves, can exert themselves more or less in self-recollection, self-attention, heedfulness, and animadvertence, in vigilant circumspection, in fortifying themselves in firmness of purpose and resolution beforehand, in carrying and pursuing steady designs of life, in exciting endeavours, in activity and diligence of execution. Now when men are commended for diligence, industriousness, studious endeavours, firmness and steadiness of resolution in good, vigilant circumspection, and blame for the contrary, *viz.* – negligence, remissness, supineness, inattention, carelessness, &c. These things are imputed to the men themselves, as the causes of things, and as not being determined by necessary causes as much as the notions of a watch or clock are.

Chapter XII

But besides internal sense and common notions, the same thing is confirmed by the Scriptures, not only apocryphal, but canonical also. The genuine sense of the ancient Jewish church herein, appeareth from this of Jesus the son of Sirach, ch. xv. 11.

> Say not it is through the Lord that I fell away. For thou oughtest not to do the things that he hateth. Say not thou he hath caused me to err, for he hath no need of the sinful man. The Lord hateth all abomination, and they that fear God love it not. Himself made man from the beginning, and left him in the hand of his counsel. If thou will to keep the commandments [and to perform acceptable faithfulness], he hath set fire and water before thee, stretch forth thy hand unto whether thou wilt. Before man is life and death and whether him liketh shall be given him.[52]

Which latter passage seems to refer to that of Moses, Deut. 30. 'See I have set before thee this day life and good, death and evil. In that I command thee to love the Lord thy God, to walk in his ways and keep

---

[52] Ecclesiasticus 15.11–17.

his commandments.'[53] 'I call heaven and earth to record this day against you, that I have set before you life and death, blessing and cursing. Therefore choose life that thou and thy seed may live.'[54] Here by leaving man in the hand of his own counsel is plainly asserted an αὐτεξούσιον, or *sui potestas*, a power of determining himself towards the better or the worse, life or death. With which agreeth Solomon himself, Prov. 16.32. 'He that ruleth his [own] spirit is more mighty than he that taketh a city.' He that is κρείσσων ἑαυτῷ, superior to himself, or a conqueror over his infer[ior] pass[ions], irascible and concupiscible. This implies a kind of duplicity in the human soul: one, that which is ruled, another, that which ruleth, or the soul to be as it were reduplicated upon itself and so hegemonical over itself; having a power to intend itself more or less in resisting the lower appetites, which cannot be without something of contingency or non-necessity. Were the soul necessarily and essentially good and impeccable, he would be above this self-power – were he nothing but lust, appetite, and *horme*, he would be below it. Now he is 'in a middle state a perfection betwixt both. He hath some power to keep under his body and bodily lusts' (1 Cor. 9.27).[55] To mortify his members that are upon the earth (Col. 3.5). To gird up the loins of his mind (1 Pet. 1.13). To add something to himself (2 Pet. 1.5). 'Add to your faith virtue, [and to virtue] knowledge.' To improve these talents which he hath received from God, and to return to him his own with usury (Matt. 25).[56] To purge himself (2 Tim. 2.21): 'If a man [therefore] purge himself from these he shall be a vessel of honour.' To 'cleanse ourselves from filthiness of [the] flesh and spirit', 2 Cor. 7.1. To keep himself pure (1 Tim. 5.22). 'To keep himself unspotted from the world' (Jam. 1.27). 'To keep ourselves in the love of God' (Jude 21). To keep himself that 'that wicked one touch him not' (1 Joh. 5.18). 'To overcome' (Apoc. 2.7).[57] In these places it is plain that the soul of man hath a reciprocal energy upon itself, or of acting upon itself – so that it is not merely passive to that which it receives from God – a power of being a [co-worker] with God, a power of

[53] Deuteronomy 30.15–16.   [54] ibid., verse 19.
[55] 'But I keep under my body and bring it into subjection' (1 Cor. 9.27).
[56] Parable of the talents (Matt. 25.14–30, esp. 27).
[57] 'To him that overcometh will I give to eat of the tree of life' (Rev. 2.7). Most of the foregoing Bible references are paraphrases, or close modifications. I have indicated those which are direct verbatim quotations, and provided the original in a footnote where it diverges significantly from Cudworth's wording.

improving itself further and further, and of keeping and conserving itself in good, all which cannot be without a non-necessity or contingency.

Chapter XIII

This faculty of αὐτεξούσιον, or *sui potestas*, or power over ourselves, which belongs to the hegemonicon of the soul, or the soul as reduplicated upon itself, and self-comprehensive, whereby it can act upon itself, intend and exert itself more or less, and by reason thereof judge, and will, and act differently, is intended by God and nature for good, as a self-promoting, self-improving power, in good, and also a self-conserving power in the same, whereby men [receive] praise of God, and their persons being justified and sins pardoned through the merits and true propitiatory sacrifice, have a reward graciously bestowed on them by God, even a crown of life. Notwithstanding which by accident and by the abuse of it, it proves that, whereby men also come to be unto themselves the causes of their own sin, of guilt, blame, and punishment – the objects of God's vindicative justice, that which will especially be displayed in that great day of judgement which is to come. The justice of which day of judgement to punish men for the past actions of their wicked lives can no otherwise be defended than by asserting – such an hegemonicon in the soul, as whereby it has a power over itself or a freedom from necessity.

Chapter XIV

It appears from what I have declared that this *liberum arbitrium* or freewill, which is properly an αὐτεξούσιον or *sui potestas*, a power over oneself, either of intending or remitting and consequently of determining ourselves better or worse; which is the foundation of commendation or blame, praise or dispraise, and the object of retributive justice, remunerative or judicative, rewarding or punishing; is not a pure perfection (as many boast it to be) but hath a mixture of imperfection in it. So that it cannot belong to God or a perfect being to have a self-intending and self-remitting power,[58] a self-improving and self-impairing power, a self-advancing and self-depressing, to deserve praise, commendation and reward on the one hand (it being observed by Aristotle that it does not properly belong to God ἐπαινεῖσθαι μακαρίζεσθαι)[59] much less to deserve blame and punishment. But to be mutable or changeable in way of diminution, lapsable or peccable, is an essential property of a rational creature. Moreover a perfect being cannot have any such power of stretching its judgement beyond certain knowledge, or of eking out the defect of knowledge or understanding, and supplying or lengthening it out, by faith and probable opinion. A perfect being can neither be more nor less in intention or being a pure act, it can have no such thing as self-recollection, vigilant circumspection or diligence in execution, but it is immutable or unchangeable goodness, and wisdom undefectible. Arius and his followers maintaining the Logos, the word and Son of God by which all things were made, to be a creature, did consentaneously thereunto assert, that he was endowed with this kind of *liberum arbitrium*, whereby he was mutable, lapsable, and peccable.[60] But the Nicene fathers, defending the true Godhead or divinity of the Logos, decreed on the contrary that being not lapsable, nor peccable, he was not endowed with that *liberum arbitrium* which is an essential property of every rational or intelligent creature. Accordingly as Origen[61] had before declared that the Logos, being essentially wise intellect itself, could therefore never degenerate into folly. And the Holy Ghost, being essentially holiness itself could not degenerate into unholiness, and so neither of them could have that *liberum arbitrium* which is the original of lapsability and peccability. And thus St Jerome, *Solus Deus peccare non potest, caetera, quia libero arbitrio praedita sunt, possunt in utramque partem se flectere.* [Only God cannot

---

58 'to be essentially and immutably Good and wise, much a greater Perfection than to be so by Contingent Freewill' – on opposite page, inserted after 'perfect being'.

59 'To be praised, to be blessed', Aristotle, *Nichomachean Ethics* 1101b10–30.

60 Cudworth refers to the Arian heresy, the denial of the divinity of Christ, which was condemned at the councils of Alexandria (*c.* 320) and Nicea (*c.* 325).

61 The name of Origen was often linked to the Arian heresy. Cudworth here reveals his own more sympathetic view of Origen, by dissociating him from Arianism on the question of freewill and the *logos*. On Cudworth's potentially heterodox Trinitarianism, see S. Hutton, 'The Neoplatonic Roots of Arianism', in L. Szczucki (ed.), *Socinianism and its Role in the Culture of the XVIth to XVIIIth Centuries* (Warsaw and Lodz, 1983), pp. 139–45.

sin. Since all other things are endowed with free will, they can turn either way].[62]

But some there are who persuade themselves that the perfection of the Deity consisteth in being indifferent to all things, altogether undetermined by any antecedent motives or reasons of goodness, wisdom, or truth, and itself to be the sole determiner of all these by an indifferent, arbitrary, contingent and fortuitous will. And this is that monstrous and prodigious idea or portraiture of God which Cartesius hath drawn out in his metaphysics.[63] That there is *nulla ratio veri aut boni* [no principle of truth or goodness] in nature antecedent to his will. So that according to him, God is both good and wise by will, and not by any nature; a being nothing but blind, indifferent, and fortuitous will, omnipotent. And all divine perfections are swallowed up into will – that a triangle hath three angles equal to two right angles, that equals added to equals make equals, or that two and two are not four otherwise than according to his will, because they were made such by an arbitrary decree of God Almighty.[64] Whereas according to Scripture God is a nature of infinite love, goodness, or benignity, displaying itself according to infinite and perfect wisdom, and govern[ing] Rat[ional] creat[ures] in righteousness, and this is liberty of the Deity, so that it consisteth not in infinite indifferency blindly and arbitrarily determining all things. There is a nature of goodness, and a nature of wisdom antecedent to the will of God, which is the rule and measure of it. But this hypothesis of Cartesius alike overthrows all morality and science at once, making truth and falsehood as well as the moral differences of good and evil mere arbitrary things, will and not nature, [and] thereby also destroys all faith and trust or confidence in God, as well as the certainty of Christian religion.

Upon this ground or principle, of God having an arbitrary contingent freewill to all things, did some of the Arian party endeavour to overthrow the divinity of the Son or Word. Because God must needs beget him unwillingly, unless he begot him by an arbitrary contingent freewill, which would make him have a precarious existence, and to be destroyable again at pleasure, and consequently to be a creature. But

---

[62] 'Arius ... *flectere*': insertion written on opposite page. Compare Jerome, *Dialogus adversus Pelagianos*, in *Opera* II, pp. 502 and 537, in Migne *Patrologia latina*, vols. XXIII–XXIV.

[63] *Meditations*, IV. See also *Principles* I.34.

[64] See also *TIS*, p. 646, where Cudworth attacks Descartes' voluntarism, calling him 'but a *Hypocritical Theist*, or *Personated* and *Disguised Atheist*'.

Athanasius and the other catholic fathers in opposition hereunto, maintained that God the Father begot a Son not by arbitrary freewill, but by way of natural emanation incorporeal and yet not therefore unwillingly nor yet without will neither, but his will and nature here concurring and being the same, it being both a natural will and willing nature. So that the Son begotten thus from eternity by the essential fecundity of the Father and his overflowing perfection (which is no necessity imposed upon him, nor yet a blind and stupid nature, as that of fire burning or the sun shining), this divine *apaugasma*, or out shining splendour of God the Father hath no precarious, but a necessary existence, and is undestroyable.[65] Whereas all creatures, having once had a beginning, cannot possibly have a necessary existence, were it only for this reason, because they once were not. But besides this there can be no repugnance, but that what once was not, might not be again; or be reduced to non-existence by that which gave it a being out of nothing. Wherefore though it should be affirmed that creatures also did proceed by way of emanation from the Deity, as being a kind of λόγος προφορικὸς of God Almighty, yet was this emanation of another kind from that natural and necessary emanation of the Son, namely a voluntary emanation suspendible. Nor can it be denied but that God Almighty might by his absolute power annihilate this whole creation. As suppose, if all rational creatures should degenerate, (as a great part have done), and continue obstinately in their apostasy (as a late sect supposeth the annihilation of wicked men's souls, after the day of judgement, concluding this to be the second death threatened), and then instead thereof create another world of rational creatures, which conceit of other worlds created before this from eternity, hath not only been owned by the Stoics asserting an infinite vicissitude and revolution of worlds, one after another, all new as to the rational creatures in them, but also hath been surmised by some of the Christ[ian] profess[ion], Origen himself having some umbrage of it.[66]

All will is generally acknowledged to have this naturally or necessarily belonging to it, to be determined in good, as its object, it being impossible that any intelligent being should will evil as such. Therefore

[65] Athanasius (*c.* 296–373) was Trinitarian defender of the divinity of Christ against Arius, a doctrine enshrined in the so-called Athanasian creed promulgated at the Council of Nicea (325).

[66] Stoic doctrine of cosmic cycles. See above, p. 161. Cudworth also refers to Origen's eschatology, which entailed a theory of metempsychosis through a series of ages, each culminating in a conflagration.

it seems both rational and pious to conceive that the best of all beings, who is essentially good and wise, should always act agreeably to its own nature, and therefore will the best, and consequently make the world in the best manner that it was capable of. Some indeed will needs pretend[67] that God does not always do the best, because they suppose this to be an essential freedom and liberty in him, to be indifferent to will either the better or the worser. Which is all one as to say he is indifferent to act either, according to his own wisdom and goodness, or not. But none of these men, nor any atheists neither, were ever yet able to show how the workmanship of God in any part of the world, or in their own bodies, could have been mended in the least thing that is. Nor can God's providence in the government of rational creatures be suspected not to be the best, by any who believe that he hath appointed a day wherein he will judge the world in righteousness, and without respect of pers[ons] render to ev[ery] man accord[ing] to his works. When Moses tells us of God pronouncing of everything that he made, that it was טוב מאד *very good* (Gen. 1.31), we are to understand the meaning to be, that it was the best, the Hebrews having no other way to express the superlative.

Notwithstanding which, arbitrary and contingent liberty is not quite excluded from the Deity by us, there being many cases in which there is no best, but a great scope and latitude for things to be determined either this way, or that way, by the arbitrary will and pleasure of God Almighty. As for instance, the world being supposed to be finite (as it can no more be infinite than it could be eternal), that it should be just of such a bigness, and not a jot less or bigger, is by the arbitrary appointment of God, since no man can with reason affirm that it was absolutely best that it should h[a]ve been so much as an inch or hair's-breadth bigger or lesser than it is. The number of the stars must needs be either even or odd, but it cannot be said that either of them is absolutely in itself the best nor yet that the number of those nebulose *stellae* [stars], that appear to our sight as small as pindust, should be just so many as they are, and neither one more or less. So likewise the number of created angels and human souls, or that every one of us had a being and a consciousness of ourselves, must needs be determined by the arbitrary will and pleasure of the Deity, who can obliterate and blot

---

[67]   pretend = claim.

any one of us out again out of being, and yet the world not be a jot the less perfect by it. However we may readily bear a part and join with the four and twenty elders in the apocalypse falling down before the throne, in that song of theirs, 'Thou art worthy O Lord to receive glory and honour and power; for thou hast created all things, καὶ διὰ τὴν θέλησιν σου, for thy will (or pleasure) they are and were created.'[68] Though all things in the universe had not been arbitrarily made such as they are, but according to the best art and wisdom, yet were they not therefore less for the will of God; it being his will to make them according to his wisdom; or to order all things in number, measure, and weight (Wisd. 11.20).[69]

Chapter xv

The instances of the τὰ ἐνδεχόμενα ἄλλως ἔχειν, as the Greeks call them, such things as are contingent or unnecessary, have been frequently given in inanimate bodies that have no self-moving nor self-changing power, and therefore can never be moved nor changed but, as to themselves, necessarily. As for example, that it may either rain or not rain tomorrow; that the wind may then blow either from the north, or from the south. These and such like inferences have been commonly given by ancient writers (as well as modern) who assert contingency against the Democritical or Stoical fate or necessity of all actions; but, as I conceive, very improperly, for though there be in nature a possibility of either of these, and there is an uncertainty to us which of them will be, yet whichsoever of them at any time comes to pass, cometh not to pass by any contingent liberty of its own, but is determined necessarily by natural causes antecedent, or without. As for that other common instance of the cast of a die,[70] here is no contingency or non-necessity neither in the motion of the die after it be out of the caster's hand, though it be uncertain to us which side will fall uppermost. But there may be an antecedent contingency in the posture, and force, or impulse of the thrower, which is to be distinguished from the motion of the die itself. No body that is by nature ἑτεροκίνητον, always moved by

---

[68] Revelation 4.11.   [69] i.e. the apocryphal Wisdom of Solomon 12.20.
[70] Hobbes, *Treatise of Liberty and Necessity*, in *Works*, ed. Molesworth, vol. IV, pp. 276–7.

something else, and never originally from itself, can have a contingency or non-necessity in its own motion, as such, though it may be contingently moved by something else, having a power over its own action, to determine the same.

Wherefore there cannot possibly be anything more senseless and absurd than the doctrine of Epicurus, who asserting a contingent liberty of willing in all animals, free from fate and necessity, derived the original thereof from a contingent declination of senseless atoms from the perpendicular, more or less, and uncertainly this way or that way.

> sed ne mens ipsa res necessum
> intestinum habeat cunctis in rebus agendis
> et devicta quas cogatur ferre, patique,
> id facit exiguum clinamen principiorum
> nec regione loci certa, nec tempore certo.

['But what keeps the mind itself from having necessity within it in all actions and from being as it were mastered and forced to endure and to suffer this, is the minute swerving of the first beginnings at no fixed place and at no fixed time.'][71]

And this forsooth upon this pretence, lest anything should come from nothing, or be made without a cause:

> quare in seminibus quoque, idem fateare necesse est,
> esse aliam praeter plagas, et pondera causam
> motibus, unde haec est nobis innata potestas,
> de nihilo quoniam fieri nihil posse videmus.

['Wherefore you must admit the same exists in the seeds also, that motions have some cause other than blows and weights, from which this power is born in us, since we see that nothing can be produced from nothing'.][72]

Wherefore for the avoiding contingent liberty coming from nothing, or being without a cause, he assigns it an impossible cause, for nothing can be more impossible than this, that a senseless atom which hath no self-moving power, should have in it a contingent liberty of moving this way or that way.[73]

[71] Lucretius, *De rerum natura* II.289–93. Translation by W.H.D. Rouse, Loeb edition (London and Cambridge Mass., 1943). Compare Cicero, *De fato*, 10.22–3.
[72] Lucretius, *De rerum natura* II.284–7.
[73] Long insertion, 'Wherefore there cannot ... that way' on previous page, running on to next.

Nevertheless it may well be questioned whether there may not be
something of contingency or non-necessity in the actions of brute
animals, though it be out of question that they have nothing of morality
or moral freewill in them. We did before take notice of a certain kind of
liberty from necessity, where blame or commendation had no place,
called by some of the ancients epeleustic, where there being an equal
eligibility in several objects without the least difference, we can
determine ourselves fortuitously to either of them. Now it is not easy to
exclude brute animals from such a contingency as this, because there
may be objects proposed to them (as of meat and drink) so exactly
equal, and placed at such equal distances for a considerable time; as that
it cannot be conceived what physical cause there should be necessarily
to determine them at last to either of them, or to this rather than that.
And yet they will not hang in suspense but certainly do one or other. So
again where they are distracted betwixt an equal fear and aversation on
one side, and equal hope or desire on the other, at the same time, as a
dog betwixt a whip and a bone, they will not always continue in demur
and suspense, though the scales be exactly even, and a perfect *isorrope* as
to motives and causes. But there will after a determination, sometimes
one way, sometimes another, which cannot well be thought necessary
without anything of fortuitous contingency.

Moreover Epicurus was of opinion, that as well brute animals, as
men, had a power over themselves, of intending themselves more or less
to their sensual or animal good, fancied by them:

> nonne vides etiam patefactis tempore puncto,
> carceribus, non posse tamen [prorumpere equorum
> vim cupidam tam de subito, quam mens avet ipsa].

['Do you not see also when cells are thrown open at a given moment, that
nevertheless the eager force of the horses cannot burst forth so suddenly
as the mind itself craves?'][74]

Where he conceived that brutes were not merely passive to their own
fancies and *hormae* but that they could add something of their own to
them more or less, and actively intend themselves beyond what they
suffered or what was by nature impressed upon them; which, if it be so,
then must there be something in brutes superior to their *hormae*, some

---

[74] Lucretius, *De rerum natura* II.264–6. The last one and a half lines are not in the original MS.

one thing, which, taking notice both of outward objects by sense, and of its own fancies and *hormae*, can intend them more or less, and add more or less to them.

And there may seem to be some further probability of this from hence, because we find by experience that brutes are many of them docible, and can acquire habits, to do many things even to admiration. Now fancies and *hormae* as such are not capable of habits, no more than of freewill. And therefore that which these habits are in, and which thus determines their motions (and their *hormae* too) must be a kind of hegemonic in the acting probably not without some contingency. However it is not easy to believe that every wagging of a dog's tail, every motion of a wanton kitling sportfully playing and toying, or of a flea skipping, hath such a necessary cause, as that it could none of them possibly have been otherwise.[75]

Chapter XVI

But whatever be the case of brute animals as to this particular, whose insides we cannot enter into, yet we being in the inside of ourselves do know certainly by inward sense that there is in us some one hegemonical, which comprehending all the other powers, energies, and capacities of our soul (in which ἀνακεφαλαιοῦται they are recollected and as it were summed up) having a power of intending and exerting itself more or less, determineth, not only actions, but also the whole passive capability of our nature one way or other, either for the better or the worse.

And I say that according to reason there must of necessity be such a thing as this in men, and all imperfect rational beings, or souls vitally united to bodies. For there being so many several faculties and different kinds of energies in them, as the sensitive perception of outward objects together with bodily pleasure and pain, sudden fancies and *hormae*, appetites and passions towards a present seeming good, or against a present apparent evil, rising up in us, or coming upon us and invading us, with great force and urgency, then the free reason of our private

[75] 'However ... otherwise': insertion on opposite page.

utility, which discovering inconveniences present and future attending them, often contradicts these appetites of a present sensual good. Again, the superior dictate of honesty, which many times is inconsistent both with the appetites of pleasure and the reason of private utility. Besides there, a speculative power of contemplating *de omni ente et non ente*, of whatsoever is and is not in nature, and of the truth and falsehood of things universal, whence it obtrudes upon us the notice of a God and His existence as the object of religion, the substantiality or permanent subsistence of our own souls after the body's decay. Lastly a deliberating power of what is to be done in life in order to the promoting of our own good and upon emergent occasions. I say there being so many wheels in this machine of our souls, unless they be all aptly knit and put together, so as to conspire into one, and unless there be some one thing presiding over them, intending itself more or less, directing, and ordering, and giving the fiat for action, it could not go forwards in motion, but there must be a confusion and distraction in it, and we must needs be perpetually in puzzle. We should be like to a disjointed machine or automaton all whose wheels are not well set together, which therefore will be either at a stand continually, or else go on very slowly, heavily, and cumbersomely. It could never carry on evenly any steady designs, nor manage itself orderly and agreeably in undertaking, but would be altogether a thing inapt for action.

If appetites and passion rise necessarily from objects without and the reason of private utility did necessarily suggest something contrary to them from the consideration of other present inconveniences or future ill consequences, were there not some middle thing here to interpose or to umpire between them we must of necessity be nonplussed and at a stand. But if either of these by superiority of strength did always necessarily prevail over the other, then would that other be altogether useless and superfluous, and so the whole a bungle in nature.

The case is the same as to the clashing and discord betwixt the superior dictate of honesty and conscience and that of sensual pleasure or private utility. If these two be equiponderant as scales in a balance, and there be no hand to turn or cast in grains of advantage either way, then must the machine of the soul be at a stand. But if one of them do always necessarily preponderate the other, then is the lighter altogether idle and to no purpose.

Again, if speculative and deliberative thought be always necessary in us, both as to exercise and specification, then must it be either because they are all necessarily produced and determined by objects of sense from without, according to the doctrine of Democritus and Hobbian atheists, or else because the understanding always necessarily worketh of itself upon this or that object, and passeth from one object to another by a necessary series or train and concatenation of thoughts. Upon supposition of the former, we could never think of anything, nor speak a word at any time but what objects of sense without did obtrude upon us unavoidably. We could never divest our own thoughts, nor stop the inundation of them flowing in a stream from objects nor entertain any constant design of life, nor carry on any projects for the future; we being only passive to the present objects of sense before us, all our thoughts being all scribbled or stamped upon our souls by them as upon a sheet of paper.

But if the latter of these be supposed, then could we never have any presence of mind, no ready attention to emergent occurrences or occasions, but our minds would be always roving or rambling out, we having no power over them to call them back from their stragglings, or fix them and determine them on any certain objects.

Lastly, if we could not intend ourselves in diligence of activity and endeavours, more or less set ourselves to pursue any purpose or design, fortify our minds with resolution, excite ourselves to watchfulness and circumspection, recollect ourselves more and less in considering all our interests and concerns, if we could not from ourselves exert any act of virtue or devotion for which we should truly deserve praise, nor any act of sin for which we should justly deserve blame, for we should be[76] but dead machines moved by gimmers and wires (*tanquam nervis alienis mobile lignum*).

To conclude, God Almighty could not make such a rational creature as this is, all whose joints, springs, and wheels of motion were necessarily tied together, which had no self-power, no hegemonic or ruling principle, nothing to knit and [unite] the multifarious parts of the machine into one, to steer and manage the conduct of itself no more than he could have made all the birds of the air only with one wing, all the beasts of the field, horses, and other cattle with three legs, for the idea of these things is nothing so unapt as that of an imperfect rational

---

[76] 'if we . . . for we should be': insertion on opposite page.

being, all whose powers and wheels of actions are necessarily tied together, which hath no one thing presiding and governing in it, having a self-intending, and self-determining, and self-promoting power.

Wherefore this αὐτεξούσιον, *sui potestas*, self-power, commonly called liberty of will, is no arbitrary contrivance, or appointment of Deity, merely by will annexed to rational creatures, but a thing which of necessity belongs to the idea or nature of an imperfect rational being. Whereas a perfect being, essentially good and wise, is above this freewill or self-power, it being impossible that it should ever improve itself, much less impair itself. But an imperf[ect] rational being, which is without this self-power, is an inept mongrel and monstrous thing, and therefore such a thing as God could not make. But if he would make any imperfect rational creatures, he must of necessity endue them with an *hegemonicon* or self-ruling power. Wherefore that which by accident follows from abuse of this power cannot be imputed to God Almighty – as the cause of it, *viz.* sin, and vice, and wickedness. Since he must either make no imperfect rational beings at all, or else make them such who may be lapsable and peccable by their own default.[77]

Chapter XVII

I have now but one thing more to add, and that is to take notice of a common mistake which learned men have been guilty of, confounding this faculty of freewill with liberty as it is a state of pure perfection, for what is more common than in writings both ancient and modern, to find men creaking and boasting of the ἐξουσία τῶν ἀντικειμένων, the liberty of contrariety, *i.e.* to good or evil, as if this was really a liberty of perfection, to be in an indifferent equilibrious state to do good or evil moral, which is too like the language of the first tempter, 'Thou shalt be a God knowing good and evil.'[78] Whereas the true liberty of a man, as it speaks pure perfection is when by the right use of the faculty of freewill, together with the assistances of Divine grace, he is habitually fixed in moral good, or such a state of mind, as that he doth freely, readily, and easily comply with the law of the Divine life, taking a pleasure in

[77] 'thing and therefore ... default': insertion on opposite page.
[78] Genesis 3.5: 'Ye shall be as gods, knowing good and evil.'

complacence thereunto; and having an aversation to the contrary; or when the law of the spirit of life hath made him free from the law of sin, which is the death of the soul.

But when, by the abuse of that natural faculty of freewill, men come habitually fixed in evil and sinful inclinations, then are they, as Boethius well expresses it, *propria libertate captivi*, knowing good and evil, 'made captive, and brought in bondage by their own freewill,'[79] and obnoxious to divine justice and displeasure for the same. Whosoever customarily committeth sin,[80] which is by his own freewill abused or perversely used, contrary to the design of God and nature in bestowing the same upon us, is thereby made the servant of it, and deprived of that true state of liberty, which is man's perfection.

The faculty of freewill is good, whereby men are advanced above the low condition of brute animals, who are under a necessity of following their fancies *hormae*, and appetites to a sensual good only, or a good of private selfish utility, they having no sense of that good of honesty, and righteousness which is of a different kind from it. But this faculty being that which is proper to creatures, and to imperfect beings only, hath a mixture of creaturely weakness and imperfections in it; and therefore is liable to be abused, so as thereby to become to ourselves the cause of our own bondage and servitude. Whereas true liberty, which is a state of virtue, holiness, and righteousness (a communicated Divine perfection or participation of the Divine nature) can never be abused.

Chapter XVIII

I now proceed to answer all the arguments or objections made against this faculty of the τὸ ἐφ᾽ ἡμῖν or αὐτεξούσιον, this *sui potestas*, or power over ourselves, which infers a contingency or non-necessity, and is commonly called *arbitrium* and *liberum arbitrium* – the foundation of praise and dispraise, of retributive justice, rewarding and punishing. And this as the matter hath been now already explained by us will be very easy for us to do.

I begin with the pretended grounds why this should be πρᾶγμα

---

[79] Boethius, *De consolatione philosophiae* V, pr. 2, line 10 reads *propria libertate captivae*.
[80] John 8.34.

ἀνύπαρκτον, a thing which hath no existence in nature, but in itself [is] unintelligible and absolutely impossible. The first whereof is this that nothing can move or act any way, but as it is moved or acted upon by something else without it. This argument is thus ridiculously propounded by Mr Hobbes, 'I conceive that nothing taketh beginning from itself, but from the action of some other immediate agent without itself.'[81] But this meaning, if he had any meaning, could be no other than this, that no action taketh beginning from the agent itself, but from the action of some other agent without it. Which is all one as if he should say that no agent acteth from itself, not otherwise than as it is passive to some other agent without it. That is, there is nothing self-moving or self-acting in the world, nothing that acteth otherwise than as it suffereth, or is made to act by something else without.[82] Now if this proposition be true, it must needs be granted that there can be no contingent liberty or freedom from necessity in nature, but all things will depend upon a chain of causes each link of which is necessarily connected, both with what went before, and what follows after, from eternity.

But it is certain that this argument makes no more sense against contingency or non-necessity, than it doth against the existence of a God, or an unmoved mover and first cause of all things. It is of equal force both ways and therefore if it do substantially and effectually prove the necessity of all actions, then doth it as firmly evince that there is no first unmoved or uncaused cause, that is, no God. And I do not question, but that this is the thing which Mr Hobbes aimed at, though he disguises his design as much as he could in his book *De corpore*, ch. 26, '*Etsi ex eo &c.*'.

> Although from hence that nothing can move itself, it is rightly enough inferred there is a first mover that was eternal; yet nevertheless it cannot be inferred from thence, as it commonly is, that there is any eternal immoveable or unmoved mover, but on the contrary, that there is an eternal moved mover, because as it is true that nothing is moved from itself, so is it likewise true that nothing is moved but from another, which was itself also before moved by something else.[83]

[81] *Of Liberty and Necessity*, in *Works* ed. Molesworth, vol. IV, p. 274.
[82] 'This argument ... else without': insertion on opposite page.
[83] Hobbes, *De corpore*, ch. 26. See *Opera latina*, vol. I, p. 336. The translation is Cudworth's. Compare Hobbes, *English Works*, vol. I, p. 412.

In which words he doth at once endeavour to transfuse and convey the poison of atheism, and yet so to do it craftily, as that if he be charged with it, he might have some seeming subterfuge, or evasion. He saith first that it is rightly inferred there is some first eternal mover, which looks very well, but then he doth not stand to this, but contradicts it immediately afterward in denying that there is any eternal immoveable mover, or any other eternal mover, than such as was itself before moved by something else, which is all one as to say that there was no first mover. But one thing moved another from eternity, without any beginning, any first mover, any unmoved self-moved mover.[84] For the first mover, if there be indeed any such, must needs be an unmoved mover, which was not itself before moved or acted by another, but a self-moving mover.

But this whole argument thus at once striking against contingency, and the being of a God both together, and which pretends to be [a] mathematical demonstration is evidently the most egregious piece of ridiculous nonsense that ever was written. For if there be motion in the corporeal world, as there is, and no part of it could ever move itself, then must there of necessity be some unmoved or self-moving thing as the first cause thereof, something which could move or act from itself without being moved or acted upon by another. Because if nothing at all could move or act by itself, but only as it was moved or acted upon by another then could not motion or action ever begin, or ever have come into the world. But since there is motion in the corporeal world, and no part of it could move itself, it must needs either originally proceed from a first unmoved or self-moving mover and cause, or else all of it come from nothing, and be produced without a cause.

But the truth is this, that these unskilful philosophers apply that to all being whatsoever, which is the property of body only, that it cannot move itself, nor otherwise move than as it is caused to move by something else without it; as it cannot stop its motion neither, when it is once impressed upon it (it being wholly of a passive nature), and from hence it afforded an undeniable demonstration to us, that there is some incorporeal being, and something unmoveable, or self-moving and self-acting, as the first cause of all motion and action, which in itself not

---

[84] 'But one ... mover': insertion on opposite page. It is a central argument of *TIS* that the mechanical concept of matter as inert, and having no properties apart from size, shape and position, must presuppose the existence of some incorporeal mover. See *TIS*, pp. 29, 162–3.

being moved nor acted by another, can cause body to move locally, and did at first impress such quantity of motion upon the corporeal universe as now there is in it.[85]

Chapter XIX

Again, it is objected, that though it should be granted there was something self-moving and self-active, and which was not merely passive to another thing without it, acting upon it, yet for all that, it is not possible that anything should determine itself, actively change itself, or act upon itself because one and the same thing cannot be both agent and patient at once.

To which I reply, first that there is no necessity that what acteth from itself should always act uniformly, or without any difference or change. That in us, which moves the members of our body by cogitation or will, doth not always do it alike, but determineth itself differently therein, acting sometimes on one member sometimes on another, moving sometimes this way sometimes that way and with more or less celerity and strength, and sometimes arresting motion again. So that nothing can be more plain than that, by determining itself differently, it doth accordingly determine the motion of the body. And it is contrary to the verdict of our inward sense to affirm that, when we thus move our body and members arbitrarily and at pleasure, no one motion of our finger, no nictation of our eyelids, no word spoken by our tongue could ever possibly have been otherwise than it was at that time, but that it was necessarily so determined, by a successive chain of causes, from all eternity, or at least from the beginning of the world, much less, as Mr Hobbes further dogmatizes, that there is no one action, how casual or contingent soever it seem, to the causing whereof did not at once concur whatsoever is in *rerum natura*.[86]

That which determineth itself and changeth itself may be said to act upon itself, and consequently to be both agent and patient. Now though this cannot possibly belong to a body which never moves itself, but is

---

[85] Half a page deleted here. The 'undeniable demonstration' is to be found *TIS* pp. 844–5.
[86] Hobbes, *Of Liberty and Necessity*, in *Works*, vol. IV, p. 267. This is almost, but not quite, a verbatim quotation from Hobbes; cf. p. 160, n. 10, above.

essentially ἑτεροκίνητον, always moved by something else without it, yet nothing hinders but that what is by nature αὐτο-κίνητον, self-moving and self-active, may also determine its own motion or activity, and so the same be said to be both agent and patient. We are certain by inward sense that we can reflect upon ourselves and consider ourselves, which is a reduplication of life in a higher degree. For all cogitative beings as such, are self-conscious. Though conscience, in a peculiar sense, be commonly attributed to rational beings only, and such as are sensible of the *discrimen honestorum et turpium* [distinction between right and wrong], when they judge of their own actions according to that rule, and either condemn or acquit themselves. Wherefore that which is thus conscious of itself, and reflexive upon itself, may also as well act upon itself, either as fortuitously determining its own activity or else as intending and exerting itself more or less in order to the promoting of its own good.

Chapter xx

But it is still further objected that a thing which is indifferent as such can never determine itself to move or act any way, but must needs continue in suspense without action, to all eternity. This is an argument which Pomponatius[87] relies much upon to destroy contingent liberty of will, and establish a fatal necessity of all actions.

And here we must again observe that what belongeth to bodies only, is by these philosophers unduly extended to all beings whatsoever. 'Tis true that a body which is unable to move itself, but passively indifferent to receive any motion impressed upon it, once resting must needs continue to rest to all eternity, unless it be determined to this or that motion by something else without. And if it should be impelled different

---

[87] Pietro Pomponazzi (Petrus Pomponatius), *De fato, de libero arbitrio et de praedestinatione*, ed. Richard Lemay (Lucca, 1957) p. 224, Book III, sect. 1. 'Verum ipsa voluntas, vel quaecunque potentia sit illa, a nullo alio determinata, indifferenter potest in actus oppositos.' *De fato* (first published 1507) is one of the most important Renaissance discussions of the problem of freedom. Pomponazzi (1462–1525) was influenced by Alexander of Aphrodisias, rejected Averroism and advocated studying Aristotle purified of non-Aristotelian accretions. He is best known for his controversial view that, on Aristotelian principles, it is impossible to prove the soul's immortality. See M. Pine, *Pietro Pomponazzi, Radical Philosopher of the Renaissance* (Padua, 1986).

ways at once by two equal forces, it can never be able of itself to move either way. Two scales put into a perfect equal poise can neither of them move upward or downward. But it will not therefore follow that if equal motives to action, equal appearances of good offer themselves to a man, he must therefore stand for ever in an *isorrope* or equilibrium, and can never determine himself to act one way or other.

Nevertheless this is a great mistake of Pomponatius and many others, to think that that liberty of will, which is the foundation of praise or dispraise, must consist in a man's having a perfect indifferency after all motives and reasons of action propounded and after the last practical judgement too, to do this or that, to choose the better or worser, and to determine himself fortuitously either way. For the contingency of freewill doth not consist in such blind indifferency as this is after the last judgement and all motives of action considered; but it is antecedent thereunto, in a man's intending or exerting himself more or less, both in consideration and in resolution, to resist the inferior appetites and inclinations to the worser.

Chapter XXI

Another argument used to prove that contingent freewill is a thing that can have not existence in nature is because it is reasonable to think that all elections and volitions are determined by the reasons of good, and by the appearance of the greater good. Now the reasons and appearances of good are in the understanding only, and therefore are not arbitrary but necessary. Whence it will follow that all elections and volitions must needs be necessary.

But Aristotle himself long since made a question whether all appearances of good were necessary or no.[88] And it is most certain that they are not so. For as we do more or less intend ourselves in consideration and deliberation, and as we do more or less fortify our resolutions to resist the lower appearances and passions, so will the appearances of good and our practical judgements be different to us accordingly. Whence it frequently comes to pass that the same motives

---

[88] Aristotle, *Rhetoric* I.vii.

and reasons have not the same effect upon different men, nor yet upon the same man at different times. Wherefore this is but one of the vulgar errors; that men are merely passive to the appearances of good, and to their own practical judgements.

Chapter XXII

Another argument for the natural necessity of all actions much used by the Stoics was this, that οὐδὲν ἀναίτιον, nothing can be without a cause, and whatsoever hath a cause must of necessity come to pass. Mr Hobbes thinks to improve this argument into a demonstration after this manner. Nothing can come to pass without a sufficient cause, and a sufficient cause is that to which nothing is needful to produce the effect, wherefore every sufficient cause must needs be a necessary cause, or produce the effect necessarily.[89]

To which childish argumentation the reply is easy, that a thing may have sufficient power, or want nothing of power necessary to enable it to produce an effect, which yet may have power also or freedom not to produce it. Nothing is produced without an efficient cause, and such an effic[ient] cause as had a sufficiency of power to enable it to produce it. But yet that person, who had sufficient power to produce an effect might notwithstanding will not to produce it. So that there are two kinds of sufficient causes. One is such as acteth necessarily and can neither suspend nor determine its own action. Another is such as acteth contingently or arbitrarily, and hath a power over its own action, either to suspend it or determine it as it pleaseth.

I shall subjoin to this another argument, which Mr Hobbes glories of, as being the sole inventor of. From the necessity of a disjunctive proposition nothing can be so contingent but that it was necessarily true of it beforehand that it will either come to pass or not come to pass.[90] Therefore, says he, if there be a necessity in the disjunction, there must be a necessity in one or other of the two parts thereof alone by itself. If

---

[89] Hobbes, *Of Liberty and Necessity*, in *English Works*, vol. IV, p. 274. Cf. *Questions Concerning Liberty, Necessity and Chance*, ibid., vol. V, pp. 382–4.

[90] *De corpore*, Book 2, 'Of Computation and Logic', ch. 9, sec. 5. Hobbes, *English Works*, vol. IV, p. 277.

there be no necessity that it shall come to pass, then must it be necessary that it shall not come to pass, as if there could not be no necessity in the disjunction though both members of it were contingent, and neither of them necessary. This is a most shameful ignorance in logic, especially for one who pretends so much to geometrical demonstration.

And yet this childish and ridiculous nonsense and sophistry of his was stolen from the Stoics too, who played the fools in logic after the same manner. Every proposition, said they, concerning a supposed future contingent, that it will come to pass, was either true or false beforehand and from eternity. If it were true then it must of necessity come to pass, if false then was it necessary it should not come to pass. And yet this ridiculous sophistry puzzled not only Cicero[91] but also Aristotle[92] himself so much as to make them hold that propositions concerning future contingents were to be neither true nor false.

Chapter XXIII

I now come to answer the arguments of those, for the necessity of action, who suppose that though contingent liberty do indeed naturally belong to all rational beings as such, yet notwithstanding the exercise thereof is peculiarly reserved to God Almighty himself only. He from all eternity determining all actions and events whatsoever according to his arbitrary will and pleasure, and so by his irresistible decrees and influx making them necessary, though otherwise in their own nature they would have been contingent.

The first ground of which opinion is this, for a creature to exercise a contingent arbitrary freewill is all one as for it to act independently upon God, wherefore this must needs be reserved to the Deity, as his peculiar privilege and prerogative, arbitrarily and contingently to determine all things, and therefore to make all actions necessary to us. God would not be God, if he did not arbitrarily determine all things.

---

[91] 'Hic primum si mihi libeat assentiri Epicuro, et negare omnem enuntiationem aut veram esse, aut falsam; eam plagam potius accipiam, quam fato omnia fieri comprobem' (Cicero, *De fato* 10.21). 'At this point, in the first place if I chose to agree with Epicurus and to say that not every proposition is either true or false, I would rather suffer that nasty knock than agree that all events are caused by fate' (Loeb translation).

[92] Aristotle, *De interpretatione* 187b ff.

But first, this is to swallow up all things into God, by making him the sole actor in the universe, all things else being merely passive to him, and determined in their actions by him. This at least is, as Plotinus intimates, to make God the immediate hegemonic, and soul of the whole world.[93]

Again, this is not the supreme perfection of the Deity, to determine all things and actions arbitrarily, contingently, and fortuitously. But to act according to goodness and wisdom, God being infinite disinterested love displaying itself wisely, therefore producing from his fecundity all things that could be made and were fit to be made, suffering them to act according to their own natures, himself presiding over all, and exercising his justice in the management and government of the whole. And since all rational creatures have essentially this property of *liberum arbitrium*, the τὸ αὐτεξούσιον self-power belonging to them, to suppose that God Alm[ighty] could not govern the world without offering a constant violence to it, never suffering them to act according to their own nature, is very absurd.[94]

This power of contingent freewill is not independent upon God, but controllable by him at pleasure, as also it is obnoxious and accountable to his justice in punishing the exorbitances of it. And were it not for this, the Divine justice retributive, dispensing rewards and punishments, could have no place in the world, nor no object to exercise itself upon.

Moreover it is certain that God cannot determine and decree all human volitions and actions – but that he must be the sole cause of all the sin and moral evil in it, and men be totally free from the guilt of them. But in truth this will destroy the reality of moral good and evil, virtue and vice, and make them nothing but mere names or mockeries.

Chapter XXIV

Again it is objected that if all hum[an] actions, be neither necessarily in themselves, nor yet made such by Divine decrees, they cannot possibly

---

[93] Plotinus, *Enneads* IV.iv.9–11.
[94] 'that God ... absurd': insertion on opposite page.

be foreknown by God, therefore we must needs either deny the Divine omniprescience, or deny contingency.

Where in the first place we grant, that volitions purely contingent in their own nat[ure] (as when the objects or means are perfectly equal, and have no differences of better and worse, being not made nece[ssar]ily by Divine decrees, or influence neither) are not certainly foreknowable *ex causis*. Since that cannot be certainly foreknown *ex causis* [from causes] which has no necessary causes.

And if contingent volitions be neither certainly foreknowable *ex causis*, nor any way else but are absolutely unforeknowable, then would it be not more derogatory from the Divine omniprescience, that it cannot know things unknowable, than to the Divine omnipotence, that it cannot do things that are not doable, or that are impossible to be done.

However, these things would not be so many as is commonly supposed. For all voluntary actions are not contingent – man's will being always necessarily determined to good, and the aversation of evil, so that there are innumerable cases in human life, in which we may certainly know beforehand what any man in his wits would do, as also many other[s] wherein there can be no doubt but that a good man would do one way, and a man of vicious corrupt principles another way.

Notwithstanding which, though future contingents be not foreknowable *ex causis*, nor we [be] able to comprehend how they should be foreknown otherwise, yet would it be great presumption in us therefore flatly to deny Divine prescience in them, because the Divine nature and perfections surpass our human comprehension. We do believe in Div[ine] eternity without beginning, and therefore without successive flux (for we clearly conceive that whatsoever hath a successive duration must have had a beginn[ing]) though we cannot comprehend this eternity.

And we believe the Divine omnipresence or ubiquity, though we do not understand the manner of it, since we cannot conceive God to be extended over parts (*extra partes*) numerically distinct and infinite, wherefore it would be pious to believe [or] conceive likewise that God foreknows all future contingent events, though we cannot understand the manner how this should be.

But many learned men and good philosophers have satisfied themselves here, that though events perfectly contingent be not certainly foreknown *ex causis*, yet they are seen and known to God by an anticipation of futurity. The divine duration of eternity, which is without successive flux, being present to the past and future, as well as to the instant now. He that calls things that are not as if they were;[95] He whose name is ὁ ὤν, ὁ ἦν, καὶ ὁ ἐρχόμενος, is and was and will be;[96] He who is both past and future, sees all future contingent events in *specula aeternitatis*, in his high watch tower of eternity, and that there is such a Divine eternity is demonstrable by reason.

Chapter xxv

But it is still further urged that, upon a supposition of the certain prescience of future contingencies, it will follow unavoidably that they will necessarily come to pass. This is the constant cry of Socinus and his followers,[97] but without the least shadow of reason, for if the prescience be true they must be foreknown to be contingents, and therefore to come to pass not necessarily but contingently. Moreover, they do not therefore come to pass because they are foreknown, but they are foreknown because they will come to pass, the certain prescience is not the cause of their future coming to pass. But their future coming to pass is the cause of their being foreknown. There is no more necessity arising from the prescience, than there would have been from their futurity, had they not been foreknown. For that which now is, though never so contingent, yet since it is, was future from all eternity, but it was not therefore necessarily future, but contingently only. Here is no necessity but *ex hypothesi*, or hypothetical. Upon supposition that it will be, it is necessarily future, but there is no absolute necessity in the thing itself. When a contingent thing hath been, and is now past, it is then necessary that it should have been; or it could not possibly not have been *ex hypothesi*. But it doth not therefore follow that it was necessarily caused, or that it was impossible not to have been.

---

[95] 'God, who quickneth the dead and calleth those things which be not as though they were' (Rom. 4.17).
[96] 'Lord God almighty, which was, and is, and is to come' (Rev. 4.8).
[97] Fausto Sozzini (Socinus) (1539–1604), leader of the anti-trinitarian sect, the Socinians, forerunners of Unitarianism.

Chapter XXVI

Again it is objected that the supposition of liberty of will is inconsistent with Divine grace and will necessarily infer Pelagianism.[98] But the falsity of this may appear from hence, that those angels which by their right use of liberty of will stood when others by the abuse of it fell, though by that same liberty of will they might still possibly continue without falling, yet for all that it would not be impossible for them to fall, unless they had aid and assistance of Divine grace to secure them from it. Wherefore it is commonly conceived that as, notwithstanding that liberty of will by which it is possible for them never to fall, they had need of Divine grace to secure them against a possibility of falling, and that they are now by Divine grace fixed and confirmed in such a state as that they can never fall.

Much more is the aid and assistance of Divine grace necessary both for the recovery of lapsed souls and for their perseverance. The use of their own freewill is necessarily required, for God, who made us without ourselves, will not save us without ourselves. We are to 'strive to enter in at the straight gate',[99] 'to fight the good fight',[100] and to run a good race,[101] we are to purge ourselves from all uncleanness of flesh and spirit,[102] we are to 'keep ourselves in the love of God'.[103] He was an unregenerated person who in the parable had but one talent given him and is condemned for a slothful servant, because he did not by the use of his freewill improve that talent which he had received and return to his master his own with usury, which had he done more would have been superadded. Our own endeavours and activity of freewill are insufficient without the addition and assistance of Divine grace, for it is God which worketh in us both to will and to do,[104] 'by grace ye are saved',[105] 'and by the grace of God I am what I am'.[106]

---

[98] See above, p. 160, n. 13.   [99] Luke 13.24.   [100] 1 Timothy 6.12.
[101] Hebrews 12.1: 'Let us run with patience the race that is set before us.'
[102] 2 Corinthians 7.1: 'let us cleanse ourselves from all filthiness of the flesh'.
[103] Jude v. 21: 'keep yourselves in the love of God'.
[104] Philippians 2.13: 'For it is God which worketh in you both to will and to do of his good pleasure.'
[105] Ephesians 2.5.   [106] 1 Corinthians 15.10.

Chapter XXVII

There is another witty objection made by a modern writer asserting a fatal necessity of all actions, that whereas liberty of will is introduced to salve a phenomenon of a day of judgement, and the justice of God in inflicting punishment upon men after this life for their actions past, this will by no means serve their turn. I say contingency will no more salve this phenomenon than necessity. For it is no more just that men should be damned to all eternity for a mere chance or contingency, than that they should for necessity. To damn men for their contingent freewilled actions is all one as if one should be damned for throwing such a cast of a die. Men could no more help contingency than necessity. Wherefore the matter can be resolved into nothing else but God's absolute power, and his arbitrary and unaccountable will, which by reason of his omnipotence makes that to be just whatsoever he will do. It seems he thinks not fit to damn men to eternity but such as were necessitated to do wicked actions before, but he might have done otherwise if he had thought good by his absolute power.

To answer this, no man shall be damned for the contingency of any action where there was no difference of better or worse, a perfect equality and one thing as much eligible as the other; there can be no fault nor blame in this case as was said before. But where there is an inequality of better or worse, a diversity of good, honesty, and duty on one hand, and sensual gain and pleasure on the other, men having a power here over themselves to intend and exert themselves in resisting their sensual appetites and endeavouring more and more by degrees to comply with the dictates of conscience opposed to them. If at the end of their lives they have run their course as that they have suffered themselves at last to be quite foiled and vanquished by the worser, it is just that they should fall short of the prize set before them, that they should lose the crown and receive shame, disgrace, and punishment.

Men shall not be damned for the cast of a die or such a fortuitous contingency. But for their not using that power which they have over themselves to promote themselves towards the good of honesty and also for their abusing that power, by actively determining and fixing themselves in vicious habits.

Glossary

This glossary lists Cudworth's unfamiliar terminology and usages. But it is worth noting that some of the earliest recorded usages of our contemporary conceptual vocabulary occur in Cudworth (terms such as consciousness, retributive, psychology, self-determination).[1]

acutangular	acute-angled (triangle)
ambage	circumlocution; obscure language
angulosity	angularity
annected	linked
anvilling	working at an anvil ('anvil' used as verb)
apodictical	demonstrable, certain
aporetical	full of doubts and objections
appulse	pressure, impact, driving against
aptitude	fitness, suitability
argute	sharp, subtle
aversation	aversion
Cartesius	Descartes
celerity	speed
circumstant	incidental; circumjacent
cogitability	capable of being thought
cognation	affinity, connection
cognoscitive	cognitive

---

[1] See Roland Hall, 'New Words and Antedatings from Cudworth's *Treatise of Freewill*', *Notes and Queries* (1960), 427–32; also his 'Cudworth: More New Words', *Notes and Queries* (1963), 313–14; and 'Cudworth and his Contemporaries: New Words and Antedatings', *Notes and Queries* (1975), 29–44. Hall notes parallels between the conceptual vocabulary of Locke and Cudworth.

colluctation	opposition, conflict
compages	solid structures
complacence	complaisance, agreeableness
complicated	folded together, involved
compossibility	possible co-existence
conative	striving, endeavour (also plural: conatives)
concinnity	elegance, neatness
concupiscible	arousing vehement desire
consentaneously	in agreement
contemperated	blended
contemperation	blending
contradictious	contradictory
contristation	sorrow
crasis	the combination of elements or humours in the animal body; constitution. On p. 89 Cudworth calls *crasis* the 'harmonical *temperature* of the whole body'
cruciating	crucifying
depinxation	term from alchemy, not found, but probably equivalent to 'tincture'
disconformity	non-conformity
docible	capable of being taught
ectype	imprint, stamp, copy (hence, ectypal)
educe	draw out, produce
eduction	drawing out, production
emane	emanate
epeleustic(k)	adventitious
epistemonical	epistemological
equicrural	equilateral (triangle)
erratas	printing errors
etymon	the true or primitive form of a word
evanid	pale
extrinsecal	extrinsic, external
flexuosity	flexibility
gimmer	hinge, joint
globulite	tiny globule
grateful	pleasant
hap	luck, fortune
hegemonicon	ruling principle of the soul

hormae	impulses, desires
iatrical	medicinal
icterical	jaundiced
idiopathy	sensation or feeling peculiar to an individual
indument	garment, clothing
isorrope	equilibrium, balance
kitling	kitten
lapsability	liability to fall
limner	draughtsman, illuminator
ludibria	baubles, objects of ridicule
lyncean	(of sight) penetrating, clear
make (*n.*)	make-up
mancipated	enslaved
mormo	hobgoblin
nebulose	nebulous
nictation	blinking, winking
noemata	concepts, objects of intellection
noematical	intellectual, mental
noetical	intellectual
novantique	new and old
obnoxious to	liable to punishment by
obstetricious	productive, 'mid-wifely'
obtusangular	with an obtuse angle (geometry)
operose	laborious
parturiency	parturient state, being in labour
peccability	liability to sin
peccable	liable to sin
peripatetical	peripatetic
phantasmatical	imaginary
phantasmatically	by the senses
phrenetical	frantic, mad
plastic	shaping, productive
polite	smooth, polished
precellency	excelling, surpassing
prepossession	possession in advance
prolepsis	anticipation
protended	protruded
protoplast	first-made thing, original, archetype

puissant	powerful
pulchritude	beauty
radicated	rooted
ray	radiate, shine
rectangular	right-angled (triangle)
renitence	resistance
sapor	savour
scepsis	doubt
schesis	relation
schetical	of scheses, relative
sottishness	foolishness
spermatic	generative, shaping
stochastically	by conjecture, probabilistically
streperous	harsh-sounding, lacking harmony or musicality
striated	thinly drawn out
sublimation	process of converting a solid into a vapour by means of heat
subsultations	leaps, bounds
superficies	surface
thetical	positive, arbitrary, dogmatic
umbratile	shadowy
undefectible	without defect
vaticination	premonition
whiffling	trifling

Index

193, 196, 205; *see also* self-determination *and* autexousion
Heraclitus 32–4, 122–4
Hobbes, Thomas xiv, xv, xvi, xvii, xviii, xix, xxi, xxv, xxix, xxxi, xxxv, 116–17n., 145, 158–9, 195; *De cive* 13; *De corpore* 198, 203, *Leviathan* 116–17, 145, 168, *Of Liberty and Necessity* 158n., 160, 163n., 190n., 198, 200, 203; Hobbesians 172
Homer 32
Hooke, Robert 107n.
hormae (impulses) 169, 174–5, 184, 192–3, 197
Hutton, S. xii n., xiv n., xxxiii, 186n.

Iamblichus 39
ideas (*noemata*) xxii, 60, 64, 66, 74, 77–8, 81, 83, 86, 90–6, 101, 103–13, 117, 125, 131, 145; cogitations 75, 79–80, 82; conceptions of the mind 81–2, 90, 111; immutable natures 10, 127, 144; immutable notions 29, 111, 113, 118, 120–1; immutable *rationes* or reasons 59, 115, 118, 120, 122, 125, 126, 136; intellectual ideas 82, 105, 108; intelligible essences, 94, 127–9, 135, 137, 144; intelligible idea 43, 75–7, 82, 84, 86–7, 91, 102, 104–6, 108, 111–16, 118–21; intelligible reasons 77; noematical ideas 106; objective ideas 76; relative ideas 80, 83–4, 90, 101; sensible ideas 56, 62–5, 69, 75, 79–80, 84, 109, 112–15; universal reasons 58; *see also* notions
imaginations 68, 70, 79; *see also* phantasms
intellect xxi, xxvi, 49, 54, 60–2, 75–7, 81, 84–8, 90–1, 94–6, 99–102, 104, 109, 118, 127–30, 146–8, 150; as active 91, 93–4, 103
intellection 54, 57, 59, 62, 73–7, 80, 82, 104, 114, 122, 128, 132, 135–6, 138, 152, 170
intellectual nature 19, 20, 125
intellectus agens (agent intellect) 82, 83, 115

Janet, Paul x
Jerome 186, 187n.
justice 12–14, 17–19, 20–2, 80, 83, 144–5, 148, 150, 156, 185, 197; divine justice 157, 185, 197, 205, 209; retributive justice 156, 185, 205

Kant, Emmanuel xxix
knowledge xxii, xxiv, 26, 29, 33, 43, 49, 54, 57, 60, 62, 65, 73–8, 87–8, 96, 99–103, 114, 116, 120–8, 130–2, 135–6, 138, 139–43, 146–8, 150–1, 174
Kretzman, N. 167
Kroll, R. xiv n.

Lactantius 12
Laudan, L. 85n.
Le Clerc, Jean x

Leibniz, Gottfried Wilhelm xi
Lemay, R. 202n.
Leucippus 11n., 38
Lipsius, Justus 11n.
Locke, John ix, xii, xv, xvi, xxix, xxxv; *Essay Concerning Human Understanding* xv
Lucian 162n.
Lucretius Carus 42, 163n., 191–2

Maccovius, Johannes 15
machine, mechanism 91, 93, 96, 99, 194–5
McCallum, H. 74
Martineau, J. x, xxxiii
Masham, Damaris xi
Masham, Francis Cudworth xii
Melanchthon, Philip xx n.
Melissus 33
Melitus 162
Menasseh ben Israel xxxi
Mersenne, Marin 23
Migne, J.P. 155, 187n.
mind xx, xxii, xxiii, xxv, 58–60, 63, 74, 76, 79–84, 86–91, 94–7, 100–12, 117–21, 125, 127–30, 134, 136, 138, 140, 146–51; as active 51, 63, 69, 73, 79, 83–5, 87, 95, 97, 99–116, 121, 134; conceptions of the mind 79–82, 90, 111; consciousness of 79; eternal mind 96, 127–130, 143, 150; mind of God 77; perceptions of the mind 81; *see also* soul
Molesworth, W. 13n. 145n.
morality, principles of 9, 12–22, 31–2, 39, 61, 75, 83–4, 87–8, 96, 98, 144–8, 150, 155, 169, 175, 176, 177, 187, 197, 205
More, Henry x, xiii, xvi, xvii, xxvi, xxxi, 72n., 74n., 93n., 150n., 151n.
Moschus/Mochus 38–9
Mosheim, Johan Lorenz ix, x n., xxxii, xxxiii
Musca, G. 162

natural instinct (instinct of nature) 53, 66, 85, 156–7
necessary nature 176, 178, 180, 181
necessary understanding 179, 181
necessity 157, 163–4, 190, 203–4; necessary cause 158–9
nominalism 116–17
Newton, Isaac xv
Nicolson, Marjorie xiii n.
noemata 79–80, 125, 127, 128, 135; *see also* ideas
notions 25, 65, 78, 87, 103–4, 106, 108, 111–12; immutable notions 111, 118; notions of the mind 75, 100, 119, 121; relative notions 82–3, 86, 92, 95, 101; universal notions 58, 114–16, 118–21

Cambridge Texts in the History of Philosophy

Titles published in the series thus far